T0003116

Praise for *The Book of Innocence*

"Throughout every historical epoch, the universe speaks to us directly through exceptionally sensitive individuals. Paul Selig is one of those individuals. *The Book of Innocence* is the latest gift in his series of intriguing channeled teachings."
—Dean Radin, MS, PhD, chief scientist for the Institute of Noetic Science and author of *Real Magic*

"*The Book of Innocence* is a culmination of Selig's illuminating library of channeled texts, enhancing the Guides' earlier teachings with an eye-opening clarity. It presents an indisputable case for dismantling our belief in separation, an invitation to recognize our true nature (our innocence), and instructions for reclaiming this divinity within us, which has been concealed by our chosen identity. If there were ever a manual for rebirth and awakening, this is it. By far, my favorite channeled book to date." —Bob Olson, author of *Answers About the Afterlife* and host of *Afterlife TV*

"Highly attuned and deeply thoughtful, Paul Selig brings us another essential channeled text. This book is a powerful guide along the spiritual path, reminding readers of their divine center and how to access this center in their lives. *The Book of Innocence* is an important book."
—Shaman Durek, bestselling author of *Spirit Hacking*, activist, and thought leader

"Both challenging and encouraging, *The Book of Innocence* is a deep ride through the heart of truth, speaking directly to the ways we diminish ourselves, and the innate ease of innocence that is always available. Beautifully written, laced with powerful insight, Selig's channeled books are the purest voice out there right now."

—Natalie Sudman, artist and author of
Application of Impossible Things

"The Guides, through Paul, continue to elevate our awareness, one soul at a time, through their profound teachings. The pearls of wisdom spill forth into a beautiful string, each more brilliant than the last. Every person who reads the words enclosed within *The Book of Innocence* will be reminded of their true essence, the power of innocence, and be forever transformed. "

—Pam Coronado, intuitive investigator
and TV personality

Praise for *Beyond the Known: Realization*

"This book is the most audacious of the Guides' teachings to date. It describes how anyone who chooses can claim the true expression of who they are; what the Guides call the Divine Self, the True Self, or the Christed Self."

—Aubrey Marcus, *New York Times* bestselling author of
Own the Day, Own Your Life

THE BOOK OF INNOCENCE

THE BOOK OF INNOCENCE

A CHANNELED TEXT

The Manifestation Trilogy: Book Two

PAUL SELIG

ST. MARTIN'S
ESSENTIALS
NEW YORK

First published in the United States by St. Martin's Essentials,
an imprint of St. Martin's Publishing Group

THE BOOK OF INNOCENCE. Copyright © 2023 by Paul Selig. All rights reserved. Printed in the United States of America. For information, address St. Martin's Publishing Group, 120 Broadway, New York, NY 10271.

www.stmartins.com

The Library of Congress Cataloging-in-Publication Data is available upon request.

ISBN 978-1-250-83379-2 (trade paperback)
ISBN 978-1-250-83380-8 (ebook)

Our books may be purchased in bulk for promotional, educational, or business use. Please contact your local bookseller or the Macmillan Corporate and Premium Sales Department at 1-800-221-7945, extension 5442, or by email at MacmillanSpecialMarkets@macmillan.com.

First Edition: 2023

10 9 8 7 6 5 4 3 2 1

Contents

Introduction: Presence and Being   *xiii*

Part I: Identity

1. I Am Known   3
2. Memory   34
3. The Truth of Being   90
4. Reconciliation   130

Part II: Innocence

5. Beyond Sin   189
6. A World Made New   237
7. True Mind   287

Epilogue   327

The following are the unedited transcripts of channeling sessions conducted by Paul Selig between August 13, 2022, and October 7, 2022, before students in Berkeley, California; Boone, North Carolina; and Maui, Hawaii, as well as in online seminars and a small group convened to receive this dictation.

Introduction

PRESENCE AND BEING

DAY ONE

What stands before you today is not only opportunity, but a new recognition of who you have been and what you may know as who you truly are. The True Self, you see, the Divine that has come as you, asks for recognition now, seeks to be seen, seeks to be realized, seeks to command the path you walk in the most perfect way you may ever know. The True Self, you see—we will call it the Monad or the Christed Self—knows who you are beyond itself. It comprehends the ideas you've held about the identity you've known yourselves through, and it has decided with you that what it may do is reclaim the life you lived in a new way.

The idea of who you were—the young woman, the young man, the young person, who has chosen to learn through her investment in outcome, his fear of this or that, the ways she has shown herself to behave with others, what she believes were mistakes, what he believes were opportunities—were all ways of comprehending an idea, an identity made in form, accrued in history, and decided with you, with your permission, to be the personality structure that you incarnate with. The idea of self, you see, is highly useful. But it is an idea. And you must understand, friends, that there is an aspect of each of you that knows far beyond the personality, comprehends itself as knowing, and seeks realization through every aspect of the self that you've accrued in personality.

Now, when we teach through Paul, we have several things we must have him know. The text that we write will be the perfect text for what is to come. And the bounty the text yields, in terms of those who read it, how they learn, how they align to the learning, and how they incarnate in a higher way, has nothing do with him at all. You must understand, Paul, that as the vehicle for the teaching you are very comprehensive. But the teaching expresses through you, and we know what we teach, and what we intend to teach is a new text in comprehension.

Now, to comprehend something is to understand, and we would even say realize in a higher way. You comprehend the idea of self you've known, the name you were given by your parents, the schools perhaps that you attended. The ideas of self accrued through these engagements are very useful for you, yes. But the aspect of you that seeks to come forth, the True Self as manifest as you, knows itself beyond structure, beyond linear time, beyond all those things you thought were insurmountable. The trajectory of this text must be comprehended by each of you as opportunity for manifestation, or the embodiment of the text that is being rendered now as the lives you live, as the body you behave through, as the identity you may now know in an altered state or higher strata of manifestation.

Now, the teaching that we bring forth today will be in two different parts. At the moment, we are preparing you for what comes afterward. And what comes prior is a comprehension of who you have been, how you have chosen, what you have known yourselves through, and how you have actually been complicit in the world that you see and all of its manifestations. You all like to think of yourselves as solvent, as separate, as having your own ideas and walking on your own solitary paths. In fact, you are of a whole, and the manifestation of reality that you see around you is in all ways comprehensive, a response in some ways to the identities held by all of you. The ideas of who you are, as manifest, conjure a world, make a world made so, render things into being, less through what you wish than what you expect. And you expect a world of challenge, of strife, and of turmoil, and you have claimed it. The lives that you live right now, and the agreements you make right now, one and all, will be part of what plays out in the landscape you share in the coming decades. The rendering of the new is upon you now. And each of you who says yes to these teachings may have a part in a new organism, a new world, a new way of being that extends beyond the old.

The Upper Room, you see, where manifestation occurs at the level we teach, is welcoming to all who would like to be here. But the world that you see today, an out-picturing of the identities of all of you, individually and collectively, is about to undergo a level of change that none of you have ever seen, nor has been seen for thousands of years. Periodically, humanity decides that it is time for a higher alignment. The alignment that is present now, and is ongoing for the next several decades, will be understood by you as the time humanity chose to re-claim its true nature. When humanity chooses to reclaim its true nature, those creations that were made in fear, those ideas that are no longer useful, those ways of being that no longer serve humanity, are up to be seen, up to be reconsidered, and up to be transformed. We say *up* because they must be seen in a lifted state for you to comprehend your participation in the landscape you have created, and what comes of it. When you view anything from what we call the Upper Room, you have the ability to perceive it in a higher strata, without the investment of fear that you have so utilized to claim a world into being. The world that you see, you understand, is a co-creation. You are all participatory to it. And you have all been reared in fear, grown through fear, and you anticipate fear. Your expectation of more of the same is what grants you more of the same. The truth of your being, the Christed Self or the Monad, does not hold fear. It is innocent, cannot hold the blemish of fear, and its realization through you, the manifestation of the Divine in form as come in humanity, is the gift of the coming times.

Now, Paul interrupts. "I understand what you say, I under-stand the premise, and it sounds like a nice invocation. But what of us and the messes we've created? I cannot imagine that we will be so changed." You must understand, friends, that everything you see before you was made, and will be remade in the higher template of the Upper Room. The usherance to the Upper Room, which will take several generations to complete, will claim itself in a much higher field. The vibration of the world you live in now, which you see before you in all different ways, must be translated, must be lifted, or transposed, as we like to say, to a higher key, a higher octave of expression than the one you have known yourselves through. Each of you here, each of you who hears these words in one way or another, is fundamental to the change that is occurring. There is no one without God, within or without. The Divine as all things is this teaching, yes, and will continue to be. The idea of self as removed from God, as separate from God, must be comprehended by you as the way that you have chosen to learn through. The realization that you are one with God, and can always be, have always been, and will always be, is a completely different level of vibrational accord than humanity has learned through thus far.

Perhaps there was a time, perhaps there was a garden, perhaps there is a myth that holds, when you knew yourself in union, when such things were so. But it is the memory of this that the Monad holds, within each of your hearts, which is about to accelerate at a level of tone that will actually dismantle many of the structures that have been erected through fear, and through the belief in the separation that you have known from Source.

When we teach through Paul, we wish him to understand that the text that we are writing now is not only appropriate to the mission of the prior texts, but the precise continuation of them. When we spoke last in text, we spoke to resurrection, and the Monad in articulation moving to a level of manifestation where reality is altered by its presence. The coming days and weeks will invoke a new text that is all about the truth of being, at its most primitive and most perfect essence. The text will be *The Book of Innocence,* and it is now begun.

We say this to the readers of this text: The text that you

are reading is an invocation to participation in a level of alignment to a level of vibrational accord where what was once known will be re-known, where what was once spoken in fear will be spoken in truth, and what was once seen as shallow, as separate, as fearful, will be re-seen in the Kingdom. And the Kingdom, as we say, is the realization of the Divine as manifest as all. Underline *all*. The Divine manifest as *all*.

Now, there are several things you must understand. Nothing can be outside of God, because nothing exists outside of God. We make nothing holy. It is already holy. You have denied the innate divinity that is in all things, and as manifestors or creators your choice to claim in fear has mandated a world that perceives itself as unholy, or outside of the Divine. The fabric of reality is actually something that can be altered, re-known, a template re-seen. As the fabric of reality is re-seen, what this reality may hold is not only altered, but reclaimed in the octave it is seen through. Everything expresses in tone, high and low and in between. When the tone is sung in a high note, when the expression of the Monad, or the Christ Truth in all of you, is sung in a resounding *yes,* the fabric of reality is altered by the trumpet, the heralding of the new song that is upon you all now. There is nothing to fear in this transition. The tribulation is the altering of reality through a new accord—a-c-c-o-r-d, a c-h-o-r-d as on a piano. The new song sung from the Upper Room claims all manifestation in the higher key. And the octave of the Upper Room, established now, may claim each of you as its embodiment. This means, really very simply, that those of you who say yes to this altered schemata of expression are calling into being the higher chord that the Upper Room announces itself through, the claim of the Kingdom—"God

Is, God Is, God Is." When the song that you sing, in its full expression, is sounded as your vibrational field, the cumulative effect of the thousands and thousands who hold this alignment is to claim into alignment thousands and then millions more. This is done through accord—not through proselytizing, not through writing pamphlets and handing them out on street corners. It is presence and being that will do the work, and the subject of this text—indeed, presence and being—will be an instruction in manifestation.

Paul interrupts the teaching. "*Innocence?* Why do you call the book *Innocence?*" Because *The Book of Innocence* is a reclamation of the truth of yourselves in its most pure state. The Christ is unblemished, and the Christ is the aspect of the Creator that is present in each of you. It is the seed of the Divine seeking its flower. It is God itself announcing itself in the form you have taken. It is the truth of your being without fear, in love, and in agreement to its Source.

We say yes to each of you, as you say yes to the path before you. Indeed: You Have Come. Period. Period. Period. Stop now, please.

(PAUSE)

What stands before you today is a recognition of the idea of self that you have utilized thus far that seeks to be repositioned, recalibrated, in the octave of the Upper Room. Self, you see, as you have known self, is a requirement for the embodiment you have chosen. You will not be without self. You are not extinguished as a personality in the Upper Room. The personality structure is realigned here to higher purpose. Your uniqueness is intact, yes. What is not intact is your desire for separation, which has a basis in fear. And your separation from your brothers, your idea of self as opposed to others, in all ways contributes to your sense of isolation—and, indeed, separation—from God itself.

Now, God must be understood as tone or sound. In the beginning was the Word. And the Word itself, the tone of God—consciousness as sound and tone—must be understood as the Source of all things. The sound of God is the experience and expression of God. The expression of God may be manifest or unmanifest. Both are equally true and valid. What you see with your eyes, what you hold with your hands, are of God. But what is seen with the eyes may also be understood as participatory to that one sound—a manifestation, a depiction, a way that sound is sown and solidified in form. What is unseen, or the etheric realities you may comprehend, exists beyond the senses, but may be aligned to through the senses. And your experiences, as we continue this teaching, will indeed include what you would think of as otherworldly. *Otherworldly* simply means that the senses that you have held, born in a sense of separation and collective agreement to separation, have not been endowed with the ability to perceive what is already present, what is always present, and may now be known.

Now, some of you say to us, "I just want a happy life. I want a little less pain, a little more joy, far less worry. Will I have that if I do what you say?" Indeed, and more. But this is a book of re-creation and recognition of who you have been. And what you have seen and perceived in the limited strata of the world you've known yourself through is necessary.

Now, some of you say to us, "Well, I have been to the Upper

Room. It's rather nice. But I can't imagine living there." There is an aspect of each of you—you may call it the Monad, if you wish—that is in full residence there, that abides there fully. The operation we undertake with our students is supporting you each in aligning all aspects of self in agreement to the Monad. We have done this through intention, and indeed attunement. When we attune our students, we simply support each of you in aligning to a level of tone that is already playing. You do not summon the Upper Room. You enter the Upper Room. It is already present. But you have been hindered from entrance through many things—the collective agreement that it cannot be so, the fear that you have of what happens to you if you go, the belief that you could become lost there, perhaps go mad, perhaps imagine the self as separate from others. In fact, when you move to the Upper Room in vibration, you are simply moving to a tone of sound, of creation, of consciousness, where the manifestation of the Christ is agreement itself. It *is* agreement. The manifestation of the Monad or Christed Self is agreement.

Now, when you align to this understanding—"I have moved to a level of tone where the manifestation of the Monad is implicit, and I am about to undergo the changes that it ensues"—you will have some comfort when the changes come, because indeed they will. Anyone who follows these teachings is going to have an encounter with the idea of personality and all of its uses and devices. Once you understand who you have been, how you have chosen, how you have overlaid a reality, an entire world, with selfishness, you will begin to move beyond it. And the gift of the times that you chose to embody in is that all are going to encounter this, and in fully realized fashion.

"Now, what does that mean?" he asks. "Not everybody is going to awaken." Oh, indeed they will. In their own good time, yes. But any sentient being will have a realization of who it thought it was as it moves to its next level of tone. Imagine you stand before a doorway. You are quite familiar with the room you live in, or at least you think you are. But when you step in through the doorway, and you turn to look back on what you had created, you are always surprised. "Oh, look at how I lived and what I thought was so." The new room, you see, is where you now establish yourself, and your alignment in the new room renders all things new.

The claim we have taught in prior texts—"Behold, I make all things new"—is the claim of the new from the one who is encountered and abides in the Upper Room. The choice to embody in the Upper Room is made in agreement with the will, and the will you hold is primarily utilized by you as the personality commandeers it. When the will is commandeered by the small self, everything that you claim will be in alignment to that self. When you lift to the Upper Room—"I am in the Upper Room"—the choice is made by you to announce the self as fully present, and that is the claim we have taught prior: "I Have Come. I Have Come. I Have Come." This announcement in the Upper Room supports re-articulation, or the manifestation of the Monad, through every aspect of self and persona that you have utilized. The will, you see, in an articulated state in a higher expression, becomes the expression of the Divine in form. And because God sees God, God knows God, in all of its creations, the aspect of you that has come will seek to reconcile itself with all things it perceives, all that is in the Kingdom and will now be known anew.

Now, when we teach through Paul, we use our language carefully as we can so that he may trust the transmission and not doubt the merit of the teaching. He is wondering, "Do we attune our students in this text?" And indeed we will, as we wish. We are preparing you right now for what innocence is, because most of you have not known it. You believe it is being unsullied, wearing white to the wedding. The idea of innocence as something a child holds is useful in some ways, but then you believe your innocence is lost, and innocence is never lost because there is an aspect in each of you that knows God, that expresses as and with God, that is innocence itself. Innocence may be worldly. It may speak a full sentence. It may know the town it lives in as it demonstrates and expresses fully as you. But when you understand that innocence itself is an attribute, an aspect, and an expression of God that seeks reconciliation with you, you will fully understand the meaning: "Behold, I make all things new." To be made new is indeed to be reborn—not, as some would have it, a denial of form, a denial of history, a denial of who you have been. The True Self, you see, is expressing love, and knows itself as love, and reclaims every aspect of you in the Upper Room as of itself.

The idea of history, and those things endured and chosen to learn through, are not only useful to you—they have been your education. And the fears you have known yourselves through in some ways have encouraged you to choose a higher path, a higher way of expressing. The Upper Room is a place beyond fear. Fear as a tone does not express in the Upper Room. The choice to embody in the Upper Room does not deny your humanity, but reclaims your humanity in the high tone or octave that the Monad expresses through. To become this creation does not deny your gender, your ethnicity, the color of your eyes, and the language you were taught to speak as a child. All of these things are of God, and expressions of same. But you know yourself beyond their limitations, beyond the ideas they presuppose you should have—"in my country," "in my community," "in my religion," "in my age group." The ways you've decided to experience yourselves are perhaps useful, but they tend to operate in separation. To align to the higher is not to exclude the lower. It is to lift the lower to the higher so that it may be reconciled. The Christ, you see, does not discriminate because it does not judge. It cannot hold fear, and judgment is of fear.

The True Self as you, in its full expression, announces itself to all. This is not done with speech or tongue, but through presence and being. And the title we are working on now, the chapter, if you wish, you might call "Presence and Being" because it will be utilized throughout this text. Your experience of being, in the Upper Room, will be the result of the alignment you claim. And your expression here, your presence here, and the being of a self in this state of vibration, claims all things that it encounters to itself for re-knowing, re-seeing, and re-articulation as well. What this means is that in the Upper Room you have become not only a doorway, but an expression of tone, an alignment in tone, that will claim all things in vibrational accord to it. The attunements we have utilized in prior texts were all requirements to support the physical self and identity you have known yourselves through to support you in what transpires next, which is a new equation, an equation being a set sequence of vibrational tones that support the recalibration of the manifest world.

Now, when we teach this, we are not teaching conjuring or magic. We are simply stating the very simple truth that the one who has come as the True Self has come for all humanity. The one that expresses at this level claims all things to its expression. And the Manifest Divine that has always been present, but denied by all of you at one strata of frequency or another, can be re-established through presence and being, and the world is made new by your knowing of it. Period. Period. Period.

(PAUSE)

What we ask of you, if indeed you are willing, is an offering of self—the idea of who you were, the idea of what you were and what you thought you were here to be—to be offered to the higher, or relinquished, if you would, in the Upper Room where all things may be made new. The choice is yours, you see. The personality structure that you have utilized here is an ally in some ways, and a prohibitive factor in some other ways. Your idea of who you should be, inclusive of the Divine Self, supports many things—an awareness of desire, or aspiration to the higher realms, that in some ways conflicts with a simple offering of self that can and will be made new when you stop meaning what you say when you say, "Give me what I want, and now."

The desirous self who seeks realization has an outline for what realization is. And its purpose, in some ways, is to create an idea of what being spiritual means, being realized means, that the small self will seek to fulfill. The True Self, you see, or the self that knows itself in innocence, will not be misconstrued.

And its desire is not of the small self, but of the Monad that seeks its realization, and will seek all things to contribute to it.

"What does that mean?" he asks. When you embark on the journey with us, everything that you meet on the path must be seen as opportunity towards higher realization. You are not designing the map for it, or even outlining what the aspect of self is that will be transformed in the Upper Room. The offering of the idea of self—who you thought you were, perhaps who you think you are—to the higher puts in motion something other. It is a release of a thought, and only one thought—that "I am not of God." Once that is released, all aspects of self reconvene to be altered, one after the next, and brought into alignment with your true nature. By *true nature* we mean the aspect of you who knows who it is, what it is, and how it serves, made manifest through you—an aspect of self that *is* innocent, that *is* the Divine, that seeks reconciliation through you with the Source of all things.

Now, when we teach through the man before you, we listen to his questions as well as we can before he asks them, and this is what he asks us now: "Am I hearing accurately? Is this in the text? Is everything you dictate going to be in the text?" This is indeed in the text, and not every word we speak will be in the text, but we will be quite clear when we are not typing or offering dictation through you. We said *typing* intentionally, Paul, because you are the stenographer, and in some ways that is what is occurring.

The aspect of self that will be relinquished here today is the idea of self that is desirous of outcome, with a mandate for what that outcome is, specifically as it relates to the journey before you. If we were to tell you, you were to go to Paris, you would expect to see the Eiffel Tower, and if that wasn't there, you might say, "I never went to Paris." But Paris exists without the Eiffel Tower, and the True Self expresses as you without your mandate for what this must look like. Trust us, we say, when we offer this to you, because the journey you will undertake will last for some time. "And the journey is to where?" he asks. Well, indeed to the Kingdom, but beyond that to a security within the self that the who and the what that you are is not only enough just as it is, but knows itself in union with its Source.

When you know yourself in union with your Source, there can be no fear because the Divine as you aligns beyond that. And the idea of self that is indeed being relinquished today is the aspect of self that would govern, would dictate, would claim or self-identify, through results born in desire. "But what is wrong with desire?" he asks. "Isn't there a use for that?" Indeed, there is. "I desire to make dinner. I go make dinner." "I desire to meet this person. I introduce myself." What we are speaking about is something other, and in fact the way we intend to introduce this is by artifact. The churches that you've known yourselves through are structures that seek to express themselves through prior doctrine. Your desire for the higher realms in most ways are informed by the church, by the synagogue, by the temple, by whatever structure you have built or erected that you believe would lead you to the Kingdom. Now, you have been taught, and correctly, that the Kingdom of Heaven is within you, and that is a key here. To release the need for desire, as it relates to this teaching, is to release the need to decide what it will look like. If you go about with a map saying—"Where is the Kingdom?"—you will miss what is within you. And we intend to bring you there, and fully, as we are allowed.

On this day we claim that all who hear these words, all who choose this teaching, this instruction, are doing so in accord to their high nature, and not through a fear or desire, to relinquish a sense of self that will instead be offered in high use in service in the Kingdom.

We say this for each of you here: The personality structure can and will be reclaimed in the Upper Room in high use. It is of you and with you. We do not vanquish it, or keep it in the lower realm. The offering you bring of who you think you are, inclusive of who you thought you were, will be the gift you bring that the transformation that is being offered here may include.

You may say this, if you wish:

"On this day I choose to allow myself to be re-known in the higher realm, and allow the personality structure, that aspect of self that I have utilized to navigate this realm, be lifted to the higher, be offered to the higher, be relinquished within the higher, to indeed be made new. I know who I am in truth. I know what I am in truth. I know how I serve in truth. I am free. I am free. I am free."

And as we say these words through Paul—You Have Come, You Have Come, You Have Come—we invite you to the journey before you. Indeed, this is the end of the introduction. The

Book of Innocence is the title. And your innocence, your true beauty, in restoration, is the gift you will receive.

Blessings to you each. We are your teachers as you wish us to be. Stop now, please. Period. Period. Period.

PART I

Identity

1

I AM KNOWN

DAY TWO

What stands before you today, by way of opportunity, is a new agreement to be, to simply be, to allow being to be the presence of your soul in its expression here. Now, the desire to do and achieve is understandable, yes, admirable sometimes, but you forget who you are in your striving, in your desires to achieve. When you allow yourself to be, at the simplest level of being—"I Am"—you actually are in agreement to all that is possible. You design a future, a template for what can be, and you try to sort through every possibility to make this thing so. Instead, what we suggest is that you move to allowance, to the state of being, in the Upper Room, where all is met by you in agreement to its Source.

Now, understand what this means. Again, there is one note sung that is in expression as all manifestation, seen and unseen. When you truly understand what this means as a principle, you align to it in the awareness that any true need will be met by Source, as you are in Source and not separate from Source. The design that you have been utilizing—"perhaps there is a God somewhere up there, perhaps I am stuck down here forever, I must do my best to climb or beseech or pray for what I need to come into manifestation"—prayer, if you wish to know, is agreement to Source, yes. But if your prayers are fearful—"Please, God, give me what I need, I need it so badly"—you are confirming lack, and agreeing to lack, because Source, you must understand, is present in all things, even your idea of lack.

We will explain this for Paul, who is questioning. As you are creators, yes, you hold principles that are agreed to by the frequency that you claim to you. "There will not be enough," a claim of scarcity, will of course be met by you because that is something you may choose to experience—or, better said, expect to experience. When something is an expectation, it is framed as a potential, and the purpose of the frame is to claim the thing into manifestation. Now, you are not thinking your way to heaven. You are not pretending there is enough when the table is bare. You are moving to a level of alignment, and manifestation, we would suggest, where your requirements are met by presence and being.

The idealization of *things* has become a great problem here. "I want a candelabra. It must fit on the table as such, and the candles must be beeswax or nothing other. Thank you, my order is in." You've looked at God as a catalog that you must be ordering from, instead of understanding that the perfect table is laid for you by your agreement to God or Source or the one note sung. When you understand that tone, alignment in tone and agreement in tone, is the action you are taking now, you will put away the ideas of what should be, and allow what can be and what will be to be made present for you.

Manifestation is understood as getting what you want, and that is confusing for most of you. In fact, manifestation is all things, are all things, all in form, seen and unseen. The chair you sit in, the air you breathe, the sky and the clouds and what exists beyond them, are all manifestations of the Divine. One is not higher than the other. The one note sung depicts itself as frequency, and the frequency in a solidified state, or what appears solid, is what you would call manifest. The chair is of God, the sky is of God, the cloud is of God, and all other things are of God as well.

Your decision that what must be of God must look a certain way, meet a certain expectation, is the point of confusion you hold. "I would love to marry a man who has so much money, looks a certain way, wants what I want, prays as I pray, and chooses what I would want him to choose." That is not how love is found, nor even how a mate is fully met. When you are openhearted, "I am willing to receive," when you are willing to know yourself as worthy of what you desire, "I am agreeing to love," love will find you, yes, because it is you that is present for it. Please stop seeking and begin allowing. You are not allowing God to be God because you are so busy telling God what it should be. And when you don't get what you want, you deny God completely. The world that you express in is in denial of the Divine. How do we know this is so? For quite obvious reasons. All of the creations you have made that are operating as limited, are chosen by you through fear—and indeed this would include war, include poverty, include famine—are creations born in the denial of the Divine, and they are your creations.

"How is that so?" he asks. When you decide where God is not, you embellish that idea, you concretize that idea, and you abandon God to that idea. You have made that idea, made manifest, a totem or an idol, a thing that you place before God. "God cannot be in that dark place." In your limitation of God, you have empowered that dark place, and your choice to deny God, an act of will, is in agreement to itself and is out-pictured in consciousness and manifest. If you don't understand what we mean, you must understand that you have will. You may choose to see God, choose to limit God, or choose to deny God, and that will become your experience. What you don't understand yet is how you contribute to the manifest world through those things. When one denies the Divine in herself, she has immediately denied the Divine in all things. If God cannot be where you are, it cannot be anywhere.

Now, you are not summoning God, making God be where you want it. God is actually already there, but is being denied by you, and that becomes the manifest experience. When one says, "I have a right to know, I have a right to be, I have a right to know myself as worthy," perhaps the door will open. But then you use will to step through: "I am in the Upper Room"—again, a claim of truth. It is the aspect of the Divine as you that resides in the Upper Room and will claim fully each aspect of self there that is in agreement to it.

When we teach through Paul, we monitor his system so that the dictation may ensue perfectly. When we teach today, we have an intention to lift the room, to lift the teaching, to lift the comprehension of the teaching beyond a kind of bias that most of you hold to what should be—your expectations and desires about how God should manifest to appease the small self's desire for a God that gives it what it wants. God is present as all things. The teaching of the Upper Room, the teaching of reception, is of course a teaching of manifestation—but manifestation through being, not getting, through alignment and reception, not stamping one's feet and shaking one's fist to the sky. "I demand what I get be as I say." If any of you got what you truly thought you needed, you might be grateful for it. But instead you find yourself disappointed because you are not receiving what you wish, what you have designed, and what you thought was so.

Paul interrupts. "There are many teachings of manifestation that say we should outline what we get." You may outline all you wish. Perhaps you will get the kitten with the long whiskers that you have asked for, but perhaps the pony would be a better gift for you. Don't preclude the pony because the kitten is what you think you need. You don't trust the Divine enough to allow it to know you. And you must understand this. You assume the Divine does not know you, does not know your heart's desire, and does not wish what you wish. So you confuse yourself in writing long lists of *gets* and *shoulds* and *must-haves* that you wave to the sky and say, "This is my list. Thank you, Santa Claus. I will go back to my business now of getting what I want."

When one knows who she is, she knows herself in agreement, in consort, with her true nature. Her true nature, his true nature, is of Source, because it cannot be other. When we say you can't make yourself holy, we are speaking to this principle. You are already of God. You have just denied it. And in this denial, you have created systems to manifest what you think you should have. But you don't understand. Your entire life, the collective world you experience, is also a manifestation of consciousness, born in expectation, claimed by desire, and through the agreement to the denial of the Divine.

A world without God is a world that operates as separate. This is not a world that requires religion. Religion can be useful as a doorway or path for some. All religions hold great truth and have been distorted through misuse of the teachings, embellishment of truth by those who would seek power—and, if useful now, are primarily useful as a doorway or permission to have a relationship with Source. But a relationship with Source is an ongoing relationship. It is not prescribed by dictate, mandate, or law. Any relationship will alter as it matures, will deepen as it grows, and your relationship with Source must be predicated on a belief and an agreement that God, or whatever you wish to call God, knows who you are—that you are not operating as a shipwreck survivor, floating on a log in the ocean, seeking God. God is the log. God is the ocean. God is the experience of all. You are always in God because you cannot not be.

Now, the choice to agree to this comes with an action. The choice to agree is a claim itself. And the claim we have offered you—"I am in the Upper Room"—is a claim made by the Monad, in agreement to will, to support the Divine expressed as the one claiming it. What this means is the choice to align—an act of will, if you wish to say it that way—is your contribution. Imagine you go to a friend's house for dinner and you knock on the table and say, "Where is the beef bourguignon, and where is the pastry I asked for?" You go to your friend's house for dinner and are grateful for what is served. What is served in the Upper Room is always in agreement to your true needs.

Many of you come from a system born in separation, lack, and fear, which supports a belief that there cannot be enough, or God would wish you to have a crumb when the one beside you gets the entire piece of cake. You limit God, because the God that you have claimed has been limited by you, in expectation, through prior conditioning and belief. To know the self as worthy of All That Is must require that you know the one beside you to be. You are not the gift of the Kingdom. The gift of the Kingdom is being and presence—and come *as* you, perhaps, come *as* who you think you are, but expressing beyond the limitations that personality would choose to know itself through.

All are worthy, you see, or no one is worthy. And the one you put in darkness will call you to that darkness, have tea in the darkness with you, until you decide to release him or her from the dark table you sit at. You may stay there as long as you wish, and many of you may, because you cannot believe that allowing another to be as of God, as all things are, will give you the liberation you seek. You would rather hold a prisoner in a cave, joining him or her in shadow, than lead her to the light that is God and freedom. The claim "I am in the Upper Room" supports all things in aligning to you at this level of choice. At this level of choice, all things can and will be made new.

Now, being made new does not mean your teeth are fixed, your face is not wrinkled, that your idea of self has improved. It means new, re-seen, reclaimed, re-known in God, of God, and as God. The tree is God, the cloud is God, and the one that was once your enemy as of God. We use the word *of* there expressly, so that you don't believe that we are inviting you to worship your old enemy. You have left the tea table by then. It simply means you hold no recrimination because you have returned to innocence. The innocent heart does not seek to punish, does not seek to rule, does not seek to gain at the cost of another's loss.

Each of you who hears these words are being attuned through this transmission, and this transmission is at a pitch or level that has not been brought through the man before you until this day. The tone that is being sung here is in restoration to divinity at a level that had been denied, not by the man before you, but by the collective that had said no. The opening is here. The window is not only open—it is open so wide that the light will not be prohibited from shining in.

The task before you now is actually a rather simple one: To make a new agreement that God knows you as you are, just as you are, with your shame, with your courage, with your predilection for this or that, with the habit you can't seem to break, with the difficulty that you address your relationships. Let all things be known. Let all things be seen. Let the great light shine, and allow yourself to bask within it. The claim is:

"I Am Known. I Am Known. I Am Known."

If you cannot allow the Divine to know you, and we suggest it already does, you will continue to seek to meet your needs, make manifest through desperate acts, longing, frustration, and damning what you don't get, or damning the one that seems to have it. Your idea of sin is doing something bad. All a sin is, is another way of denying the Divine. Sinfulness is not what you think. It is not a terrible thing. It is usually unconscious. "I am so jealous of him and what he has." The envy that you seek to employ in that interaction is the denial of the Divine—again, born in lack, that there can't be enough, that you have been given the crumb while he eats happily the cake.

Each of you here who see these words, who hear these words, who comprehend these words, will be known anew. But to be known anew, you must be seen, you must be shown. You must rest naked to the Divine, resplendent just as you are, to allow the Divine permission to receive each aspect of you so that it may move to itself in a higher state of frequency. "What does that mean?" he asks. When you offer your shame to the Divine, it is transformed. When you offer your longing to God, it is known anew. When you offer the belief in self and personality that demands she gets what she wants when she wants it, you are met in true need as they occur.

Imagine living a life where what was required was met by you, when what was chosen by you was chosen in alignment with a higher will, when the receipt of good, or requirement of good, was known by you because it *was* the expression of the Divine, operative as all things, that you had begun to experience. You see, the Upper Room is not a store, but it is a place without lack, and a level of consciousness where it is the father's or the mother's good wishes to grant you the Kingdom. We said *father* or *mother* to impose an idea, known through religious tenets that are in fact true, upon a world that is confused by them. "How could God allow this terrible thing to happen?" is a confused idea. You are creators. You choose your world. You made war. You made famine. You starve your brothers and sisters in a belief that there will not be enough for you. But when you lift to the Kingdom, beyond separation, beyond the mandates of separation, you are welcome to receive the gifts of the Kingdom as they are present. You become the gift of the Kingdom through this alignment. And it is your presence and being that support all others in requiring their own mandate for development and growth.

Now, in our texts we have supported an agreement for the entrainment to the higher realm through progressive instruction. We have no expectation that all will read these texts, but we have great expectation that those who attend to them will become the doorways for many who follow, because it is the alignment you hold through these teachings that supports the window opening wider and wider. As each one of you awakens to your true nature, you awaken a thousand more by nature of presence. And this is how you be—how you show up at your job, how you teach your class, how you wash the windows to let more light in. The being that you are, in the Upper Room, from the Upper Room, claims a world made new, because the level of vibration or tone she holds will lift all things to it by presence and being.

We will take a pause for Paul. Please be quiet. We will resume speaking in two minutes. This is indeed in the text. Period. Period. Period.

(PAUSE)

The world that you see before you is actually shifting to a new level of frequency, a new expression. When something changes, there is great disruption. When you are changing the stations on a radio, you may encounter static. You may understand yourself in a space of change now, where what was known is not present in the ways that it has been, and what seeks to be born is not yet confirmed by your experience. This is a useful time, and a very necessary time. When you are cleaning a closet, you must take a look at what is about to be discarded, understand why you no longer require it. And the closet is being emptied now, and the accumulation of debris, that which must be relinquished, is being experienced by the collective. The choices made in fear, known by each of you as what you have known yourselves through in fearful acts or in collective agreement to fear, must be re-seen so that you may choose anew.

When we speak to will, we speak to the aspect of the Divine that operates as will. Some of you foolishly say, "I have free will. I will do what I want." And of course, while that is true at a certain level—indeed, you have free will, it is cherished— even this is of God because all things are of God. The restoration of will to its divine nature does not deprive you of choice. It supports you in a higher choice than perhaps you would have made prior.

To understand choice is to understand desire. When desire is met in the light, it may bloom in beautiful ways. When desire is held in the shadows, it may be malformed or confused in its requirements. Some of you say, "I think I know who I am. I desire to know myself more." If you give this desire to Source—"I allow my growth to be under the purview, in the benediction, of True Source"—you create a path in light. If the spiritual path that you choose is one of achievement—"I must be seen as spiritual, I must have a dais to sit upon, I must be the miracle worker, and no one else"—you have claimed a path in shadow masquerading as light. There is no one more spiritual than the one beside him.

There are different levels of amplitude and vibrational accord that one may align to through progress. But the progress itself, whether or not you know it, is primarily the byproduct of allowance and surrender and gifting will to the higher realm so that it may be employed. To understand the self as in the employ of the Divine is to allow the will to be utilized in a high way.

He interrupts the teaching. "Well, lots of people believe they are doing God's will and chaos ensues." That is not what we are speaking of. We are not speaking of any other calling than being, presence and being. You are still in choice here, but this choice is made by alignment. And the choices accrued in this place of being will always teach you what you require and provide what you require, be it a lesson that one must learn or a choice to care for the self in a way that is necessary, which will be met by the choice met or guaranteed in reception by you.

Some of you say to us, "Well, I pray all day long, I get nothing." Your expectations of what you should receive must be understood anew—your idealization of outcome, your belief in what you should have, precluding what might be gifted to you. The five-year-old child wants a car. He watches his parents drive. His feet don't reach the pedals. This child cannot have a car. Terrible things could occur. Instead, the child receives the toy car, enjoys it for a time, and then one day, years later, he or she may drive. You understand yourselves as such. When you strive for the high place spiritually, without understanding the level of alteration that you must undergo to maintain the high tone, you can create confusion. While we support our students in their learning to the level that they may hold the frequency and choose in high ways, we do not rush this process. We would rather you keep your feet on the ground, with your head in the clouds, than be blown by a wind to a level of tone that you cannot manage psychically, emotionally, or physically.

"What does that mean?" he asks. Each text we have given you has supported a level of attunement that may be maintained in manifestation, and maintained, supports you in accruing the next level of vibrational tone and the awareness that accompanies it. As you progress, the texts fall away. The need for the attunements are gone because you have embodied at this level. When you are aligned in the Upper Room, the progress that occurs is still happening, but without the level of chaos or drama that you have known yourselves through in the lower field. That does not mean that you don't have challenges in the Upper Room, but it does mean that you meet the challenges in very different ways. You have stopped denying the Divine, you have moved to a comprehension of the reality that you are aligning in, and you do understand that each encounter is supportive of your learning, even if it is not what you would choose, in the higher level you have aligned to.

Many of our students, know it or not, embody the teaching and don't know they do. They expect to be turning water into wine. They expect to be receiving dictation as the young man does before you. In fact, *being* this teaching is being as love, is being as compassion, is being as truth, and knowing those before you as of God, or Source, if you wish, regardless of your expectations of what they should be or how they perhaps should act.

When we say these words now, we are saying them for all who will ever hear them: The Divine will not lie. It will not exclude. It cannot. Truth cannot lie, and God cannot be in deceit. To move to this level of agreement is to reclaim innocence, or a purified state of expression. This does not mean you don't like your back rubbed or your nice drink before dinner. It does not mean you are a saint. It does mean you have claimed the Kingdom, and indeed are the expression of it, and your presence and being will be available to all who hear the sound of the song of your expression. The claim "I know how I serve," which we have taught in prior texts, is the claim of expression. And the being that you are, at this level of tone, is the window, is the doorway, is the illumination, that transforms the world you see.

Thank you for your presence. Stop now, please.

(PAUSE)

What stands before you today is opportunity to release and to recognize your participation in the ideas that have held you, claimed you in separation. The identity that you have known yourself through, forged through separation, wishes to know itself in a higher amplitude, and its consent is participatory to the action you are now engaging in. When the personality has said, "Yes, the idea of who I am may be moved to a higher strata of vibration," the aspects of self that would demand to be seen, demand to be seen anew, will come forth to be re-seen.

And the claim we make today—"It will be so"—is the Manifest Divine supporting this act of re-creation.

Some of you say, "I like who I am. There is nothing I wish to change, thank you." This is not about changing. It's about recognizing where aspects of self have been ruling a small country and mayhem has ensued as a result. The higher alignment will guarantee one thing—that you are no longer choosing in fear. And this choice alone, to hold this level of tone, will alter the landscape you express through. The idea of self, you see, known through and born in separation, equivocally claims itself as separate from Source because it holds no other bounty. Why would not the one who believes there will not be enough scavenge for further, for more, and gain more only to realize the fruits are nothing?

When the True Self claims things or moves towards manifestation, it is operating from a different sphere, a recognition of Source and abundance in Source. And the True Self, when recognized as the dominant source of your experience here, will begin to claim many things that you did not believe you could hold. "What does that mean?" he asks. The one who feels denied in love may know love in a new way. The one who believed she would never be recognized for her work may discover recognition, not in a way that appeases the structure of ego, but in a way that supports the identity and further sharing of her abilities. Each of you says yes at the level you can hold, and the manifestations that occur from the Upper Room are always congruent to what the identity knows and has agreed to.

Now, some of you desire wealth. There is not a thing wrong with wealth. It is not a bad thing or a good thing. It is simply something else you might learn through. You might as well begin to understand that any teaching of abundance need not exclude wealth, but if it is a true teaching, it is not *about* it. Wealth may be an occurrence, but the true teaching is the comprehension that Source is all things, and all things may be claimed in Source. But you are not striving for wealth. You do the work before you, perhaps, if there is work to be done, in an awareness of the fruits of your work. But you are not doing this work in order to achieve as much as receive. And once you understand the difference here, it is far easier to partake in the great banquet that is laid before you.

"What does that mean?" he asks. Well, imagine there is a table where everyone may be fed, where there is no lack. The awareness of this table is the awareness of bounty. When you take a seat at this table, you have what you need. You don't pile your plate too high. You don't shove some food in your pocket to save for a later day. You understand that the table is there, and all who have agreed to this table are present and partaking of the bounty therein. When you comprehend that what expresses at this table are all things that may be known, you will understand that what is before you is what is required for you for the day you sit in, or the moment you sit in. The idea of the day as a period of time is useful primarily in metaphor. "Give us this day, this time, this experience of being." It is not sunrise to sunset as much as the moment you sit in, which is of course the only moment that God may be known.

Now, when you understand that the gift of the Kingdom is not what is in the Kingdom, but the experience *of* the Kingdom, you will not put the cart before the horse any longer. Those of you who strive for things, who believe God is a gift that gives what you want, will be surprised with the ease that manifestation occurs when you have simply gone into agreement with Source as itself, and the alignment to Source provides what is required. What is required is in many ways the byproduct of your expression, of the being you are and the necessities, requirements, that are needed at this juncture, in this moment of receptivity. When you ask us questions—"Will my marriage last?" "Will my child be happy?"—we answer as we are allowed. We do not intervene in your personal lives as much as remind you who you are and what you may claim therein.

Your ideas of who you should be are meritful in some ways. "I should be a nice man, do good things." "I should be a happy woman and give myself joy so that I may share it with others." These are fine in their own ways. But understand, friends: The joy that you seek is a state of being, being in joy, and the claim of being kind is actually replaced by recognition of truth of the deep love of God for all of its creations. When you have aligned in the Upper Room, you have no need to be nice, to try to be kind. You are not efforting good manners. You are being, at the level of amplitude where the transmission you hold cannot judge and does not fear. When you are not operating in judgment or fear, the consequence is simple. You see truth. You see the struggle of the one before you. You do not judge her for her struggle. You claim the truth of her being through the resonance you hold.

Now, in prior instruction, you were taught to state the claim—"I know who you are in truth, I know what you are in truth, I know how you serve in truth; you are free, you are free, you are free"—and this is always appropriate. But at the level of alignment you are coming to, you are moving into expression as the Monad. In other words, friends, the truth of your being is transmitted by being. The statement of expression—"I know who I am, what I am, how I serve"—*is* who you are, so you no longer are required to state it. And because you hold this, the co-resonance of your field is a blessing to all you encounter.

Now, in this case, by *blessing* we mean the presence of God upon the thing seen. You *are* the presence of God upon this thing seen. You are no longer trying to fix people, which in almost all cases is your idea of getting them to resemble what you think they should be. The truth of your being expresses differently. The being that you are, at this level of presence, occupies a space in vibration. This space extends to wherever your consciousness may land or agree to go to. You believe you are here in this room—this floor, these walls around you. You are actually in the Upper Room, receiving this dictation from there, and you are elsewhere as well. You are with yourself in other lives, in other days in memory, in your idea of the future as well.

Consequence of creation is not limited in linearity, by linearity, or by your ideas of what can be conceived. The consequence of being, at this level of tone, is that consciousness is available in experience beyond your idea of what can be. So you are in multiple identities in multiple ideas of time, and the expression you hold as the Monad is in radiance as all of them. In other words, friends, you don't fix the problem on the corner of the block by going to the corner of the block. You stand where you are, you know yourself in fullness, and you claim the presence of the Divine upon what you see. You are not fixing.

You are not renegotiating anything. You are aligning what you see, or may be held elsewhere, to the truth that is infinite, that is ever-present and always. Your idea of where you can be and what you may know are in almost all cases limited by the ideas that the collective has chosen to know itself through. The claim we offered you prior—"I am free, I am free, I am free"—lifts you beyond the old, beyond the parameters of false agreement, to a level of agreement where what is true is always true, and what you may know may be aligned to in truth.

Some of you say to us, "Well, I want to know everything. Let me know all things." If you were to know all things, you would no longer have the experience of learning that is required of you. And even in the Upper Room, in a higher state of expression, your learning ensues—in somewhat different ways, but it continues. You have made many things in a lifetime. The reflection of your past creations surround you. You are accountable to these creations, yes. And as you re-see them from the higher template of the Upper Room, they will be re-known.

Now, if you understand that everything in manifestation is in energy, and concretized by thought, named and held in solidity by all who have agreed to the name—"That is an institution, we call it a bank," "That is something of nature, we call it an ocean or a tree"—when you understand that these things are all in tone, in oscillation, and your lifting of the self to the Upper Room claims your agreement to what you see in the higher octave that you experience, "all things made new" is the act of recognition of the Source of all things as demonstrated by one who knows who he is, what she is, and how she serves.

Each of you before us say these words, "I know who I am,

what I am, how I serve," in a slight comprehension of what they truly mean and signify. If you understood only one of those phrases in full realization, the consciousness you hold would be completely transformed. But you learn what the meaning is experientially as you can hold it. To understand or realize the claim "I know who I am in truth" would qualify you for sainthood by your own admission, and that is not the purpose here. When one truly knows who he is, he knows who all others are, and he loves them because he cannot not love them.

The instructor you knew by the name of Jesus was trained in this way. This is not a new teaching, and anyone who has walked this plane in a realized state has been indoctrinated by the instruction you are receiving. We have taught for a very long time, if you wish to use time as a structure or frame, and how we teach has never altered. It has always been in vibration and tone, but in the ways that were appropriate for the cultures and times we chose to teach through.

Now, before you sits a man who is in training still, not very different from the rest of you, but he is here to learn who he truly is, as are the rest of you. All the students of these texts are here to learn who they truly are. When the old personality self has fulfilled its use, it is actually discarded. You do not carry a personality from lifetime to lifetime. There are degrees of comprehension through similarity, but the tone of the soul is what moves between lives. And it is the tone of the soul in acceleration that mandates change, or an altering of the structure of being.

You are altered by these teachings. You like to think of

changed as improved, but in this way it's rather different. We have never improved anything. We have restored many things. We have seen many people on many paths with the same deep yearning for reconciliation with God, and because we know who we are, we may show you who you are. The truth of our expression has come by different names in different times. You may know us as Melchizedek. You may know us as the Christ Truth, because that is how we define ourselves as a teaching. We are not human beings, although some of us have known ourselves through form. Indeed, we are your teachers, as you choose to be taught.

Heresy, you understand, is not claiming you are Christ. Heresy is claiming you are the only one. And we cannot be, because each of you are as well, all of you are as well, but unrealized yet because you have been so moored in the trenches and the gallows of the lower field that you no longer look up at the sky and experience your self in wonder. *Your self in wonder* is correct. "I am of that sky and of all things in that sky and of all that created the sky and the earth below me. I know myself as one with the Source of my being, and as I know I claim all things in agreement to this."

The path before some of you may feel arduous for a time. "Why am I dealing with this again? Why am I fighting that battle yet again?" Everything is an opportunity to learn, and there are things that you've ignored, said, "I will get to that someday," and then chosen to ignore your own statement. Your letting it lie in the wayside requires you to claim it and offer it again. The offering that you made in this teaching already—the personality structure brought to higher use, aligned to Source—does not dismantle personality as much as it reclaims it. And the aspects of self that you require an encounter with are about to be seen.

Now, if you perceive this as a gift, you will encounter many things very quickly and move into a higher way of experiencing yourself. If you keep trying to push things back into the darkened room where they just escaped, you will have a battle before you. There are aspects of all of you, forged in pain, disassociated from your true natures, that require sight and response and realignment.

You will say this, if you wish:

"On this day I choose to allow every aspect of myself that requires sight to be seen in loving ways. I give myself permission to see all things so that they may be made new in equivalency, in truth, in the high light of the Upper Room."

When you agree to this, you support the process you are engaging in now.

He interrupts the teaching. "Will there be a time when we are no longer looking at the old? Will there come a time when I am no longer worried or ashamed or frightened?" In fact, Paul, it is already here. Much of what you do is born in your tainted memory. Self-perception as the one who should worry or be afraid continues to claim you because you rely upon it. But what is no longer true is that you are no longer energized by it. It is a passing thing. "I will eat the piece of chocolate off the countertop although I know I should not." In fact, you had no need for the chocolate, but it was there and you ate it again. You understand, yes.

Now, many of you say, "Can this happen in my lifetime?" We will give you the same answer. It is happening now. It is always now. This lifetime is an idea, a sequence of exchanges known through time, or your idea of time, under a label of a personality, that was educated perhaps, reared in love or anger—it matters not. What you learned is what you learned, but who you are expresses well beyond this lifetime and always will. In other words, friends: It is now. It is now. It is now. And presence and being is the expression of now, at whatever level of amplitude you are choosing to learn through and by.

"What does that mean—*by?*" You learn *through* your experiences and you learn *by* your choices. What you choose creates experience, which becomes your instruction. When the motives of one have aligned to the higher, you learn in higher ways. When you perpetuate the old idea of self who demands to be seen as the only one, the highest or the lowest of all, you claim the old again and again and again. Your liberation is here, and for one reason: You have said yes, and this great *yes,* this wonderful *yes,* will claim you on a path that will carry you forward, with escort, to the Kingdom as your experience.

We will take a pause for Paul. We will return in two minutes.

(PAUSE)

Each of you says yes, with the agreement in participation to what is about to begin. *About to begin* is correct, Paul. Each of you are present for a re-knowing of self beyond the structure of personality that you have learned through thus far. If you allow the Divine to know you in fullness, you would know yourselves in an altered state. The blemishes that you carry, the thumbprints on the faulty glass that you hold before the world, may be made new by your agreement to it. The gift of this morning's teaching was reconciliation with the truth of your being. This time we offer you something other—the claim of knowing as may be invoked beyond any creation you have known yourselves through.

We will explain this for the students here. Your idea of something that once occurred becomes your idea of history, and you claim identity through the history you have carried and invoked. When you claim, "I am Word" through this or that, you claim the action of the Divine upon this thing or that. "I am Word through that memory of my pain" is actually far more effective than what happened, because what you carry is the memory, and it is the memory of the thing that taints your perception, less so than the thing itself. When you lift yourself to the Upper Room, the claims that we offer you here—"I Have Come; Behold, I make all things new; It will be so; God Is, God Is, God Is"—are all claims of truth that may be recognized and realized from this level of tone or vibration.

The work prior was supporting you in this alignment that you may now hold and choose to hold. The claim of the day—"I Am Known, I Am Known, I Am Known"—is again a statement of truth. You are not asking God to know you. You have been denying that God knows you all these times, all these lives, through all these agreements to separation. But on this day we choose to support each of you in the alignment that may be claimed by you in this moment of time, or your understanding of time.

You may say this after we speak the words, if you wish:

"I Have Come. I Have Come. I Have Come. Behold, I make all things new. It will be so. God Is. God Is. God Is."

Now, align to the truth of the last statement:

"God Is. God Is. God Is."

You are not invoking it. You are not desiring it. You are claiming its full presence as and through you, and as and through all things.

And now, when you say these words, we invite you to experience the full meaning of them:

"I Am Known. I Am Known. I Am Known."

Let this be claimed for you as well:

You Are Known. You Are Known. You Are Known.

And allow every aspect of yourselves to be known by this. We thank you each for your presence. Stop now, please.

DAY THREE

What stands before you today is a new agreement: "The idea of who I was has served a purpose. I have utilized it as well as I might. And I am ready now to forsake the idea of self that was so indoctrinated by fear." The choice is yours, you see.

You are not leaving yourself. You are reclaiming yourself in the high order of the Upper Room. The triumph of this teaching is indeed a world made new, and the gift you each bring to this world is the identity you have reclaimed in the Upper Room as the True Self.

Now, understand True Self. This is not a structure of identity that has been manufactured. It is the essence of yourself, the true nature of your being. And to ascribe it properties of personality would in many ways be to contaminate it with an idea claimed from the lower realm. The Upper Room, you see, is Christ consciousness, and the aspect of self that manifests here is indeed the True Self or the Monad. Its ascriptions, its province, is being. And its presence and being, at this level of amplitude and tone, is what reclaims the world. To assume that your True Self is polite, is nice, does what she's expected to do, would be confused. To comprehend that the aspect of you that is in allowance here, and is reclaiming every aspect of you in true nature, is the aspect of God come as you will announce it in truth. Who said that God was polite? Who said that God likes its tea at the afternoon hour? The Monad as you—Who Has Come, Who Has Come, Who Has Come—is in decree of a great tone and sound: The great "I Am," yes, but not "I am Sheila" or "I am Roger." "I am the True Self that reclaims all things in the true nature of being."

Now, personality exists here still, but do not confuse it. Your idea of self, the masquerade you have been playing, has an anchor still in the lower realm. You know your favorite television show. You know your best friend's name. These things exist. They are yours to partake in. But the claim that is be-

ing made for you now—"I am in the Upper Room; I Have
Come, I Have Come, I Have Come"—claims all aspects of
self, and then all aspects of the world, in the high order you
have moved to equivalency with.

Equivalency must be understood again. Everything operates in equivalency. As you reincarnate, and we use that word
intentionally, as the Monad or True Self, the architecture of
being is actually translated and the vibration you echo consol-
idates the Monad and reclaims what it encounters in truth. In
truth a lie will not be held. And the announcement of being,
from the Upper Room—"Behold, I make all things new"—is
the announcement of the Creator upon its creations through
the vehicle that the Creator is utilizing, which is the incarnate
self.

Now, the change you undergo through participating in this
act has nothing to do with what you think. Your idea of what
you will be in this high strata is relatively confused because
your bias of what should be holy, what should be claimed, announces you in defiance of the Monad. We will explain this
for Paul, who is asking. Your structure of personality, the idea
of self, extends into your imagination. So your idea of who
you are in a re-articulated state, the Monad as physical self, is
endowed with your ideas of what that must be. The moment
you relinquish these ideas, the alchemical process of manifestation will claim you in perfect ways, but if you are still ascrib-
ing meaning—"In the Upper Room I wear chiffon," "In the
Upper Room I have a date," "In the Upper Room everything
comes as I say it must"—will demand that you partake in the
lower realm for more instruction.

There is much to learn in the lower realm. We do not discard it. We translate it. Imagine you've known a language where every other word was informed by the idea of fear, and you claim a new language that does not speak in fear, does not invoke in fear. Then the manifestations of this world, without fear, will align you to your true natures, because you are no longer operating in vibrational accord with the old self entrenched in fear, seeking to absolve itself of guilt, so that one day you might be ready for entrance into the Kingdom. The Kingdom, you understand, *is here, is here, is here,* and can be entered through the expression in vibrational accord of the Monad.

Now, the action of the Monad, once incarnated in a realized state, is the alchemical act of manifestation. And the act of manifestation from the Monad is re-articulation and the lifting of all things to the one note sung—the Word, if you wish to call it that, or the true nature of all things. The disfigurement that you have all engaged in of self and of others, the defilement of the manifest world sown in greed and denial of the Divine, will be re-seen, and can and must be re-seen, from the Upper Room for the manifest world to claim itself in truth.

Now, what is not in truth is that which denies the Divine. Most of you think of heresy as speaking out against the church or a religious idol. Heresy, in fact, is the innate denial of divinity in what you see and experience. To understand that all things must be of God, whether or not you agree with them as a personality self, is an enormous step for most of you. Because you have been taught to judge in fear so much that you re-articulate fear at every opportunity, you contaminate the world with more and more of the same. The choice must be yours now. The progression of this teaching has finally en-countered itself through you, and each of you, as you are on the cusp of a new life, in a new accord, for the benefit of all you encounter.

Now, those of you who say, "Oh, this sounds lovely, let me get my good outfit on so that I can go about blessing the world," would be quite confused. The action you express at this level of intonation is in accord as and with the Monad or the Christ vibration. It is the Christ that does the work, not Sheila who has dressed for church. It is Josh who arrives and says, "Here I am, I offer myself in fullness," and it is the aspect of Josh in an aligned state, in a reclamation of true identity, that claims his world in all ways as the truth of being.

"What does that mean?" he asks. To reclaim the truth of being in what you see is to know who you are and what you see as of one Source. The denial of the Divine is in opposition to this. "That terrible man cannot be of God." "That terrible event cannot be of God." Now, God did not create the event. Perhaps you did, or someone acting in fear. But to realize God where the event has been is to reclaim manifestation or the presence of the Divine where it has most been denied. Where God has most been denied is what you see as suffering, is what you see as poverty, is what you see as disease. When God is love, when God is known as love, many things will change, because love will not harm, love will not defile, and love knows itself in innocence.

"What does that mean?" he asks. Love knows itself in a purified state. The Christ expression is pure, untainted by fear. The manifestation of this innocence upon the material realm is not only a cleansing. It's a reclaiming of what was once laid in waste, what was once defiled, what was once left in ruin, to be re-known in love, and consequently resurrected. The idea of judgment, that you are judged for your sins and will pay penance for them, must be reinterpreted now to understand that what you would call your sins, or the denial of the Divine out-pictured by you, is the reason you suffer. When you no longer claim these things, when you allow them to be reclaimed in the high octave of the Upper Room, all things are made new, and you are reborn in innocence.

Now, understand what innocence does not mean. It does not mean you don't have a temper. It does not mean you don't enjoy physical pleasure. You have a body. You need to feed it, you need to bathe it, and please, hopefully, enjoy it on occasion. The Divine as you, expressed through you, also knows itself in form. And the schemata you have engaged in—"The bride must wear white," "You must take the veil and forgo the flesh"—is in all ways confused. One may choose a celibate life. One may opt for a life where there is no conflict around desire. But to understand that the Monad expresses in form supports realization of the material realm. Most of you believe that as you ascend in vibration you no longer want what you've wanted, and there is actually truth to this. You no longer want what you've wanted in the way that you've wanted it, but you enjoy a good meal, and you may make love, and you may participate in the great dance of being alive with all the gifts that it offers you.

We will say to the new students: You are encountering yourselves through these teachings, like it or not, and the bias you hold for what should be, anchored in the personality structure, will be unanchored and unmoored. And, indeed, there will be times when logic will fail you here. Your understanding of who you have been is about to be altered, because when memory itself is reclaimed as the Monad, the taint that memory holds, the fear that memory has held, may be known anew.

Now, when memory is known anew, it does not alter fact. Yes, your father died. Yes, your wife left you. Yes, you lost the dog and never found it again. But your agreement to what these things mean and how they have shadowed your experiences is re-known, because you comprehend them, first and foremost, as result of choice, and agreement to fear, and perhaps what was required to be learned at any time in any life. All must be seen as new opportunity. And the reclamation of memory is something we intend to teach, because it has gone on too long that you have suffered at the hands of faulty memory, designed wars in retribution of faulty memory. Because you forgot who you were, all memory is based on a false premise, born in identity that has been manifested in a fearful realm. And the taint that memory holds must be understood as the result of this entrainment.

"When we release our memory," Paul asks, "what happens to what we think?" You have clear vision. You are not seeking to rejoin some idea of self that experienced something once upon a time. You comprehend what was, but you are in the present moment. And the present moment, we always say, is the only moment where God can and will be known. Period. Period. Period. Stop now, please. Indeed, this is the end of the chapter.

2

MEMORY

What stands before you today is not only opportunity, but a release of an idea that has impeded your progress, impeded your recognition of the Divine Self as the actuary, the expression, of your life. Most of you have believed that you are the result of things that happened, and in some ways that may be seen as accurate. But far more than what happened, you are the result of the choices you have made.

When one of you comes before us and asks why something happens, there are many ways to answer. "You chose to learn through the opportunity that you co-created" might be a way we would answer, or you were participatory to a collective belief that you were so entrenched in that there was no other opportunity. An example of this would be a collective event. Each individual participates in the actualization of the collective event, but certainly not by an intention that you would think of as conscious. When one comes before us and says, "I demand things be different," we would often say to them are you willing to *be* different to *receive* the different answer, the different experience? Are you willing to know who you are beyond the obstructions that you have so encased in necessity that you make them so? "I will not be changed," you may say, and then we may answer that is your choice.

Now, when you go to the Upper Room and announce the claim "I Have Come," indeed you put in motion a new way of operating. The strata of vibration that has been the lower realm has been your schoolhouse. When the Upper Room becomes your schoolhouse, you are given new lessons, new ways in which to learn. Some of you would say, "But I know the old way, not the new." In many cases, what is experienced in the Upper Room holds a mirror in the lower. Much of it depends on how you interpret it, which is, again, how you choose. When you choose to learn through fear, you continue to claim opportunities for fear to be your instructor. In the Upper Room fear is not operable. The energy of fear does not express here, so the mandate becomes that you learn in a new way.

The idea of who you were is what we have been addressing thus far, the idea that you may be known anew, that the Divine knows all things, knows your true nature, because it expresses as you. When you deny the history you have held, you create chaos. "I know how to walk to work. Now I don't know how to walk to work." We don't ask that you deny your history. We do ask that you reclaim your memory beyond the institution-alized thinking that you have inherited in familial structure and in collective agreement.

What collective agreement means here is that there are

ways of seeing a world that are mandated by the collective that become entrenched, institutionalized, and consequently you do not understand yourself as expressing beyond them. "There will always be war." "There will always be an economic system that oppresses some." "There will always be religions that disagree." When you claim these things, or simply adhere to them through your expectations of their being there, you understand yourself as in consort to the structures that would inhibit you.

The claim "I am free, I am free, I am free," invoked prior to entering the Upper Room, is the agreement to be free of all of the things that would tether or bind you to the lower strata. The Monad *is* free. She exists, he exists, it exists, beyond time and space as you have known them, and *is* free and is not contaminated and blemished or obstructed by these things of the material realm. What you don't understand yet is that by lifting to the Upper Room you become participatory to the eradication or reclamation of the very things that have hindered the collective.

Now, personal memory can be understood as interpretation. "My father left us when we were ten. My mother never got over it. We didn't have nice clothes. I didn't go to the good school I wanted to. I have a life that is a reflection of the things that I incurred." You may comprehend yourself in such ways, but what you are actually interpreting are events, the ramifications of events, and you have made choices in agreement to them. *You are not your history. You are not what happened to you.* You are who you choose to be, and a result of the choices you make at the level of personality. At the level of truth, you are actually liberated even from those choices because the Monad will not be limited and cannot be limited by personal history.

Paul interrupts the teaching. "I can think of many instances where personal history limits somebody. Somebody has an illness. Somebody has been through something that harms the body and the body no longer operates the way that it might." How you interpret any situation and decide its merit or lack of merit will inform the life you live, yes. But the aspect of you that we call the Monad is not even limited by these things.

Now, you inhabit a physical plane. It is a shared expression of what you believe a world should be. The world that you express through is what the collective has agreed to, and all of the challenges of the physical realm that you experience are indoctrinated by belief and by the expectation of them. You anticipate strife, you anticipate war, and you are not surprised when they arrive. When the collective emerges from the transition it is beginning to undergo, it will not claim the old because the old will have been moved, it will have been released—in some ways easily, in some ways with difficulty—because the collective has chosen to move beyond them, and this must include the institutions that now inhibit you.

Because an institution is no longer present as you have known it does not imply that there must be chaos or ruin. You may have a new structure that may meet the need of the collective in a way that will not be moored in fear, because the collective is moving beyond fear and beyond a race memory that it has held that has been so moored in separation that humanity does not understand itself as of its Source. That is the great gift of the times you are beginning to experience, and will continue to be for several generations. But the pulse of humanity has already made a choice to withstand change, to claim the new. And in order to claim the new the idea of memory must be addressed culturally, which you are beginning to see now.

There have been fraudulent histories perpetrated throughout time, generally to control, or to claim a narrative that a victor of a war would like to perpetuate. When you understand yourself as moving beyond lies, you must also understand that you may experience these lies, have to perceive them, because whether or not you like it, you are indeed participatory to them. "Why is that?" you may ask. Indeed, you are participatory to everything you see and have ever seen. Their creation is not mandated as much by your presence, as your presence contributes to their manifestation.

Now, when a culture has been indoctrinated in a lie, when they perpetuate that lie, that lie will be seen, and there may be chaos as the new seeks to be revealed and the old may be understood as a creation. Everything that has been created in fear will have to be now re-created in the higher template of the Upper Room. And this does not happen by bypassing, by pretending it is not so. It *is* so that you have oppressed your fellows, and karmically you are responsible for all of your creations.

Now, when we say you are participatory to all that you see, in fact you are making it so by your claiming it, by your recognition of it, and by the announcement of it as so. How you decide what something means colors it, gives it form and meaning. And the realization that all things are of Source is impossible for some of you, because you have invested so heavily in your idea of evil that you make the separation somewhat immobile. "There will be good and evil, and I will find the right side to fight on." You may perpetuate any war, in any time, by the faulty use of this logic. When you realize that how you endow something with meaning claims the thing in manifestation, you will understand how responsible you are to your experiences. The choice to know yourselves through memory can be utilized in a very high way or a very destructive one.

We have always said that one incarnates in this field as an opportunity to learn, and in the Upper Room the learning continues, but in a somewhat different way. Your idea of who you are as a person, the identity you have claimed, has always been the way you have comprehended identity within the collective. *Within the collective* means you place yourself in the field with others. You compare your abilities, your physical appearance, your eagerness or lack thereof, to the ones beside you. And you equate your worth with a hierarchical meaning of worth and the legacy of worth that in fact you've inherited. When you know yourself as free, you move beyond even these things, and beyond the limitations that they imply.

"What are those limitations?" he asks. Well, every ceiling that you would ever encounter has one purpose—to keep you within it. And separation itself, an idea of separation, if you wish, that has been made concretized through the collective agreement to it, is not true. It is a vast lie that you have aligned to in such a way that all identity holds within it an agreement to a structure that was no longer true, was never true, and can never be true when it was first invoked. What this simply means is the limitation of what you're allowed by way of true knowing, true expression, and true being has been prohibited by a lie.

Now, the collective memory of separation is a radical one. It has been invoked through every religion, with perhaps a keyhole that you may find your way through to the truth of your expression. Every religion may operate as a doorway, but one must have the key with which to know the truth and enter therein. The teaching you are receiving is actually the basis of all religion, however misconstrued they may have become. There is an aspect in all of you that remembers this information, that knows it to be so. And its equation, which means its alignment to the manifest world, can only be invoked through the True Self, or you may call it the Christ or the Monad or the Universal Self, that holds the knowing and is the key, is the way forward.

The realization of the Monad you may call enlightenment, you may call awakening. We prefer the latter. To move to an awakened state is not to sit on a dais and be the soothsayer. It is to be the person you are in a realized state. Realization is knowing, and when you operate at this level you are known and knowing at the same time. In other words, you are not excluding the Divine from any fabric of your expression, because the cloth that you are made of is the Divine, has always been, and can only be.

The awareness of this is gradual for most of you. To awaken too quickly would unmoor the idea of identity and displace it, prior to your aligning at the level that we are claiming you at. The level that we are claiming you at is the highest level humanity can receive while maintaining form. But to abolish the old with the stroke of an ax would leave you bleeding, would leave you terrified. And we do not teach in fear. Some of you have experiences in the higher octaves that you cannot assimilate, and you get confused or find yourselves lost or struggling with information or experience that you cannot process or utilize in productive ways. What use is it to know the truth if you cannot operate in truth? What is it to know the Divine when you are still hungry for the things of the world? You must move towards these things in receptivity, and indeed trust that the level of tone that you may hold is the level that you can align to, and productively, because as you align at each level and you assimilate the information that is received therein, the bounty that is actually available to you at each level, the residual affect of the transformation you undergo, is far easier than you would ever make it by trying to embark on this journey with the personality as your ammunition.

The personality self, you see, is reinterpreted, re-known, in the Upper Room. It exists, but in an altered state. And while your will is required for this journey to ensue, because the alignment of the will to the high will is what aligns you to each stage of your development, it is not the one that is triumphant that is personality, but the Monad that has claimed all things made new. We will explain this for Paul. We have already addressed the deification of personality, but the belief that you must strive or must imbibe something to have access to a higher level of consciousness is actually faulty. You may have those experiences, but they must be utilized in a high way, or they operate merely as experience and not instruction. You may learn instruction by walking headway into a door, or you may understand the door needs to open, or you may continue to bang your head. Unless you realize that the door opens, the experience of bumping one's head has not been meritful.

Now, the egoic structure may operate in a healthy way.

Comprehending one's true worth—no better, no worse, than the one beside you—is highly useful in this endeavor. It is the distortion of the egoic structure that is so challenging for all of you. And when we begin to retrieve memory, true memory, aligning memory to its true nature, beyond interpretation but by simply being and allowing what was so to *be* so, you will begin to comprehend the who that you are without requiring yourself to rest so very heavily on anecdote, on experience, and an entrenchment in the meaning that you have given to your personal lives and the events you've experienced, and the collective as well.

As the collective lifts and encounters the creations it has agreed to, be it enslavement of another, be it the misuse of hierarchy, the abuse of economic structures and religious teachings, humanity will comprehend how the use of these things may have been employed once in productive ways, but how the distortion of them became institutionalized. When this is recognized, be it a political system or a religious one, new choices can be made. Not reactive choices—it is never our presence to teach punishment or vindication—but a new idea that will be born through the collective desire for the new to be made new, to be made so, to be comprehended and seen as so.

We will take a pause for Paul, only two minutes, and we will continue for a brief time.

(PAUSE)

Recognition of what you have chosen and how you have chosen will become a requirement. You don't get a free pass, you see. Your creations surround you. How you have chosen, what you have chosen, what you have decreed be so, is in fact the life you are living. You would seek to excuse your own behaviors. "I didn't know any better." "I didn't mean to be so" this or that. And while those things may be true, you are still required to see your part in any experience. You cannot do this work and blame your brother or sister for your misfortune. To do so is to enable separation.

This does not mean that you don't recognize where you are harmed, how you were harmed, or who brought the harm forth. It does mean that you understand that you are actually complicit to the events of your lives. These are opportunities to learn choices that were made, or in some cases karmic experiences that you are seeking to utilize to learn. Nothing will be learned until it is first seen. Nothing will be recognized when you are seeking to deny it. And nothing new will be chosen when you are demanding the old menu, based in prior circumstance and history, be what you order from.

The gift of this teaching in memory will continue later. We are going to teach you what memory is not, and how to align to truth at the cost of the small self's desire to interpret what once was through a faulty lens with a basis in fear.

We thank you each for your presence. Stop now, please. Yes, in the text. Period. Period. Period.

(PAUSE)

What stands before you today is a new choice: "I am willing to absolve myself for the memories I hold that have incorporated as personality that deny my True Self. I am willing to release an idea of what I have been, known through memory, that claims me in separation. I am choosing to know myself in the high order of the Upper Room, wherein all things are made new."

Now, the choice is yours, and the idea of forgiveness of memory is actually useful here. You've incorporated ideas shrouded in history, known as memory, that claim you in separation, and you align through memory to realities beyond what you see. In other words, friends, when you move into the present moment and you understand that all things are now, you also understand that memory is a way to transport the idea of consciousness outside of your idea of the present moment and confirm an identity that is no longer true. You are no longer two years old, or perhaps twenty or forty. There is an aspect of you that *is* two and twenty and forty, but your memory of two and twenty and forty is actually in agreement to the idea of consciousness and identity that you held at the time. In other words, the memory is faulty. It is perceived through the eyes of the one who experienced through a claim in limitation. What this means is that the two-year-old cannot comprehend, or even the twenty-year-old cannot comprehend, what the Monad or True Self can claim as new.

Now, when something is claimed anew, it is not eradicated. It is re-seen and lifted. And in the offering of memory to the Upper Room to be claimed anew, you are simply aligning the ideas that you hold, born in linear time, about what once perhaps was to a new sight, a new way of being and seeing. The inherited structures, the ways you were taught to perceive, inform how you see most things. The ascriptions of others, the choices others make, that become codified in a life, that inform individuals' choices, ways of being seen and seeing, can indeed be made new once you understand that the idea of self, informed by memory, can indeed be reclaimed beyond the old, beyond the old ascription, beyond the old identity, that while useful at one time mandates its old claims be sorted through in the present moment.

Paul interrupts the teaching. "I think I understand what you mean—I am not sure. Can you re-state this, please?" The idea of who you were has been inherited through collective agreements, the structures of reality that you have been taught through. Much of what you believe yourself to be is actually informed by these things, and memory is accrued in relation to these things. You remember yourself as a child wishing to be older. Now you are older, you wish the self to be young again. Your ideas of who you are, are in most ways relational. And the obstructions to realization that we are teaching you now are artifacts in memory that can and will be reborn or re-seen from the Upper Room.

We will offer you this now, if you wish it: There is nothing that was once seen that cannot be re-seen from a higher perspective. We do not invalidate the view from the first floor, but if you go up to the twenty-fifth floor, the view of what was lower is seen from a very different perspective. We are re-identifying you each beyond the ideas of self that you have utilized to foster identity, and reclaiming you each in a new way. When you are relying on memory to tell you who you have been, you reinforce these ideas and you re-create them unintentionally. The small self knows itself through history. It has been appropriated by history. And all that stands in the way of the present moment is your memory of what was and how that plays out in your idea of present time.

Now, there is memory in the Upper Room, but it is not tainted. It is not meaning to claim you in different ways. You understand what was. You accept what was. You have made choices based in this, and indeed will continue to, but you are no longer framing your reality through an identity that was fostered in shadow. If you understand that the one who has known poverty and continues to fear poverty is making choices in fear, the one who believes he cannot be loved holds his history of lovelessness and his memory of it as a shield that would stop him from receiving the love that is already present. When you release the idea of who you have been, you are not releasing what happened. You are releasing the misidentification of self through a trajectory born in memory and agreed to in a collective way through a culture that ascribes great meaning to an idea of what was.

We will explain this further if we are allowed. Any history that you may hold invokes the identity of others as participants in the same play—"my father's legacy, my mother's legacy, and their parents', and their cultures'." The legacy of the collective indeed informs your idea of present self. We don't deny these things. But when you have continued to claim a history born in a faulty narrative, one that was claimed by others in agreement to what they were taught, when you release the need to perpetuate an identity born in accruing misinformation about self and who others have been to you, when you release the need to claim identity through past ideas, you move fully into the present moment, where indeed all things may be made new.

Now, the claim has been taught prior: "Behold, I make all things new." It is not the personality structure that is capable of this claim. If you seek to prove this, you will find out very quickly that the best that the small self can do is rearrange the furniture, perhaps paint the walls a brighter color. The idea of something being made new in the Upper Room is the alchemical act of re-creation, of lifting what was, held once in shadow, to the higher vibration where it may be re-seen and re-known.

The idea of personality being made new is not about improving personality. It's about re-comprehending the essence of your being, and aligning to the higher, and allowing the lower to be in service to it. Again, freedom will come when the throne relinquishes its king. If the king is sitting in the throne and it is the throne of the personality, that small king will claim a very small kingdom. When the True Self sits in the throne, the king or the queen claims all things made new because it is the purview of the Divine Self to render all things new.

Each of you before us, each of you who hears these words, who reads these words, one day will know this. The idea of who you are is as a character in a play, and the play that you are enacting is engaging with others who are also engaging in their own plays. The characters you choose are useful ways of experiencing the manifest world. But when the costume is discarded and the mask is released, when the masquerade is ended, what is there in truth is resplendent—the Divine Self, who does no longer require a mask, who allows her full expression to be claimed, made known, and consequently claim all she sees in the high octave she now experiences herself through.

Paul is interrupting. "Are you going to do an exercise in

this? Is this lecture nearly done? What is happening now?"
When we teach through Paul, we listen to his concerns. We
placate some of them and we continue regardless. The text that
is being written is actually not for Paul. It is for the reader. And
the speaker of the text, the man before you, while a student
of the work, is not always the intended audience. Now, when
we teach through him we also comprehend his concerns. He
doesn't understand the teaching of memory yet. "How can we
be without memory?" You are not without memory. But what
you are without is the embellishment of memory in such a way
that disfigures identity, and *disfigures* is a fine word.

The one who was left in shadow as a child, who has been
grown through shadow, who has known herself in shadow, an-
ticipates shadow. She is comfortable there. The memory of
shadow actually informs every day she walks. It may be the
brightest day ever, but she knows herself through shadow. The
Divine Self operating as this being will seek to reclaim every
aspect of her, and in doing so must release the belief that she
is known through shadow only. And as memory perpetuates
this, memory must be claimed in the Upper Room. It is not
that it did not happen. It is true that it is not who you are.
What you thought you were, even who you think you are, is
an idea, and every idea may be re-known in the Upper Room.

You may say these words very softly after we speak them,
if you wish:

"On this day I choose to allow all aspects of self to be re-
known, and I comprehend myself beyond any memory I hold
that would disfigure the identity I choose to learn through.
As I agree to this, I offer memory, and every memory I have

ever held in any time, to be re-known, re-seen, from the
high octave that is the Upper Room. As I say these words I
give permission to the Divine Self to reclaim all memory,
all misidentification, and support myself in this agreement
with the following tone. I know who I am in truth. I know
what I am in truth. I know how I serve in truth. I am free.
I am free. I am free."

[The Guides tone through Paul.]

Let yourself be known. Let yourself be seen. Let yourself
be claimed as you can only be in truth. Period. Period. Period.
Stop now, please.

Indeed, this is in the text.

DAY FOUR

What stands before you today is recognition of what you were.
The idea of the manifest form, who was once two years old, or
twenty, or more, the idea of the body as known through memory, may also be re-known in the Upper Room. Now, form itself is elastic to thought. When you go higher in vibration, the
idea of who you are is altered in many ways because you are no
longer in a construct that is born in a negotiation of the denial
of the Divine. When you lift beyond that denial, you become
the True Self, or express as True Self, and the mandate of form
at this level of tone and vibration is that it aligns you through
itself to a level of recognition of the manifest world as of God.

Now, to understand what this means is that as you align
in a higher template, a recognition of what is always true, as

the body itself acclimates to the new recognition that it is also not separate from God, your perception of form itself is transformed. Now, you know what a chair is. You know what a cloud looks like. But the comprehension of chair and cloud, indeed altered in perception from the high perspective of the Upper Room, is re-seen as what it has always been—an outpicturing of the Divine now known as chair, now known as cloud.

Each of you before us has known form in prior incarnations—or, better said, other incarnations than the one you sit in now. There is an aspect of you that truly knows that form is elastic, that consciousness dictates form. The alignment in the Upper Room reclaims you beyond a kind of solidity—and we say *a kind of* intentionally. If you stub your toe, you will hurt your toe. That is nonnegotiable. But your comprehension of what the toe is, what the internal organs are, what the skin is, what every hair follicle is, is actually altered.

"Altered how?" you may ask. When one denies the Divine, one creates a kind of overlay or a systematic reproach to what is seen. "That is not of God because it cannot be." You may take an example that you wish: "That horrible event. That painful ordeal—that is not of God." The one who encountered that ordeal, who is in negotiation with it as a kind of reality, is in co-resonance with that idea of separation. "That cannot be of God because I am perceiving it as outside of God." But because the perceiver claims identity in what he or she witnesses, she has aligned herself outside of God through that claim.

The altering of reality, as you perceive it now, has been known in gradation. Everything lost its luster through the denial of the Divine. The claim of the body that we have taught in prior texts—"I know what I am in truth"—is an actualization of the realization of form as may be known by the one who has indeed come in manifestation as the Divine Self. You cannot exclude form from the equation and anticipate, expect, or agree to a higher level of tonal alignment. If the body is excluded—"that awful body, that glorious spirit"—you have created separation yet again. Now, the memory of the body is actually an interesting thing to consider. When you are born, you don't know yourself as separate from anything around you. You experience yourself as in a sea of vibration, and as the sea, simultaneously. The idea of separating from the mother is actually a useful metaphor. The child in the womb, who knows itself as of the mother, is initially startled to realize it is no longer in the womb. But the realization of a new environment, at this stage of development, is also the realization that the container that the child was in is of a larger one. In other words, the mother is within the whole as well, as are all things.

As you are acclimated to the self that believes itself as separate, which is done through conditioning, the world is altered for you. And what was once a fluid experience of perception becomes expressed in a rather delineated way. You are given the names of things. You negotiate space, what you can reach for, what you cannot. As you begin to align in an awareness of form—"I am in a body, the body is hungry," "I am in a body, the body needs warmth," "I am in a body, and the body is in pain"—you begin to concentrate on the manifestation of form and confuse it with who you are. It is a confused action. You are of the body, you express through the body, but you are not the body.

Humanity, in most ways, believes itself to be either the

body or the intellect, rarely the spirit because you don't experience spirit in the manifestation of the lower vibrational realm as you may in the higher. The sage may comprehend that there is more than the body. The thinker may comprehend that there is more to life than the mind. But most of you fall into one category or the other. The realization of form as of God, or the realization of the body as holding its own divinity, is an important step for all of you. It is so easy to deny the body its true nature when it doesn't do what you want, look as you wish it to look, heal as you think it should, or move about as you would like. The one who cannot walk is in a body that is as holy as the decathlon runner. The one who stands tall and claims the light is as holy as the one who grovels in darkness. Form is holy regardless of what you think.

Now, memory of form must be understood in two different ways: The body you have grown up in, and the memory of the body at different ages, as well as the prescriptive memory of what a body should be that is inherited by you through interaction with the collective. And the claim of the body as its true nature, which knows itself beyond time.

We will explain this for Paul. He has memory of the body at early ages—his fear of the body, his pleasure at the body, the experience of swimming in the ocean, or hiding in fear from an angry parent. The body holds memory. And the identity that has been moored in body qualifies its sense of safety through the physical realm. The one who knows itself in spirit does not discount form, but is unafraid in the ways that the small self might be. The articulation of form as of God, indeed a process you undertake, is not the divinization of form. It is the reclamation of form as of God. Because you hold memory, and have claimed memory of the body as separate from the Source that is actually held in the vibrational field, even the tissues and the organs hold memory of what they have been claimed as.

Now, each lifetime is an opportunity to develop, and we say the word *develop* because it is what you do. You come out a small infant, you grow into an adult form, perhaps an aged form. This is how you progress through form. You are always growing, whether or not you know it. The recognition of divinity augments this growth, and then ultimately replaces it, because once you truly comprehend the innate divinity of form, form is no longer a requirement for your expression. When the body is seen as Source, an aspect of Source, if you wish, vibrating at a level of tone in congruence with its true nature, the body ceases to express as a necessity.

Now, we operate through Paul, who is in form, and the form that he has taken has known many challenges. He would have preferred not to have a form, because there is an aspect of him that remembers vividly the freedom that comes when one is no longer trapped in an experience of density. We use the word *trapped* intentionally, not because it is an accurate assessment of embodiment, but because it was his experience of finding himself in a body and then wanting to be elsewhere. You will not align in a higher template when the body is being eschewed. You cannot align in the Upper Room if you have relegated the body to the cellar. The memory of the body as separate must be realized as another illustration of indoctrination through separation. We are not negating your memories. We are not wiping the blackboard clean. But what we are doing with you is releasing the grime that has covered the mirror of your experience, the distortion that you have experienced yourselves through. And you will not align in the Upper Room in a new state of comprehension if memory itself seeks to occlude the divinity that is always yours.

What does it mean to know the self as Divine? What it does not mean is that you are having a happy day and you say, "Oh, I must be in the Upper Room. There is not a cloud in the sky." And the moment something difficult happens you deny God in the experience and in yourself. Your realization of divinity is in fact a restorative act. Understand this, all of you. You are being restored, reclaimed, and resurrected. You are being granted the Kingdom. But you cannot embody in the Kingdom when memory itself serves to distort your true nature or what you perceive, and the body itself known by you in memory—"that freckle I always disliked," "that challenge that I never got over," "the perfection that I aspire to that I can never meet," all held by memory and all informing your experience of being. *Your experience of being.* Underline that phrase. It is at issuance here. Some of you mandate that what you have known must be correct because you have invested time and energy into it. If you believe a lie hard enough, that does not make it true, and many of you would rather invest in a lie than be reclaimed, or offer the self to be reclaimed, in what we call the Upper Room, and for the very simple reason that your sense of identity is predicated on the lie that is born in separation and seeks more and more evidence to confirm itself as separate from its Source.

The True Self, you see, already comprehends this. And the body itself also comprehends what it is formed from. But you must align to that knowing, not in an intellectual way, but in a realized way. Realization is knowing, and the knowing of the body as of God does not dismiss your experiences, but it washes away the residue of the dark wave that has tainted your idea of form. Imagine you are a pure being, an innocent being, a being that knows who and what it is. And imagine a dark wave, claimed by separation, manifesting, caressing, and then overtaking. This is not evil, although evil may be known by this wave. This is denial of Source. As soot from a factory chimney that overtakes the town, separation has claimed the manifest world, and memory invoked by this separate self will always continue separation because it will always have a thousand examples of why God cannot be.

The claim "God Is," which we will instruct in very shortly, is the Manifest Divine as claimed by you as and through all things. It is the antidote to the denial of the Divine. And the claim of "God Is," the realization of truth where the lie has been held, will wash you clean, renew you, if you wish. Now, to be free of sin, if you truly wish to know what that means, is to be free of the denial of the Divine. It has nothing to do with what you might think. An action that one might believe to be sinful simply may be how something has been described by the collective. But your idea of sin—be it gluttony, pride, avarice—may all be seen as ways that you deny the Divine. When you know there is enough, you don't grab for more than you need. When you know your inherent worth, there is nothing to be jealous of. The transformation you undergo is not towards sainthood. It's towards the recognition of who and of what you have always been.

Now, because the body holds memory, and the energetic field claims manifestation in accordance with expectation and most of your expectations are known through memory, the reclamation of memory is an essential part of holding and maintaining the tone or vibration of the Upper Room. The reclamation of memory is not denying what happened. It is knowing what happened in a true way.

He interrupts the teaching. "But it has been said that the manifest world is an illusion. How far do we go? We can't be floating about in the ethers all day. We have work to do, bills to pay." We will address this differently than you would like. The truth of the reality that you know yourself through, or the octave of experience that is the collective world that you have known yourself in, is implicitly in the denial of the Divine. The idea of a fall from grace was simply the re-articulation of the manifest world as separate from its Source. We are working towards reconciliation, initially with those who read the texts. But the operative act here *is* reconciliation. And as each one of you does this at the level you can hold, you reclaim what you see and what you experience at this higher level of alignment. The truth of your being, you see, when not held by a lie, not bridled by fear, not claimed in fear, will light the world. And the light of the world, come as each of you, is the resurrected Christ that may be known in form.

Now, to remember who you truly are is a significant act. Some of you move this in ways that are confused. "Well, I recall my lifetime thousands of years ago when I was the pharaoh," or "I perceive myself as having a simultaneous lifetime on that star system out there." We would much prefer that the manifestation of the Divine, come as who and what you are, is in the eternal now, which is the only truth you may ever know. Everything else is an idea. The body itself, whether or not you know it, is primed for the present moment. It was created for this. And when you are no longer moored and tethered through false memory, a false idea of who you have been, what you have been, how you have served, the truth of that refrain—"I know who I am in truth, I know what I am in truth, I know how I serve in truth"—will sing through your expression, and sing to the world, so that it may be sung to and lifted by your presence and being.

When we return, we will continue with a teaching on the body and the memory of form, and support you in the recognition of its re-acclimation. In the text. Period. Period. Period. Stop now, please.

(PAUSE)

What stands before you today is recognition and choice. The moment something is seen as it has always been, a new choice may be made, a new opportunity may be claimed. And the realization that the body itself, indoctrinated through separation, holds memory that would seek to reclaim separation, may give you the amplitude that you require to make the choice before you now. To know the body in a higher way, to align the body to a level of truth which will dispel or reclaim or recognize the lies that it has held, will support each of you at a level of maintenance in the field of the Upper Room, more so than you have known thus far.

Imagine you have a scratch, an itch on the body, ever present. You enjoy your day, but there is that nagging itch and need to scratch it. A memory in the lower field that would seek to claim you back to it is just such a thing. Now, some of you would say to us, "I wish to remember everything." You are not forgetting anything. Underline that. *You are not forgetting.* You are re-seeing and re-knowing. You are wiping away the mirror, the residue that accrued over lifetimes of neglect and adherence to a belief that the form that you have taken cannot be of God because God is only spirit. Everything is spirit, including the body. It is just operating at a lower level of vibration.

When something is claimed in form, when something is named and claimed, it oscillates in a lower field. When you move beyond naming and you move towards allowance to what is, your experience of matter is altered. In some ways you return to that infant self who perceives all things as one, without leaving the level of awareness that is required by each of you to maintain a sense of self in an operative way. Knowing that you are one with Source does not mean you neglect the body. Knowing you are one with Source does not mean you may eat off your neighbor's plate without his or her permission. Comprehending yourself as one with your neighbor, with the elements, with God itself, will merely claim you beyond the illusion of separation. And separation is an illusion that has been made fact by your agreement to it. Nothing exists in this world without your agreement to it. Understand that, once and for all. You did not make the hurricane, but you agreed to it. And to confirm it through your agreement is to claim a level of alignment to it.

The broadcast that you are receiving this morning is happening in two ways. While you hear the language and you operate in your discernment about the ideas being offered, you are also being claimed by us as a wave of vibration—a wave of vibration that reclaims memory, tainted in a false belief in separation, accrued through time, and agreed to through collective experience. The amplitude of the wave we are about to bring you far surpasses what many of you have experienced thus far. So we are preparing you for this. The tone that we will sing, and we alone will sing, will claim each of you at a level of alignment where the invocation of the release of false memory held by form and energetic body may be completed.

Now, this is first completed at a level of vibration. Your acclimation to this and realization of it will come in stages. You need to know where your mailbox is. We are not taking away your memory. But because you have codified your experience in this realm through a memory and an agreement to separation, so much may change when this is moved that it must be moved in stages. We don't wish you disassociating from the experience of being. We wish you claiming it in fullness, without the taint of fear, the agreement to separation that memory must mandate, and not because memory wills it—memory does not have will—but because you utilize memory to claim vibrational accord. "That is that woman who was rude to me one day. I will stay far from her." The idea of memory as predicating action is easily understood by all of you. Even with the new claim that we are making on your behalf, you may choose not to take her company. That is up to you, and an act of will. But the act of will is no longer informed by the mandate of separation that the small self was reared in.

On this day we claim that all who hear these words will be re-known in a higher template of agreement, that form itself may be realized beyond any agreement to a memory

in separation that distorts one's true nature as expressed, as
realized, in the Upper Room. We sing your songs for you
so that you may learn the words. And as we sing on your
behalf, we sing the truth of your expression and what may
now be known.

[The Guides tone through Paul.]

Behold, I make all things new.

Allow the body to be received. Allow the memory of the
body to be held in this high frequency. And allow the idea of
self, moored in memory of form, through all time be reclaimed
in the high octave that is the Upper Room.

We will say this now to all of you, to memory itself, as the
Divine Self that we come as on your behalf:

God Is. God Is. God Is.

Allow the body to receive. Allow the energetic field to receive. And know the self as whole.

God Is. God Is. God Is.

Period. Period. Period. Stop now, please. This is in the text.

(PAUSE)

What stands before you today is a new recognition of what
you are, the Divine as manifest in flesh and blood, in all things

you see or may ever encounter. Some of you say, "Well, perhaps this is so, but what is my experience of it? How can I know that this is true?" The authority you actually hold to recognize this is implicit in your expression, how you be. The recognition of the Divine Self that has come as form is expression as may be known in the manifest plane.

Now, while you are aligning in what we call the Upper Room, which is the octave above the one that you have known, your exchanges are still present in what you would know of as a lower field. You are operating as the Upper Room, and your claim of vibration, "I Have Come, I Have Come, I Have Come," has enacted you towards a realized state of manifestation. The being that you are, in her expressed life, in his expressed presence, indoctrinates by level of vibration or intonation all that he or she encounters. The residual affect of this is twofold. What is encountered by you is transformed, or lifted to the Upper Room. And your realization of this manifestation serves as counterpart.

Now, your experience of this is individuated, but there are comparable experiences for all who walk on this path. While we have often said what you bless, blesses you in return, you do not yet understand that you become this blessing. Your active presence serves as conductor for the upper realm to transform or translate—if you wish, transpose—what is seen and encountered to the high octave you are operating from. The residual affect of this is the announcement of presence from what is seen by you. Imagine you are saying hello to something and it is now saying hello back. You understand the simple principle that the Divine sees the Divine in all of its creations. But when something is recognized as it truly is—"I know who and what you are in truth"—the energetic field of the one called, or the thing called, will move to conversation with you.

Now, this is not a conversation in language, but in tone and vibration. When we speak through Paul, he serves as conductor, but he is present as conductor without our speech through him, through the acclimation of his vibrational field in the Upper Room where it claims all things. He operates in ignorance of this, unless he is working with us. Most of you are the same. You serve as conductor through the alignment you hold. Now, this is always true at whatever level of alignment you hold. You are serving as a conductor to the level of vibration that you are manifested as. The one who knows herself in self-pity or great rage is claiming that vibration in all of his or her encounters.

The great difference in what we teach is that we have moved you beyond the octave that you have known, which claims all things through fear—not by intention, but by the omnipresence of fear or the infiltration of fear through this octave. In the Upper Room, the manifestation that you may claim, which does not hold fear, will never be in resonance with it. So from this place of expression you are claiming all things made new by presence and being, less so through intention.

Now, when you are the light, you don't have to walk around announcing it. You simply are. When you are the light, you do not seek to illumine things. Things are illumined by your presence in a tangible way. Underline the word *tangible*. This is an experiential teaching. To comprehend the Divine as idea is one level of agreement. You may agree to any idea you wish.

But to realize the Divine, or to know it as what you experience, calls to you the benediction of the things seen. Again, the idea and the true claim: What you bless, blesses you in return.

Now, the choice is in all ways yours. Your expectation of what this might mean is that you walk on water, you turn the clouds inside out and upside down. In fact, it is so simple that you don't understand it. The realization that you hold about divinity, what is always true, is met by you experientially, not through effort, not through practice, but by presence and being.

Now, the accumulation of experience through presence and being will translate your idea of self in significant ways. But until this becomes manifest in ways you may know, you are embarking on an adventure, an experiential one, in what it means to know and to realize the Monad as form. Now, when we speak of the Monad, we are speaking to the aspect of the Divine as you, come as you, informing every aspect of you, and then everything that you experience, because the Christ is not limited by form, although most of you would like to confine it because you can comprehend it more readily. The energetic field you hold, in this translated state, out-pictures itself as all things seen and unseen. In other words, all things are re-claimed to Source through your presence and being, individually and collectively. The residual affect of this is the return of the vibrational field, the thank-you, the acknowledgment, the Divine saying yes to its resurrection through manifestation.

Now, you may begin with yourselves. When you claim, "I am Word through my body, Word I am Word, I am Word through my vibration, Word I am Word, I am Word through my knowing of myself as Word," the invocation of the Monad as identity, as form, and as expression is experienced by most of you in a palpable way. You feel the current of vibration where it is invoked. "I am Word through my hand." "I am Word through my back." "I am Word through what I see before me."

The energetic experience of this invocation is the gift of the experience as may be known by the systems you hold that are experiential. There are levels of experience that you will not attain while moored to this dimensional reality through form, but there are ways of understanding and comprehending the experience of the Divine as manifest. In the Upper Room, you are not as precluded from these experiences because you are moved beyond fear, and your experience of self as manifest as matter is challenged only by the idea that the Divine cannot express as it must, which is always your own decision—that God is limited and cannot know itself as form.

Your triumph, the triumph of the True Self in a resurrected state, is the claim upon all things it sees: "Behold, I make all things new." It is the Monad, or the Word expressed as form, that announces this as so, because at this level it is always true. It is not the light trying to be the light. It is the nature of being and presence, through invocation, that aligns what it encounters to the divinity that was ever present, but had been denied.

Now, some of you say, "Well, where's the magic here? I want to feel the magic. Give me some more magic." There is no magic here. There is realization, and the alteration of form through realization. Now, your form is altered, know it or not, through your recognition of your inherent divinity. Because now this is available, because you may perceive it, you will now embark on the realization of the material realm beyond the density that it has accrued through the alignment of the lower field. You must understand that the tree and the brook express in the Upper Room, but in a more refined state, because the eyes that perceive the tree and the brook are the eyes that perceive the Divine, and the brook and the tree claim this by their own recognition of your claim upon it.

Now, you may speak the words "Behold, I make all things new" and feel the affect of them. The residual affect is translation from one octave to another, or the realization of what was always so, but had been denied. The juncture some of you stand at is that you want this, but you will not accept the potential of it until proof is given you. And while this is understandable at one level, it precludes experience because you are denying what is already true. What is already true is that the one before you is of God, that the bone and the marrow in the bone are of God, that the sky and the sea and the earth are of God—the oscillation of vibration of the tone of the Divine at varying levels of experience.

Now, when you move beyond the dense plane and you are no longer denying the divinity of self, the agreement is made to the divinity of all things. Agreement is not consent. It is accord. When you get off the elevator at the fifth floor, you are in accord with all that expresses at the fifth floor. You are not consenting to be there. You are there because you have aligned and agreed to it. *In agreement* means vibrational accord. The vibrational accord that is the Upper Room, the Christ consciousness that has always been available to humanity, but has been heretofore denied in spite of great instruction that has come at varying times in history, the agreement to be re-known, reborn if you wish, at this level of oscillation, claims all things made new by presence and being.

When we teach through Paul, we monitor his body, what he can hold and how long he may speak for. We have one thing we wish to contend with before we stop this lecture for the time being—the agreement to fear that you cherish, the agreement to fear that you hide in your back pocket, the agreement to fear which we would suggest, finally, is treasonous to the Divine Self. Some of you would seek to sneak fear into the Upper Room and contaminate your idea of it as well. "You see this awful Upper Room, there can be nothing here for me"—the words of fear claiming you in a climate that is informed by itself. When this occurs, you are not in the Upper Room. You are in an idea of it, because fear will not express at this level of intonation. We said *contend*, Paul, because we will not negotiate this. The choice must be made to support a new agreement that the requirement to fear, the belief in fear as necessity, must be moved for the energy that has been fear to be moved again, or re-known in a higher way. We said *re-known* intentionally. We will say it again. Fear is of God, but seeks to deny it. It is the aspect of self that would say, "Don't go there. You will get lost. You will not be as you wish. You will be decided upon by others." If you are willing to release the agreement that fear is your ally and your protector, you may cross the threshold.

Now, Paul interrupts the teaching. "Are there times, though, when fear is useful? It propels us to run from the bear. It keeps us safe in harmful situations." Your reaction may be fearful, but in the Upper Room the awareness of what is operates quite well without fear serving as its catalyst. Do you understand this? You may move from the bear in an awareness of the harm that the bear may bring you, but that is not necessarily fearful.

It is prudent, it is true action, and you must begin to trust that the Divine Self knows what is for your highest good, and will support you in moving from danger when danger appears.

When we say these words to you now, by way of agreement to you or accord with you, we are supporting you in the choice you may make as you wish it:

On this day we claim that all who hear these words may recognize their participation in claiming fear as an ally and make a higher choice—to release the mandate that fear accompany them to what they believe to be the Upper Room, in an awareness that fear will always lead them to a confused state, a small idea of what God might be, where fear can claim itself as sovereign.

As we say these words for each of you, we claim you in liberation with your consent. Underline *with your consent*. We cannot take something from you that you do not wish to offer, but we will support you in this release as you are willing to receive it.

Each one who may hear these words will now be met in the true nature, the true expression, of their own divinity, which will vanquish the fear they have utilized or restore them and what they have held in darkness to a higher state of liberation and comprehension of presence and being. We know who you are in truth. We know what you are in truth. We know how you serve in truth. You are free. You are free. You are free. You are in the Upper Room. You Have Come. You Have Come. You Have Come. Behold, I make all things new. It will be so. God Is. God Is. God Is.

Blessings to each of you. Stop now, please. Yes, in the text.

(PAUSE)

What stands before you today is recognition of what you once thought you were, the memories accrued through those experiences, and the identity that you may now hold, unembellished by the treasonous self, which simply means the aspect of self that would deny your inherent divinity. The realization of the accord that you may now hold will come in stages. The availability of the individual and the consciousness therein must be attended to in stages, lest the idea of self fragment in such a way that distortion occurs. We are cautious in this teaching that the amplitude that an individual may attain be welcomed by them in adherence to truth. And what that means is you cannot carry more than you can hold. You cannot lift higher than you can manage.

Some of you say, "The Kingdom is here, I want the Kingdom." And, indeed, the Kingdom is here, and the realization of the Kingdom is what comes through the progression that we are taking you through. Now, *taking you through* is an interesting idea. It is not an obstacle course. In fact, the only hindrances are your own creations, and the creations that the collective has maintained that you give credence to. When you stop aligning to an idea that was claimed in separation, when you are no longer supporting it with a sense of identity that demands that it be there, you lift beyond it. It loses significance. The meaning is altered.

Now, the idea of the Upper Room as a place where all things are made new is for some of you a dream state, a fantasy landscape where your father didn't die when you were young, where your wife did not leave, where things happened as you wished. In many cases, what occurs in the Upper Room is that the demands that things be as they should be is released, because the aspect of self that *shoulds* is the aspect of self that has been born through history. When your attachment to outcome is released—who you think you should be in the Upper Room, what the Upper Room is—you find yourself simply being, and expressing at a level of tone where what you require is met by you in perfect ways. The docile nature that some of you hold seeks to command that this be about comfort. This is less about comfort than receptivity. Imagine your driveway is full of snow. You require a shovel or help with the shoveling. You may discover the shovel that was hidden in the back of the garage, or the neighbor who comes by and offers a hand. You are not clamoring or frightened. You trust the Source to meet those needs as they can be met by you. And if you must go to the garage, please do so and discover what might be there.

The trajectory of the text we are writing is embodiment, yes, but it is the fruition of embodiment at a level of tone where realization occurs. The chapter on memory that we will be completing soon is in some ways a requirement for what comes after, because as long as you are maintaining a sense of self born in coherence with a false idea of who you are, and a false idea that the collective has foisted upon you or been in agreement with, you will be deterred. You will instead fabricate an idea of a self that *should* be in the Upper Room, and decide what the Upper Room *must* be, and design it as you think it *must* be to fulfill the small self's wishes. The small self does express in the Upper Room, but it is aligned to the soul, and the Monad restructures it so that it may be utilized in a full way.

Some of you say, "I have things I can't forget," or "The world has seen terrible things that will not be forgotten." Again, nobody is asking you to forget anything. It is useful to remember that the rattlesnake is poisonous and avoid stepping upon it, but there is no need to be frightened of what may occur when you leave the house and walk around the corner. The realization of the Monad in fact claims a path for you, defines a path for you, in accordance with high will.

Now, high will or true will must be understood. Divine Will is not a separate idea from self. It is the self that knows who it is, operating in accord with its truth, or a high truth that expresses beyond memory or edict born through collective reason. In other words, the will that expresses at this level is in a high alignment and will not agree to a platitude, will not agree to a collective choice, if the collective choice holds a bias born in fear. The will that you have known, personal will, if you wish, is of course integrated here. It is always the braiding of the will, the true will and the will of the personality structure, in a true aligned state that expresses Divine Will and will lead you on a course, direct your path in perfect ways.

"What is a perfect way?" he asks. "It sounds lovely, but what does it mean?" A perfect way for you, Paul, would be a way where the realization of self is gained in accord with what you can hold in alignment in perfect ways. It is realization, as can be manifested and maintained. It is not a rush to a higher state of experience or consciousness. Too many of you, these days, mistake a higher experience for a higher alignment. You can go out and watch the fireworks, but when they are not going off, all you have is the memory of them. To achieve a higher state, through any means, must support you in an awareness of what that experience was. But unless that experience is utilized in a high way, it has been something less than the fireworks display. It has been an experience, fleeting perhaps, that did not leave a thumbprint that can be responded to and realized through in your daily lives.

While we offer experience in these teachings, and in some ways promote one's own experience of the teaching as the way to know the truth of them, the experience is the byproduct of the teaching and the integration of them, not the purpose of them. You will all reach a level of vibration in this incarnation or another where the idea of experience is replaced by being. You are not seeking experience. You are *being* at a level of tone where all things are made new, and your recognition of this is not much different than your awareness of the color of your eyes or the brilliant night sky. These things simply are. You are in agreement or accord with them because they are the manifestations of the level of consciousness that you have aligned to.

Earlier in this text we spoke of striving, or the small self's need to propel itself forward for acquisition, even in the spiritual realms. This is a stage of development that all may pass through, but there is little sustenance there. It keeps you striving, seeking the next peak experience, the next experience that you can decide is of spirit. When you understand yourself as of Source, all experience qualifies as this. The walk to the store, petting the dog, enjoying the sunset, weeping over a loss—all are holy states. And the one experiencing them is no less holy than he or she would be in prayer upon a mountaintop, or experiencing something that he or she would decree is of a higher realm.

The one who lives on the mountaintop is not striving to be there. She simply is. He simply is. You simply are. We love you as you are because we cannot do other. We know *as* you are, what you are, how you express, because we become who you are when we know you, and understand what it means to fear or comprehend the self as separate. But understand that we do not live there. We have lifted. We rejoice in where we align to, but we rejoice for each of you at every stage of alignment, through any experience that you learn through, because that is your gift, your undertaking, your expression, as you move forth in the alignment and progression that we support you in.

Thank you each for your presence. Stop now, please. Period. Period. Period. Period. Yes, in the text.

DAY FIVE

When you wake up every morning to a new potential, a new opportunity to realize the self, you will have choices. "How do I navigate the day?" "How do I know myself in the Upper Room?" "What are the requirements of maintaining this vibration?" The questions are useful. The opportunities to meet these questions will occur in the day. Every day is an opportunity, yes, for a higher level of tone. One does not aspire to this as much as align to it. And the requirement of each day is presented to the individual as she walks her path, as he says yes to the path before him.

Some of you say to us, "Well, this is all well and good in

theory, but humanity will not change. We will destroy ourselves eventually." And this is the aspect of self that contributes to that destruction. You may have this, if you wish. You
may choose this experience, if you like it. But we will suggest
otherwise. The choice humanity has made to move beyond
a system of separation is an arduous one for the personality
structure, and a very simple one for the aspect of self who
already knows who she is. And this aspect is present in all of
you, regardless of whether or not you adhere to it or not.

The subject of the day is preparation. The subject of the
talk is how one chooses. And how one chooses will be met by
you only at the level of consciousness that you have aligned to.

Now, each of you says yes to a potential here. "I may know
myself in a higher way. I may choose in a higher accord." But
the opportunity to choose is offered to you each day. And the
small self, still knowing itself by memory or prior adhesion,
prior choice, prior predilection, will seek to maintain the
structure of identity that it has known. When you say yes to
the new, you must be willing to receive it. You cannot say yes
to the new and claim the old concurrently. It will not support
you. You will end up with the old and deciding that the new
could never be had.

When you have an opportunity for change, you must weigh
this opportunity by the requirements it holds for the small
self, and the opportunities to grow that may be presented to
it. But you must also understand that when you have moved
to the Upper Room in your alignment, every choice you make
becomes the opportunity for a higher degree of presence. He
interrupts the teaching. "You are speaking of higher degrees,
as if we are to aspire to this." Not so at all. This is not about

aspiration. It is about what occurs when you release the density of prior choice, claimed by memory or adherence to the collective.

Each of you who says yes to this teaching begins by balancing, in a way that feels unsupported, the two levels of reality that you may know yourself through. You may call it higher or lower, but we will talk about it differently. The aspect of self—personality, yes—reared in the lower realm, has all the evidence he or she could ever require that this is the only way they may know themselves, and everything else seems like a potential that may be realized by few. When you move to the Upper Room in vibration, it is not a tightrope, although you may experience it as such because the old—still present through habit, adherence to memory, prior choice, and collective agreement—will seek to call you back. You keep one eye on history and one eye on the potential. When you move to the present moment, which is the only moment that God may be known, you walk right forward. You walk claiming the new as what is—not what may be, but what is.

Now, *what is* is different than you think. Imagine for a moment you are on an escalator. You don't know what each floor lands as. You don't know where you stand until you disembark. Such is the same with the Upper Room. The experience of operating here, in tone and vibration, is simple alignment. As you become steady here, as you are not tempted by fear or by the rules of the collective to maintain the old, you begin to move in an escalation of vibration.

Now, each octave that you may realize yourself through has low and high notes. If you look at the world you have known yourselves through, with its joy and despair, you may find equivalency here. The greatest pain humanity has known, the highest degree of separation, which culminates in war, self-abuse, harm to others, are the low notes that may be played, if you wish, to learn through. But in this octave you know yourself through, there is also joy, there is also love, there is also great beauty and splendor. The Upper Room is an octave of its own.

Now, we call the Upper Room a space or level of consciousness that is the entryway to what we have called the Kingdom, which is a vast level of consciousness that you may discover, once you grow comfortable in the foyer, or the Upper Room. The balancing act is released very quickly when you begin to realize the simple claim "God Is." You are not invoking God. You are claiming the presence of God where it has previously been denied, and the alchemical effect of that claim is a new agreement to what has always been so.

The opportunity is present today to move into this octave and leave your baggage downstairs. You wish to bring your baggage to the Upper Room. The work that we have done with you on memory will support this release. If you don't remember where your bags are, you won't drag them upstairs with you. When you begin to comprehend yourself as liberated from the old, you will no longer seek to reattach to an archaic idea of what you have been—the separate self, the one who is in fear, the one who operates in shadow and pleads for God to save her. To allow God to be God is to be known by God, and the claim we have offered prior—"I Am Known, I Am Known, I Am Known"—is a high decree of truth.

Now, the validation of any claim we offer you must be in the experience of it. To utter the words without intent is to string together vowels and consonants that have no accord with what exists through the intention they hold. When you make a claim that we have offered you, we are in support of the claim as the claim is held. The intonation of the claim is momentary, yes, but each claim will offer you a level of vibrational accord that you may align to. Maintaining this alignment is not arduous. You are radios. You are always in broadcast. Your broadcast is your consciousness. When you turn the station to the Upper Room, that is the level of accord that you may play. When you switch the station to the old pain or fear, you align to the old pain or fear. Switching a station is a simple act.

We have claimed for you the affect of each record that we play. And the record that we play—"I know who I am in truth, I know what I am in truth, I know how I serve in truth"—will support all of you at a level of alignment that can be maintained, even in the common field, as you prepare yourselves for the affect of manifestation in the Upper Room. Manifestation in the Upper Room. The agreement to be without the conditioning that you have utilized to navigate a plane fraught with fear. The agreement to be here is in conjunction with the personality structure, not in opposition to it. The will that you have known yourselves through is utilized every day in choice, and the personality self claims will, as does the higher. When the two work in union, when a claim is made in a high tone—"I know who I am, what I am, how I serve"—will is utilized in accord with the vibrational tone that you have aligned to.

We have attempted to make this very simple for all of you. This is not theology. This is an agreement. And agreement is alignment, or vibrational accord. To support you each in this work we have utilized language to support comprehension, but the texts that we write exist beyond language, and you can align to them, and the true meanings of them, through the choice to know who and what you truly are. The idea of this is not done by personality, through personality, or as personality. The choice to align may be in agreement to personality, but the level of alignment that you may claim as the texts, through the texts, exists beyond language as a template that may be adhered to.

"What does this mean?" he asks. Every text we have offered supports a template of recognition through echo and tone. The tone of each text is what you are aligning to. The information a text holds is what supports you at a level of agreement in comprehending the experience you are undergoing. We don't tell you what to feel, but we offer you the reasoning behind it. Imagine you woke up in a strange country, didn't know the language, didn't know the rules. The texts may support you in comprehending where you have come to—the Upper Room, not a physical place, a level of tone and consciousness that supports your alignment and the reclamation of the manifest world in the light, beyond the shadow, beyond the decree of separation that humanity has chosen to learn through.

Each of you here, by agreement, is responding to this text at the level of adherence that you may hold. Each of you who learns holds the vibration of the text in the energetic field through the claims of truth we offer. The choice you make in this alignment is to become the doorway for others. Now, this is again not done through proselytizing. It is done through presence and being, or the agreement to be, in the Upper Room, which supports the doorway, or alignment with all, for all, and to all who encounter the doorway. You as the doorway. You are not choosing this as much as being this. And the invocation of the claim that we have taught you thus far—"Behold, I make all things new"—is the agreement to re-see, to re-know, all that one encounters from the high order that is indeed the Upper Room.

On this day we have two intentions: To claim you as you have been and often denied, to allow you the knowing to realize this for yourselves, and to support you each in maintaining the balance that the Upper Room offers, so that you may not be frightened of falling away or releasing the new in favor of an old structure, which even though painful is familiar to you.

We thank you each for your presence. Stop now, please. Period. Period. Period. Indeed, in the text.

(PAUSE)

What stands before you today, in recognition of memory of what you have known or believed yourselves to be, is what may now be claimed. The idea of being, simply being, from the high level of tone that we instruct you in, must be comprehended by each of you, not as a potential, but as a reality. You have been indoctrinated to believe that you may not maintain a level of self-identification that is in coherence with the Divine, and for several reasons. You have created an architecture where the soothsayer, the rabbi, the priest, the shaman, has access to what you do not. And the petty experiences that you may receive or understand yourselves through are going to be the product of their benevolence.

When you understand your birthright—"I Have Come, I Have Come, I Have Come," the Divine as you claiming all things into manifestation—you will entrust the life you live to the Monad, or the Christ Truth, that dwells within you each. The doorway is present through the activations that you have invoked through these teachings. The affect of the manifestation of these claims must be evidential in the lives lived by each of you. The triumph of this teaching for the world is the template that has been wrought, that is now present, that anyone may align to. And we say *anyone* intentionally. The Upper Room is not the purview of our students. The Upper Room is the divine gift of experiencing God as the beings they are. *As* the beings. Not in some other world when you've lost your bodies, but as you walk the earth in accord, in agreement, to what is only true. Underline the word *only*.

Self-deceit will seek to carry you to a shadow land, where one moment you are in the light and the next step you are back in darkness. That is how most of you have operated. The idea, the possibility, that you may claim the light, be in the light, and as the light, is not only foreign to you. It feels to some blasphemous, and to others impossible. We are telling you something very different. The gift of the Kingdom is the gift of being. It is not aspiration. It is not deciding what must be so. It is knowing what is. Knowing and realization are identical, and the experience of the Monad as the one who knows you, and giving the memory of what you have never been to the Monad, supports the incarnation or expression of the Divine that seeks itself through you. Hear those words, friends. *Seeks itself through you.* You *are* the light. You just don't know it, and you have denied it.

Now, to maintain the vibration of the Upper Room is to know who you are, and it is not to understand the mechanisms of the Upper Room, or a rule book that will keep you looking at your feet. We don't want you looking at your feet. We want you walking forward as the self you are, the Christ that has come as Mona, as Gerald, as Anna, as Joan, the Divine that has come as Phillip, as Oscar. As direct expression occurs, you know yourselves as this, as of this, and by it, while maintaining identity at a new level of evocation, vibration, tone, and being. What this means is what is extraordinary becomes the ordinary, because it is Oscar in the Upper Room, it is Anna loving others, it is Joan going to the store and seeing the ones before her as they can only be seen in truth.

Some of you desire a system that you can maintain through identity. "Give me the right mask to wear so I may stay up here." You must be here without the mask. You don't need the mask. You need to allow the truth of your expression, made manifest as you, to support the awakening of the aspects of self that require the love, the light, and knowledge of their true nature. Any aspect of self that is being denied will and must be brought to the light to be re-seen. The idea of the collective undergoing such a passage is imperative that you understand. The idea that humanity itself is dislodging the bullets that it has accrued through pain and suffering, born in separation, that humanity itself is ascending to a new level of tone, and comprehending itself through its choices to abandon itself to shadow, will give you a comprehension of the passage before humanity.

"Well, how do we maintain the Upper Room in times of great upheaval?" Upheaval does not express as the Upper Room. The idea of the Upper Room as consciousness may give you the understanding that what is experienced here is re-seen as the Divine Self, so it is not fraught with fear or judgment of others. You are not passive to change. You are carried by the wave of change. You are not fighting the tide. You are riding the tide. And you are claimed, as all one day will be, on the high shore of a new realization of who and what you have always been.

The indoctrination you have held in support of separation is being addressed here. The causation for this separation, as we have taught prior, is an agreement to it born in a belief in scarcity. And there could not be a God who would allow pain, or a choice to deceive the self and claim God as the source of pain. God as the one note sung, or Source of all things, is not the executor of pain. It does not support suffering. But it does allow choice. And until humanity's choice moves beyond separation—the need for war, the need to keep others captive through small self will—humanity will be challenged.

The operation now is revelation. Things are being revealed so that humanity may see them and move beyond them. The moving beyond is the process of ascension that has been discussed, or the lifting, incrementally, to what is always true. Maintaining the vibration of the Upper Room is not about pretending things don't exist. It is about what exists being seen as of God, or lifted to God where shadow has held in abeyance or ruled.

We will suggest this for Paul. Stop trying to listen as we speak. You interfere when you do. We continue now.

The passage this class, these students, these readers undergo is an agreement to the soul. It must be. The will that you utilize to turn the pages of the text is the same will you've utilized to agree to this teaching, and to support yourself through the process of engaging with it. The process of engaging with the text is the agreement to what is already true. You don't have to strive for that, nor are you giving authority to what you don't agree with. To claim what is always true is always the essence of the thing, or the tone, the one note sung, the Word that is God itself.

The passage you will now undergo is not a reflective one. We are moving beyond asking you to reflect on what you thought you were, and become who you truly are. Misidentification—through cultural design and through agreement to collective agreement of what you think should be—is being addressed here.

We will take a pause for Paul. We are still continuing the chapter on memory. That may be the title. We will tell it to you later. Period. Period. Period. Stop now, please.

DAY FIVE

When we speak to you today about resurrection, we are speaking of the aspect of self, the True Self, the Christ or Monad, that is resurrected as you. Now, the Divine Self does not hold the record that you do of your indiscretions. It does not care if you cheated on a test when you were ten. It is not looking in your bedroom, deciding whether what you are doing is safe or lovely or holy or not. The Divine as you is the expression of God.

Now, the claim we have offered you prior—"I Am Known"—the True Self that does know you does comprehend these things, but not at the level that the personality structure does because the Divine Self does not hold the moral antenna that you believe it does. There is always a record of action. You may call it a karmic record. You may call it a record of identity and choices made. When we claim the term—"You Are Known"— you are are indeed known by the Divine as all things, through all ideas of time and personality that you may have ever encountered.

He interrupts the teaching already. "Well, you just said the Divine isn't looking in the bedroom. The Monad doesn't care. Then what is the Monad knowing about our indiscretions or our fears or our lies?" We will say it differently for you, Paul. Once again you impose identity upon the Creator through mythological structure. "The Divine that knows what is good and evil sends some to heaven, some to hell." There is no God that operates as thus. That is a creation. But we must say, like all creations, that will be your God if that is the God you wish, and you will continue to torment yourselves or believe yourselves to be sinful and unworthy. We have spoken of sin as the opposition to the Divine, or contrary to high purpose of the True Self. But sin is not bad behavior. Sin is simply the denial of the Divine. When we say the Monad doesn't care, its action is always the same—reclamation and resurrection.

Now, the teaching of history, the teaching of memory, personal and collective memory, as informing the world you live in is necessary for you to understand, because you reenact old battles, you claim old wars, and you build Gods out of the ashes of statues that fell thousands and thousands of years ago. There have been many Gods that have ruled this plane. Some have been high, some not high, but whether or not you wish to believe it, any God is one God masquerading as something other.

Now, when we say you create God, you create the tenets of

a God, the attributes of a God, and you behave in accordance with those tenets or attributes. "We will not eat this kind of meat. We will always pray at this time in a certain fashion. We will do penance thus. We will tithe as thus. We will do these things in agreement to a structure to appease a God that has been created and serves that purpose." When you claim a deity that is beneficent, that is loving, your experience of the Divine is such. When you claim a vengeful God, you will claim all attributes of vengeance and decide what this God should despise because it is what you wish to see. These are false Gods.

Paul interrupts. "You said all Gods are one God. How are they false?" They are identical to the level of consciousness that created them. But because all things must be of God, even the totem, even the angry God, has a presence as an evocation of Source. The release of memory, as we have instructed you, is actually inclusive of this, the denial of the Divine that comes in pagan form. Now, we do not mean *pagan* to eschew a religion that may be called pagan. We are simply speaking of a structure, or an idol, or a way of understanding through delineation what an aspect of God might be, and praying to that aspect—be it the God of revenge or the God of love. When you move beyond these structures and the need to replicate them, which you do unintentionally—"I must grovel before my God, I must stand tall in my God, my God must know what I require as I say it should"—must support you in an agreement to what you believe.

The challenge for some of you now is that you will believe you are without God if the Gods you have utilized are moved away from you. We do not move away a God. We lift you to the

Infinite, to Christ Truth. Christ is not God, but it is the aspect of God that is known in form and the level of agreement to itself that you may adhere to, in and from the Upper Room. The challenge now, as we said prior, is how do you maintain the tone and the benefit of alignment through the Upper Room? It's really very simple. To gift the self and the will to the Divine is to allow the Divine a reclamation of the will. To gift the self in offering to the Source of all things is to be re-known. Again, the claim "Behold, I make all things new." In fact, you are reborn, and what *reborn* is, is re-known in a state of innocence, which has been interpreted to mean without blemish and without sin.

The idea of Christ being without sin is misunderstood. The Christ *is* without sin, but the Christ come as Joseph or Marianne or Philomena may have done awful things and enjoyed every moment of them. The Christ, come as her, incarnates as and through, and she is made new through this interaction. We are calling it an interaction because in fact it is. If you think of a flow of lava encountering all that it touches and creating something new from it, the invention of expression at this level must be seen as a new invention—beyond the old, beyond the chastising God, even beyond the loving God that you think looks into your bedroom, and perhaps disapproves of what you do.

The idea that God simply is, *is all things*—that it knows what you require because the aspect of you that it is in an encounter with is claiming its needs in ways the True Self understands—takes the hard work out of maintaining the Upper Room. You are not sitting impatiently in your chair, saying, "God, you know what I need. Why isn't it here yet?"

The True Self, you see, in comprehension of one's true needs, in collusion with the soul, in agreement to the soul, supports manifestation because you are not operating in separation. The Kingdom, you see, offers all, holds all. Because it holds all, all things may be known here. The denial of the Divine, which is indeed the source of lack, is not present at this level of tone, so what is claimed here is already yours. Do you understand this? You are not claiming to God, "You forgot about me and what I require." Instead, you are claiming, "I Am Known." Now, the idea of being known, for some of you, still, is decided by the aspect of self that wishes to hide things behind her back, speak ill of her neighbor, and assume that is not known. In fact, you are already known.

Paul interrupts. "You spoke of a record. What happens to this record? Is it expunged? Are we forgiven? Is that what forgiveness is about?" In many ways, yes. Now, if there is something you require learning through, you will have that lesson. But the idea that you are already forgiven, that God cannot hold a grudge, nor deny you entry to the Upper Room, is mostly unfathomable for most of you, because you still hold a God that is wagging its finger and saying, "Do it my way, or else."

He interrupts yet again. "But you spoke of our need to forgive others. Isn't that a requirement?" It is not God's requirement. It is your own. As we say, what you put in darkness, claims you in that darkness. When you stop putting things in darkness, you are released from it. There is nothing sanctimonious here. It is extremely practical. "But it's not easy," he says. It is easy when you stop attaching to outcome, your idea of what should be. "He should pay for what he did." "They should be told what's right." The small self is vindictive, and vindictiveness masks itself in self-righteousness, which is why you have armies amassing to commit atrocities in the name of God, and it has been thus for a very long time. You create the God that will give you what you want, and if what you want is suffering, that will be what you get.

Now, a loving God must be understood as being released from your prescriptions of what a loving God is. "A loving God is gentle, merciful as I say it should be. It is a gentle breeze. It is a loving whisper." God is also thunder. God is all things, not what you wish. But love as the essence of God, as the true tone of God, must be comprehended by you as beyond the personality structure's idea of what love is. You romanticize love. It is a white pretty kitten. It is a happy child playing in the street. The weather is God. The ocean is God. All things are God at different levels of oscillation.

He interrupts again. "Then what are we praying to if God is the ocean, God is the sky, God is the thunder?" You are praying to the knowing of the one presence, the one true consciousness that expresses as all, and we say consciousness, intelligence, high truth, and love. You are not embarking on a journey to atheism. On the contrary, you are claiming a realization of what God is through the direct experience of it. Again, the claim "I Am Known." When memory is known in offering to God, when the record of your past acts is offered to God, you are not suffering, beseeching God for forgiveness. You are aligning to God and restoring what was always God.

Nothing is outside of God except that which you have placed there. The identity you hold, in a resurrected state, is of God and in the experience of it. This is the teaching of equivalency. The tightrope many of you experience is the first stage of learning a new language, learning a new expression. And then you understand what you thought was a piece of twine that could barely carry you is a plateau, and that that plateau holds within it high tones that may be understood, explored, and experienced.

We sing your songs for you so that you may learn the words, and we say these words now on your behalf:

You have chosen to come. You have offered yourselves. You have said yes to the release of memory as would damn you or keep you from the light. And we say this now as we sing your song: Not only are you known. You are loved.

Period. Period. Period. Stop now, please. In the text, yes.

(PAUSE)

When we speak to you about God, we speak of infinite presence, that which has no beginning and no end. Each of you are part of this, the Eternal Self that is the Christ, the Monad in expression, aligned to what she can hold. The teachings that will ensue, as we complete this text, will be about innocence, and what innocence truly is.

Each of you here has been participatory to a transmission in vibration that is beyond what the man before you has held thus far. And your equation to it, which is the calibration you now hold, will support you in what comes before, what comes after, and what comes during your experience on this plane.

"What does that mean?" he asks. When you begin to move beyond time and linearity as a way of comprehending experience, all things are included—that which was, which is, and will one day be. They all express in the eternal now. The chapter that we have completed you may call "Memory." It is done.

We thank you for your attention to our words, and the tone we sing in. Period. Period. Period. Stop now, please.

3

THE TRUTH OF BEING

DAY SIX

When we speak to you today about what will be, we are speaking both to the individual and the collective. The transition humanity is undergoing will take time, but we grant you each this much trust. What will come is what is required, and what is required is a level of change that you cannot fathom. Why can't you fathom it? Because you have no context. The residual idea that what was will be, which has dominated this plane, has allowed for incremental growth, at times large steps, but in all ways you have carried your history with you. When you stop carrying your history with you, what is present for you is what can only be in truth.

Now, you look at the world you've created, the challenges that you have, the physical challenges, the cultural challenges. All these things are what you have known and expect to know. We are not erasing the blackboard. We are changing the blackboard. And there is a very different comprehension when something is replaced, as opposed to re-stationed.

Now, when something is re-stationed, it is the same thing viewed from a different perspective. And while the Upper Room holds high perspective, what humanity requires now is a transition to a level of tone where it will stop replicating fear, stop demanding fear, and stop contaminating all that you encounter with choice born in fear. Can this happen? It will. But the transition will not always be graceful.

Now, the individual encounters this in her own way. "I understand who I was when I was twenty. Who I am today is rather different. I identify with the ideas that I held, but I no longer seek to replicate them." This is maturation, and you all undergo this. But when a template is transformed, or the expectation of what life is and should be is altered, the transition that an individual undergoes is much greater.

"What does that mean?" he asks. Well, imagine your idea of self was predicated upon who you thought you were, and then one day you discover you were never what you thought, you believed a lie, and now how do you go about your business? You go about your business in an awareness that everything has been altered, and that you are up to the task of meeting the new as it aligns to you. Now, *to you* is important. Again, you must remember that at the level of the individual all things that you encounter are in agreement to your energetic field, which holds expectation, your idea of history, what you expect to see and get. The transition you are undertaking here is to reclaim the energetic field without the ties to history, or a faulty sense of identity, which would continue to perpetuate an idea of separation that is born in a lie.

The template is transformed when you align in the Upper Room, and grace is present. The presence of God and the alignment to God claims your experience with you. Underline the word *with*. Will is still present, but it is operating in a higher tone. And the choices available in the Upper Room are rather different experientially than what you have known in the lower. When you choose in the Upper Room from the place of agreement to Source, you are not claiming lack, you are not in despair, nor are you desperate for the answer. You have faith or trust that what is required will be met by you in a perfect way. And, indeed, if there are actions for you to take, you will undertake them. The truth of your being, expressing at this level, aligns all that you encounter to the Source of all things, which is indeed how a world is made new.

Now, the collective has known itself through fear, through deceit, through agreement to anger, and the opportunities that war presents to increase a belief in separation. When a collective template is moved, the transition is not always graceful because the myriad opportunities for change will be met by individuals at the level that they can hold them. If you have a consciousness that denies the light, refutes grace, agrees to fear, and demands more of the same, the entrenchment in fear is a great challenge. Because you have will and may operate from will at any level, the one born in fear, seeking to indoctrinate others in fear, will do what he or she can to maintain an idea of a status quo that she has known herself through. Even this human being will be moved, will be lifted, but it is not a graceful passage. The one who seeks to stay asleep will do everything he can to stop the daylight from encroaching. But, of course, it will.

Now, the transition that humanity undertakes will take several generations, and for one reason. The residual affects of what you've created are still being reclaimed. They are being re-seen. But the movement of these creations to the higher octave has not occurred yet, and there is a reason for this. The reality that you have known is still the reality that you require because you would not know who you were. Kingdoms do not need to fall in a moment. It is always generational. The societies that you have built, that you give great power to, are not all born in fear. But there are aspects of all cultures that are steeped in the denial of the Divine, and these are the aspects that will be moved. You will begin to operate in an awareness of change beyond what you could fathom. "Well, we didn't think this would happen so quickly," or "I knew it would happen one day, but not in my lifetime." The challenges that you face as a collective are all born in the agreement to fear. Underline that. *The challenges humanity faces are all born in agreement to fear.* And the transition beyond this fear requires that you agree to something other.

Now, imagine this: There is a small piece of wood floating on the surface of the ocean. It is not a very glamorous piece of wood. It's an old piece of wood, splintered, perhaps with stuck nails. Imagine that the boat that you have been in is beginning to sink. Some will swim to shore. Others will say, "I must be carried." And if the only thing that you can grab is the thing you never thought you would, perhaps you will. And God, for all of you, or a true God, the one Source of all things that realizes itself through its creation, will be the thing you cling to.

When the intellect fails, when science fails, when economic systems are falling and being reclaimed in different ways, the challenges are many. But this does not need to be a collapse. It is a resurrection. And as long as this is known, the movement forward is actually guaranteed. You will not have a seed grow out of the earth without disrupting the soil around it. And you are the seed. You are growing. The scent of the flowers you are informs the world by nature of presence and being.

Now, we will say this to the students in this room only: The energy that you have been experiencing is lifting in amplitude. What you experienced today and in the days prior through the dictation of this text is the energy that humanity will be experiencing as time progresses, or your idea of time progresses. The shift in frequency requires that all who encounter it are moved beyond what they have been steeped in or claimed in fear. When you allow this process, the movement may be graceful. When you deny the process, you will find yourself very confused. It's as if you go to the market and there is nothing on the shelves that you recognize. It's as if you go to bed and you find that sleep is not what you thought. To surrender to the times does not mean you need be passive to them. You may raise your voice. You may be heard. You may offer others the help they require. But the true work is done at the level of the True Self, who lifts all things to its resonant tone.

Paul interrupts. "You said, 'for people in the room.' Is this in the text?" We will tell you when we complete the lecture. The teaching that is being received now is actually required to provide context for both the reader who is experiencing this text as energetic transmission, and the ones who were present in the field that was created for this dictation to ensue. Indeed, a field was created, and the release of history through false memory was the requirement of the class we have undertaken. But the text is several classes, and will continue to be. There is much to teach. There is much to learn. But more than that, there is much to be—far more than you know, and far more than you would claim through the idealization of the small self and her idea, his idea, its idea of what divinity is.

You *are* divine. You are all divine. You cannot aspire to divinity. It is your true state of expression. Everything else is accrued detritus—a filter, if you wish, that holds the light that would shine as you from expressing fully in the world. As the energetic field, and the body itself, lifts in resonance, the field is exposed. And because it is always in union with its Source, it becomes the expression of God as humanity faces its next chapter.

Thank you for your presence. Indeed, this is in the text. Stop now, please.

DAY SEVEN

What stands before you today is opportunity to re-see the limitations you have utilized and decided upon that have claimed you in a reality that defines you in separation. The idea of freedom must indeed be seen as moving beyond these boundaries, these walls of separation, that you have all been in agreement to. Some of you say to us, "Well, I'm not really free. I pay my taxes. I have to have a career. I have my children, my parents," this situation or that, that claims you in agreement to it. In fact, these things are in agreement to you through co-resonance. And how you hold anything, how you describe anything, how you claim anything, claims you in accord with the expectation these things hold.

Now, you do need to be responsible to your creations, but how this occurs is actually very different than what you presume. Almost all of you decide to work in a structure—the idea of career, the idea of salary, the idea of earning a living—and you decide whether this is worthwhile or not, granting you what you wish or not, supporting you in the ways that you require. And while this may be all well and good at a certain strata of vibration, it is actually claimed in limitation because there is always a ceiling, always an idea of how much and when and what will be that you are claiming in accordance with the collective. Everybody who has a job that seeks the promotion. Everybody in an office who wants an office on a higher floor. Everybody who decides what is meritful and what is not based on common agreement. A worthy career. A mediocre career. Not a career at all. When you release the idea of career and you see yourself on an adventure in liberation, your needs may be met, yes, but perhaps in ways that you hadn't thought of or agreed to prior. The choice is always yours, you see, because you understand yourselves through the common field where what has been established by your forefathers, foremothers, is entrenched in a kind of logic that you hold and you agree to. "It must be this way. It cannot be another."

Now, the common field, or collective agreement to reality, is indeed so. But you don't perceive it as elastic, and in fact it is. The elasticity of form must be understood by all of you now, because freedom is claimed through this elasticity and never through common agreement to limitation. Here are some examples of limitation: "I can only go so far." "I can only be loved this way." "I can only be respected if I do this." "I may only know God if I appease God." "I may only know myself as worthwhile if my fellows confirm this worthiness." All of these are limitations. In fact, none of them are true except that you make them so.

Now, we are not suggesting that you walk away from your jobs. But you must understand that you can. We are not saying leave the marriage. But understand that you can. Your idea of being a good husband or a good wife in all ways is claimed through the common field and what *good* or *valuable* means. And the agreements these things hold pin you in some ways, or strand you in other ways, to a life that is not holding potential, true potential, expressed potential.

Now, the Upper Room is indeed a place where you may know manifestation through, but if you don't align here and you keep trying the old way, perhaps the old way will serve you. You will get the higher-floor office. You will get loved the way you think you should. But if you move to the Upper Room as a place of agreement, which means co-resonance here, you can become the receptor of it. Now, the idea that God already knows your needs—and, indeed, that is the claim "I Am Known"—you may begin to trust that you are not left outside the doorway while others may receive. That is an old paradigm, deeply entrenched, that the Divine must favor some over others, and that could never be further from the truth. You deny your gifts because you don't receive them. In fact, most of you push them away or deny the gifts that the Divine has offered you with, the beautiful voice you sing with, the sense of laughter you bring to any encounter, the joy that you do things with, whatever it may be. The moment you begin to acquiesce

to your true gifts, your true high expression, a path will continue to unfold for you. Underline the word *will*. Indeed, it
will happen because you are confirming it, not through trying
to make it so, but through the allowance to it from the Upper
Room where the old interference is not operative.

"What does that mean?" he asks. Well, you understand your
world through the denial of the Divine. "That awful man."
"That awful event." "Those awful people." You begin to trust
the awful things, which means expect them more and more,
and any calamity you face suddenly makes you in confirmation.
"There can be no God. God can never know me if such a thing
could happen in my life."

To release the old—or the expectations born through fear,
through the neglect of your true nature—offers aspects of you
beyond limitation that have been entrenched and known in
form through the denial of the Divine. Anything that you hate
you are denying the Divine in, be it the body you hold, the
behavior of another—it really matters not. To hate something
is to define it through separation. To hate another and create
a plausible reason why may be useful in a certain way. Perhaps
you rediscover self-esteem through the refusal to allow another to hurt you. But the gift you are truly offering the other
is the release of an expectation of who and what they should
be. Then there is nothing to hate, and the act of restoration
may ensue in the Upper Room.

To move to the Upper Room in vibration is to allow the
Upper Room to be. And we say this to all of our students, new
and old: If you don't move here in vibration, you will not receive the gifts of the Kingdom. Now, the gifts of the Kingdom
may not be what you wish, but they will always be what you

require to support you in the movement or new agreement towards unification—unification with the Monad, the aspect of you that claims, "I Have Come," and the universal truth that must be called God.

Now, God as universal truth is a very interesting concept for some of you because you've already decided what is true and what is not, and in every case those decisions are made in a kind of limitation and agreement to what cannot be. "That woman will never be who I want her to be." Well, that is perhaps a personal truth, and we will not deny your right to choose it, but we must say to you the one who invokes that is not operating in the Upper Room. She may pretend to be spiritual, but her investment is in separation. You need not like anyone in this room. This has never been about the personality. But it is about the recognition of one who has become the recipient of God, who knows herself, himself, anew. And the challenges that he or she faces, from this new bias, is the agreement to truth where truth is not convenient, where it is not what you want to hear or agree to.

Now, to understand God as truth does not dismiss God as love, does not refute God as knowledge, and the blessing God brings in all its facets. Each of you are saying yes to a realization of who you have always been. Underline *always*. And because this is who you have always been, you may know yourself in truth, realize yourself in truth, but don't for a moment agree to a preposterous idea that truth is sanctioned by personality. In prior lectures we have discussed memory and the attributes of memory, the way that an individual may frame an experience accrued in separation and seek to banter, recruit through that belief, that memory, that has been so eschewed in fear. Because the memory holds fear, or the agreement to separation which holds its basis in fear, all of you who choose this end up recruiting yourselves in fear and releasing the potential that is already present for a higher level of manifestation in the Upper Room.

Because we know who you are, we also comprehend the idea of memory as you have utilized it. And the offering of memory to God, and to the God of truth, is incredibly useful now, because all of the beliefs that you hold that you are separate from God have been known through separation, which finally, we suggest, is a great lie. The opportunity here is to be re-known in high truth, accepted in high truth. And, in the Upper Room, what you require to grow through, which perhaps can show up in any form, will be available to you through your agreement to the potential that exists beyond the lower realm.

Now, some of you say to us, "Well, I pray all day and night. I believe God wants what I want, but I'm not getting what I want, so what does God want from me?" Perhaps the will. Perhaps a surrender to something higher. Perhaps the corner office or the idea of great love would bring you great shame and pain, and the other opportunities available to you, which you may indeed learn through, are actually higher and being proffered—but you tend to refuse. None of you accept what you don't think you can have, and almost all of you deny what is offered to you, because you have an idea of what it should look like and express as.

In the Upper Room, humanity may know itself in a higher way. And God as God—not God as the man in the cloud, but God as truth, God as love, God as expressed knowledge—may be met by you in the ways that you may hold him. "But how do we hold it?" he asks. "This sounds quite lovely, but what do we actually do?" You forgive yourselves for not being where you think you should be. You stop denying yourselves what you can have because it doesn't resemble your idea of what it should be. You stop creating totems in the sky of a God that is Santa Claus and that will give you how you have written and outlined your desires.

"Is there a place for that?" Paul asks. Indeed, there is, and indeed you will learn through this. But we have said this so many times: What aspect of you wants what you want? The one who wants the promotion, desires the great love as he said it should be, is generally claiming through the personality structure. While this is not wrong—it's how you have been taught to be—it holds limitation as its expression. Do you understand this? The lower realm or octave, the schemata of reality that you have known yourself through, indeed has a ceiling—until you make the claim "I am free," claimed as the Monad, which is your passport to the higher realm or Upper Room. Again, the claim "I am in the Upper Room" claims you in accord with potential beyond what you would choose as a small self.

"Can't we have an idea of what we want?" You may be divinely inspired, yes, to take actions in the higher realms that you would not offer yourself to in the lower field because you have mandated what it should look like. The one who is moved to paint a picture, write a play, propose marriage, may be operating in high inspiration. The one who offers herself to God, himself to truth, is always acting in high accord, because the offering holds promise beyond the dictates of the personality and what you think it should look like.

Paul interrupts this teaching. "Is this teaching for the text?" Indeed, it is. We are continuing the last chapter and would like to continue a little more.

The promise of the day for all of you is an agreement to the Upper Room as a place where you may be claimed, and every desire your heart has ever held may be claimed there in union. You are not abandoning the claim. You are offering the claim to the Divine, the great wish to God, so that God may do what it wishes. It's not that you are not ready to receive. It is that you don't know that you are allowed. And you are so busy grasping that you have forgotten how to say yes to what might be offered to you here.

We come in the name of the true Christ. We come in the name Melchizedek, the archetype of the Monad that may be expressed as form. As you align as this teaching, you become as us—beyond the tarnished window that you have sought a world through, beyond the acclimation to separation that memory has chosen to know you through. Each of you here is being received now, is being claimed in the promise of the new.

We thank you each for your presence. Stop now, please. Period. Period. Period.

DAY EIGHT

What stands before you today is a way of experiencing the self beyond the parameters that you have utilized to distort reality. We use the word *distort* intentionally. Indeed, it is your idea of who you are, operating in distortion, that acquires information that you agree to. This coherence with a false narrative, a false idea of who you are, placates the small-self structure, but requires it to operate within the confines of a false kingdom. We say *false kingdom* intentionally.

Now, the reality that you know yourselves through, indeed operable, indeed useful, is the best that you can manage, but it only requires you an insignificant portion of your expression to realize yourself through it. You understand, yes, that the personality structure, in coherence with the manifest world, claims all things in accord to it. And in the higher expression, all things are called to the Monad, or seen or realized as and through the Christed Self, the Monad Self, the Eternal Self, that operates in a high Kingdom. When you understand this, the expression that you hold is actually unbridled, unfettered, and not operating in distortion. You have peered through a window with smoky glass for so very long that you assume that what's beyond it is based upon how you see it through this lens of distortion. When you operate in the higher, the agreement is made to the higher, and the unfoldment of what can be experienced will be known by you in stages.

When those of you who enter the Kingdom first align here, you are somewhat surprised that you are not operating in fear—that the choice to fear is present, but it is not enacted upon. There is nothing there. And you begin to accumulate data through one's experience to support this realization. This is how knowing occurs. When you comprehend the self in safety in the higher strata of vibration, the episodic nature of reality that you have become accustomed to is actually altered. An unfoldment begins, or a fluid experience of presence and being. And it is not that you don't know when Tuesday is or what time the clock says. You are actually experiencing the self beyond these ideas but inclusive of them. Another calendar becomes apparent, another timepiece is present, and we will call these things agreement to eternity. You may be in Tuesday, but know the self in eternity. You may meet your four o'clock appointment, but be in eternity in the same time.

Now, the True Self expresses beyond time, and without that one border what becomes available to an individual in vibration is vastly different than you have known. The ideas you've held about what should be are almost all born in agreement to time—"my four-year college," "the marriage that lasted five years," "the child that is now twenty," "the body that is now seventy." You understand the evidence of time through the agreement to it, which is the parsing of vibration in a diluted sense that must be comprehended as the result of the lower field. It is not that you do not age in the Upper Room. The body may indeed age. But the aspect of self that is ageless is actually announced and is operating in a higher coherence. So the stages of decay, how you have believed you would be at seventy, after the five-year marriage, after the four-year college, is altered because your agreement to time itself, while present, is also operating in a simultaneous state of now—of eternity as now.

Now, the comprehension of eternity is less understood by the senses than by the entirety of the vibrational field. You are reliant upon the senses, and to a certain degree you will be, as well, as you hold a body. But the senses operate differently in the Upper Room. They are no longer held in abeyance by *should*, or the prior expectations through inherited structure— what seventy must be, what winter must be, what the idea of self must be through the confines within the old borders.

Paul interrupts the teaching. "But how do we be in the world but not of it? Winter is winter. If I need a sweater I need to know it's winter." We will say this somewhat differently than you would wish. Your idea of winter is part of a common agreement. Even your idea of cold is born in an agreement to what should be. It is not that you move beyond these things, but you do move to a higher coherence, and the level of realization of this coherence actually re-establishes you in the high strata with new requirements. Indeed, if you are cold, get a sweater. But it is your expectation of cold, your expectation of how time passes and the affect of time, that entrenches you in a certain kind of logic born through the collective agreement of what should be. When you move to what truly is, and always is, you are beyond this system.

The alignment to this system—the Upper Room and beyond—must be understood by you as where you align as you can align to it. You must understand that if you put your hand in a fire you will burn, not only because your expectation is such, but because the rules of the physical realm will require it be so. Alignment in the higher is not avoiding these old rules, but comprehending the self beyond them.

Now, this is not akin to a young man who believes he can fly and then tumbles out the window to a broken arm. This is a realization that consciousness is informing manifestation. And in the high consciousness that we are teaching you now, what is available to you expresses beyond the normalcy, solidity, expectation, that you have endowed things with. You understand that snow will melt and become water. You understand snow is cold, but you know that water may be any temperature. You have some understanding already about the fluidity of form.

What you don't understand yet is how much more there is to know and be in experience with.

"What does that mean?" he asks. To be in experience with something is to learn through the alignment to it—not what we teach, but *how* you become aware and how you move to agreement through the fact of presence and being. "What does that mean," he asks, *"the fact of presence and being?"* Well, the being that you are operates in multiple realities. You may know yourself in this dense field in the Upper Room, which is significantly lighter and completely untethered to a body, which in some ways you do in dream states, in some ways you do when you travel to other ideas of planets or systems of time, alternate realities that may be experienced in you and through your body. But the body is still held or tethered in many ways to its requirements for well-being. Presence, you see, is eternal. But how you realize yourself in presence—how you *be*, in other words—may have many different ways of understanding itself.

Each of you who comes before us has his own requirement, her own requirement, for unfoldment. One size does not fit all here. Imagine that there is a ladder and there are different steps on this ladder. To move to a higher step is to move beyond the lower, and you must steady yourself at each step, become comfortable there before further ascent is helpful or possible. We say *helpful* because you may attempt to strive upwards and fall back down. To grow comfortable at each stage is to align to the lessons that come here, and the lesson that each initiate faces will be altered by his or her requirements.

"What are the requirements?" he asks. "This is one great journey, isn't it? We are all one, aren't we? Don't we have the same experiences and lessons?" You may all look out the same window and have completely different experiences of what you see. You may all know love, but know love in different forms and textures. The individuated experience is actually present in the Upper Room, but when we move to an eternal truth—what is true is always true—you also comprehend that the individuated lens is contributing to the large, vast picture of comprehension of God.

"I don't understand this." He asks for an explanation. We will say this: Each of you looking out a window has prescription for him or herself and what he or she expects. When you go higher, these expectations are altered, perception is altered, and what is received in perception is altered. Some of you say, "I know what God is." But you only know God at the level of agreement you can come to. No one can truly know God because it is unknowable in its vastness. But you may be known by God and experience this vastness at the level that you can hold it. As we said, you require time still, although you may be able to move beyond it experientially to know the self in timelessness, beyond the rubric of time and the mandates of time that you have been indoctrinated in.

When we teach through Paul, we must listen to his concerns. "Is this in the text? I heard a stumbled word. Will this be in the text? Are you going to let me know?" Indeed, this is in the text. We just let you know. And now, if you would permit us, we would like to resume our lecture.

The teaching of the day is actually on infinity, where God is known at the level that God may be received. While you may know God in Tuesday, at the eleventh hour, at four o'clock or two, your experience of God is always in infinity, because God is beyond time, and in your moments of knowing you are beyond time as well. To live in the Upper Room, or in the presence of the Divine, is to move to a strata of vibration where you may be in the world, yes—"I made my four o'clock appointment"—but not of it—"I know it is always now." The eternal *yes* sung to God, the eternal agreement to God, is actually ever present for you here because you are not denying it.

When you stop denying the Divine, even the idea of time moves to its divinity and may be utilized as such. Yes, you take your medication twice a day. Yes, it is wise to know when to pick your child up from school. But the comprehension of self as infinite allows you alignment to infinity. You believe this must happen in meditation or in some prayerful stance. What you don't understand now is that you are already in infinity, and the illusion is time, the illusion is the manifest world. It is all God, it has always been God, and can only be God.

Each of you who comes before us asks this question: "Why am I here?" Because you cannot be anywhere *but* here. And you are here, in all ways, and everywhere else simultaneously. This speck of consciousness that is your agreement to this entitlement of identity that may be named Jonathan or Bill or Freda or Alice is present in all ways. But you are so vast that you don't understand who you can be. So our desire is to move you now beyond the borders, beyond the entrenched systems, that have claimed you in limitation. And we say these words now on your behalf:

"On this night I claim that all that I have known in limitation will be made new, that I give permission to move beyond the borders of consciousness that I have inherited or

erected, that I am willing to be on this journey to what is beyond the Upper Room, and may know myself in fullness as this is my birthright. I know who I am in truth. I know what I am in truth. I know how I serve in truth. I am free. I am free. I am free."

Thank you for your presence. Stop now, please. Period.

DAY NINE

What stands before you today is recognition of what you thought you were, what you believed you could be, and how you claimed an identity in potentials based upon prior construct. The idea of self, even, is a conflagration of ideas, many ideas that create a composite that you utilize as identity. Some of you say, "I am a worker." Some of you say, "I never work." And you define yourself through actions and ways of being seen in consort with the whole. The big change that is upon you now is a reclamation of presence and being as the expression that you identify through. If you know how to use a hammer, use the hammer. If you know how to climb a tree, climb a tree. But you are not identified through hammering, through climbing, but through presence and being.

Now, the gift of this teaching for some of you is a new utilization of the idea of self beyond the construct that has determined outcome. The one who identifies as the one who hammers seeks to do the job he has been called for. The one who believes she cannot be loved claims lovelessness because it's what she has claimed, and consequently expects to claim. When you move beyond the rubric of prescription based in history, many things fall away immediately. It is the habituated behavior—the idea of self encroached by thought, predetermined by memory, which supports you in a kind of stasis. You believe yourselves stuck. You have never been stuck. You believe yourselves limited. You have never been limited. But you have agreed to limitation, and predetermined outcome through it.

Now, when we teach through Paul, we comprehend the limitations of his body and we work beyond them because we don't agree to them. We understand what he believes, what can be claimed through the identity he has used, which has been expanded quite enormously to support the work he does with you. But our reconciliation with form is to form as limitless—at least by the standards that you would utilize. Now, the body will one day die, yes, only to its current form, and be re-known in another way. But while holding form, the escalation of vibration can continue beyond what you believe.

Imagine you have a very small house and you light a candle in the middle of the room. The room will be lit well. You may see the corners, perhaps, by that one flame. But now imagine this same house is expanded, and expanded again and again. One small flame may be built upon. A great fire may fill the house. A fire of light. A fire of truth. A fire of God. And as your house, which is your expression in form and beyond form, is moved beyond the old ideas of what's possible, not only do you illumine the world, but everything that you encounter is illumined by presence and being. This is a radical teaching, and we have spoken about this in texts, but never in the ways that we intend to now, and for one simple reason. We had to pull the roof off the house, and that has been the claim "I am free, I am in the Upper Room, I Have Come." The manifestation of these claims is what expands the house, or reclaims the house in the Upper Room without predetermined ideas that would limit its expression—*it* being form and how form can be re-known.

When you encounter us speaking through the man before you, you encounter an idea of a man, an idea of a voice, and ideas coming from the mouth of the man speaking. You actually don't know the man. To truly know the man is to know what has created the man. To truly understand the language we use is not to listen with your ears, but to move towards comprehension of presence and being. If you were all to take a moment now, wherever you sit, and allow yourself to be informed by the man speaking, with no predetermined ideas claiming you in expectation, you may have an agreement to begin to know the man beyond the structure he has claimed. The light that the man holds is actually in high radiance, and this is an affect of our work through him. But as one candle lights another, all will finally be lit by the presence of all who have been reclaimed, who are listening with their being, and knowing with their souls.

"What does that mean," he asks, "*knowing with their souls?*" To know with your soul is to move beyond the idea of substance in ways that you have utilized substance. Form is useful, but, as we say, form is vibration operating at a dense level of focus, intonation, and resonance. As the field is lifted, the soul which is present in a re-articulated state through the presence of God or the Christ Self or Monad experiencing soul, all things are made new. And the vehicle that you are—soul, Monad, in expression in alignment in the Upper Room—is operative beyond time and space, and inclusive of form, but beyond form as well. In other words, you know where you sit, you may describe the room you sit in, but you may also see beyond the room, and see beyond time, and comprehend the self beyond the old structures that humanity has utilized to negotiate a landscape claimed in shadow and separation.

The one who lives in the valley knows the experience of the valley. She understands the sky through the trees. She understands the breeze as it comes. The one who lives on the high mountain experiences the world differently, and perhaps without shadow. To experience a world without shadow does not mean that there are not shadows in the valley. Indeed, there will be. But the view from the mountaintop is in escalation, and the one above the clouds perceives what's below the clouds and lifts what is and has been there to itself in a higher expression. In other words, you are translating reality through the accord you hold.

Now, the experience of this, as we have said prior, must come in stages. We will not lift you too quickly, but we will lift you, yes, or at least support you in your choice to be lifted. We say *be lifted* intentionally because you are not lifting yourselves. Quite simply put, you cannot. But you can align to the Monad—which is lifted, which operates in the higher field or mountaintop or Upper Room—and lift all things to it because it is what does the lifting.

The claim "I Have Come," the initiate's claim of reconciliation with Source, the agreement of the Monad or the Christ to be reborn in humanity, has not only come, but is moving obstacles so rapidly that you believe that the dominos are falling and must come to an awful end. When many things are brought forth at once, self-deceit and communal deceit, the agreement to deceit and to engage in deceit, deceit is what you will see. And those things claimed in deceit, known through shadow, born in agreement to separation, can and will be met in the Upper Room through agreement in tone.

When we say this, we quite simply mean you are not trying to fix anything. In most cases, seeking to repair is only to bandage the old, put a new shingle on the leaking roof. The roof and the building need to be lifted to a level of strata or frequency where what was once lost is reclaimed or re-known. And here we speak of truth. We have said for many years that in truth a lie will not be held. Truth is an expression of God—as is love, as is wisdom, as is charity. The evocation of the Monad in form as truth quite simply means that there are levels of alignment you will not attain until you move beyond the lies that you have partaken in. There are many lies you have partaken in unknowingly, without awareness that they were untrue. The agreement to time is a lie only in that the idea of time can become an obstruction to the Divine when you make time a totem or an idol that God cannot exist beyond.

To understand the self as in liberation from things that you've agreed to must be understood now. Imagine you have never taken a shower, bathed in a waterfall, stood in a thunderstorm. Imagine that the experience of the water washing the form that you have taken was completely foreign to you. In likelihood you would run from the shower, seek a cover, seek to reclaim the body in its old state. The washing away that is occurring now removes, yes, but not before it reveals. Paul is seeing the image of someone standing in a shower. He sees the mud pooling at the person's feet as the body is washed clean. The mud that is washed away is actually present in un-consciousness, and much of what you will be dealing with in the coming years is the residual affect of unconscious agreement and unconscious choice.

"What does that mean?" he asks. It means that you are unaware of how you contribute to fear, how the bias you hold claims separation, how your predilection to favor one over another denies many the love that would be present for them. When you understand that the expanded state that you are claiming now cannot be limited by the old, you will understand the process you are engaging in. It is not a house of mirrors where you see the distortions one after the next. It's the quiet awareness of how you partake in injustice, and perhaps relish separation, and contribute to the structure of separation through your acquiescence to it.

Again, a great wind comes and moves many things. Again, a great cleansing occurs and washes clean many things. The one that is present for this in an awareness of what is occurring may contribute to the good of the whole. The one that seeks to deny these things—"Get the hammers and nails out, build a shed to protect from the rain, hide from the wind"—will find themselves failing, because the frequency that is present on this plane now will not abate for some time. Go back to what you had? It will not happen. Claim what you would desire in the old way? It cannot occur. What occurs in its place is a reconciliation of all that the Divine has been denied in. This cannot happen without your witness. The simple claim you have been instructed in—"Behold, I make all things new"—is a claim of reconciliation. But as your alignment increases, it is presence and being that operates as the reclamation or the redeemer. And we use the word *redeemer* intentionally. You are redeeming what has been enshrouded in shadow. You are bringing it to light because you will not hide from it. You will not claim another in darkness because there comes a point when you simply cannot. It is not possible.

You understand the idea of the Upper Room more than the experience of being here. If you were to take ten minutes a day in simple meditation—"I am in the Upper Room; I Have Come, I Have Come, I Have Come"—and allow the Christ Self to operate in reconciliation through you, you would be blessed by the outcome, perhaps not as you think, but as you may hold the frequency. The operative word here is *hold*. Now, to hold is, yes, to maintain. But the maintenance of the Upper Room cannot be an arduous task or no one will undertake it. Finally, it is not a balancing act. Finally, it is a simple state of expression, presence and being, as the Christ Self announces itself to all that it encounters, may see and know, and redeem.

The truth of expression—"I am in truth, I am aligned to truth, I perceive truth, I speak truth, and I know truth"—will claim you in a coherence that may be instilled in the field. As anything is instilled in the field, it is seeded. Once something is seeded, it is made presence and known. And its expression as you, and as the field you hold, is what you claim in this teaching.

On this day we claim that all who hear these words may be re-known in truth, announced in truth, aligned to truth, expressed in truth, with one intention: To know and be known by the Divine as it can be known, to experience the Divine at the level that can be held while maintaining

form, with permission to move beyond any limitation that
you have utilized to deny God in self, in others, and in any-
thing and everything that could ever be.

We thank you each for your presence. Indeed, this is in the
text. Stop now, please. Period. Period. Period.

DAY TEN

What stands before you today is opportunity to realize an aspect of self that has been hidden from you, or denied by you.
The truth of your being, you see, must express at the cost of
the old: "Behold, I make all things new," inclusive of any aspect that has contributed to shadow. Some of you say to us, "I
am as I am," and indeed you are. But to be as you are in the
Upper Room cannot contain the old that will deny the light.
So the reliance on the old, the claims of memory, the claims of
self-deceit, are being addressed here intentionally. To turn to
true innocence is to reclaim the truth of your being at the cost
of what has encased it, what would deny the light, what you
would call to yourself in fear.

Now, the aspect that is being addressed today is the need
to be right, the need to be sovereign, through a distinct idea
of what the will is. To understand what we are saying is not to
deny sovereignty. Indeed, it is the Divine Self that is sovereign
within you. And the alignment of will that we have addressed
prior, the realization of will as of God and contributing to
good, must be claimed as what you are doing now. What we
are talking about is the aspect of self that has defied the light
and claimed every reason possible for it. "I will be right at the

cost of this because if I am not right what could I possibly be?" The choice to be right, to deny another their will, or at least their own authority to choose, is always a mandate of the small self.

The challenge humanity faces now is that it has decided to move beyond an old system while applauding much of the old system, or clamoring to it for the old answers. When a world is made new, self-justification, which is a form of the denial of the Divine, must be laid to the wayside. You must claim the True Self at the cost of the idea of what you think should be. Now, anything that you think may have merit, may be useful. "I think I will hang the picture there, plant the roses there, say hello to this one or that one." You may think whatever you like. But to comprehend the self as right at the cost of another being wrong is to decide who they are to you.

Paul interrupts the teaching. "I don't agree with this teaching in the least. If I say, 'Two plus two is four,' and the one beside me says, 'Two plus two is six,' I am correct. There is nothing to argue." Perhaps, Paul, there is a universe where two and two are six. Perhaps there is an idea of self that is progressing through an old system, and utilizes the old system to confirm a reality that she has been indoctrinated in.

Imagine you are walking a path. You understand the view from the third mile, and you will say to the people behind you, "When you get to the third mile, there will be a tree" or "there will be an orchard" or "there will be some dust in a pile and you will recognize it." As you continue on your path, you have no idea what waits for the ones behind you. Your presumption for them—"They will see the tree," "the orchard," "the pile of dust"—is based on your idea of what you saw, equivalency born in memory. And what they may perceive, through whatever eyes they have or whatever reasons they hold, may appear differently. Perhaps the tree has been cut down. Perhaps the orchard was razed. Perhaps the pile of dust has been dispersed by a breeze. You cannot contain an idea of what should be, based in a premise that may not hold true anymore. And self-righteousness, we always say, is indeed the small self trying to prove itself correct, and always at the cost of another being wrong.

Now, an opinion is an idea that has been formulated into a theory. If I believe that this will happen if I do that, I have a theory. If my opinion of you is that you are not this or that, because of past experience or behavior, I am demarcating who you are through the same idea as that tree or that orchard. What I saw two days ago must be true today, because the eyes that saw two days ago seek to perpetuate what they knew. When a world is made new, everyone will clamor for an idea to sustain them.

This world is being made new in a high way. This world is falling, collapsing, can never be the same. Many will hunger or thirst. No one will hunger or thirst. How humanity views the experiences that are before them will actually contribute to the manifest world through the simple premise that what one damns, or what a collective damns, will always damn it in return. Now, we are not telling you that if there is a famine there is plenty of food on the table. But what we will say is your realization of the Source of all things will actually claim beyond a famine and a reliance upon plenty. This is done by the one who knows who she is, what he is, and how he serves. You have been taught stories about loaves and fishes. You have been taught stories of water into wine. But you don't understand that the basis for these stories is a simple understanding of the mathematics of Source. In Source, two plus two is always a thousand, or a million, because the math that exists in the Upper Room does not confirm to the math that you have known, which is in most ways born in agreement to systems known in scarcity.

He interrupts again. "First of all, I don't like math. Second of all, two plus two is four. How can it be a thousand?" Paul, imagine there is one mirror before you and you see that one reflection. You are facing reflection in a singular way. Now, imagine there is also a mirror behind you and suddenly you are perceiving infinite reflections, ongoing into infinity. The idea of the one mirror containing one reflection must be abandoned when the rules are changed. Now, if you wish to argue that it is an illusion, we will remind you that the manifest world is also an illusion. Everything is in vibration in tone and expression through tone. The idea of a reality that is elastic to thought has begun. But you don't understand the agreement that is available to you in the higher octave. Each and every one of you seeks to place the mathematics, the rules of right and wrong, in the Upper Room. And the moment you do this, you call the Upper Room back to the lower field. Imagine the Upper Room had pink curtains, and you go up to the Upper Room and say, "Oh, lovely pink curtains." And then you damn your neighbor, and you say, "Well, I put a pink curtain up downstairs so this must be the Upper Room." That would be the self-deceit of the pious, the blasphemer, the one who claims that God is there to do his or her will because it must agree to his or her politics or opinions.

When you move to the Upper Room in vibration, you have begun a journey, and a great journey, in elasticity and the product of the elasticity of a consciousness that has not been born and raised in limitation. Now, you understand what a room is. If we were to ask any of you what a room is, you would say, "Well, four walls, perhaps a doorway, and a ceiling." And then you would say, "I have a room." The idea of *room* is what codifies this experience. When the idea of *room* is released, inclusive of Upper Room, you have an expanse of potential. You don't realize that the idea of a room may encase an entire universe, have no walls, no boundaries as you have known them. When you listen to music, you actually assume that when the song is over the music has stopped. In fact, the music is present always. Once a note is sung, it is always heard. Those of you who have the ability to read what you call the past or the future are actually tuning in to the music that still lingers through the idea of time and space. When time and space are re-known and re-seen— again, the simple claim "Behold, I make all things new"—reality itself, the very fabric of reality that you have known, may be transposed, which simply means sung and expressed in the high octave, where indeed all things are made new.

He interrupts the teaching. "You began talking about self-righteousness. How is this still a teaching on that?" Every opinion you hold that is indoctrinated through an idea of self born in limitation holds limitation within it. Do you understand this idea? Now, imagine that there is a prison, and a prison with walls and doors. You know yourself in this prison, unable to exit. You qualify your experience here as what you have known, and any idea of what exists beyond this prison can only be an idea. When you realize, which simply means *know*, that the prison itself is the construct of an idea made manifest, and that all that comprises the prison is that one Source, codified and made permanent in idea, you may re-know the prison, and you may move the walls. But you will not do this when you have decided you are right and another is wrong. All of these opinions are born in a reality that celebrates separation. Indeed, you like being right—not nearly as much as you like making another wrong. And this gives you a sense of importance, which is how the small self seeks to rule. Again, we must say that the small self, who rules a small kingdom, has every investment in being in authority, which is its idea of sovereignty. Now, the Monad or the Divine Self is the true sovereign self, and for one simple reason: It does not operate through the old structure. It cannot operate through the old structure. This prison that we described is not present in the Upper Room because it has already been made new by the aspect of self that is free, is free, is free.

The teaching we offer you now in elasticity is actually a requirement for where we intend to take you, which is a return to innocence or to your own Christed nature. Permission is necessary. But as long as the small self is seeking to dictate the terms of this, your experience will be one of limitation and self-deceit. Paul interrupts the teaching yet again. "I understand, I believe I understand, what you are trying to teach us. But how is this possible for us? This sounds too implausible, or too far-reaching. How can any of us return to a state of innocence?"

Through presence and being, and the gift of presence and being in the Upper Room, which is the manifestation of the true Christ that makes all things new, inclusive of the doubt you have held, the self-deceit you have utilized to get your idea of your way, and your understanding of what it means to be, which is actually rectified, reclaimed, in the high octave once you claim your true presence here. We say *here* intentionally because we are teaching you in the Upper Room. It is where we move to from a higher field for this instruction. And the aspect of any of you that already abides here is welcoming the aspects of self that would deny the truth, seek to maintain a lie about self, or who another should be, based in a false premise known through separation. Understand we said *through separation.* When you have a lens in a camera, the lens claims what is seen. When the focus of the lens is changed, what is seen is other. When the lens of separation is not present, when the filter is gone, what is expressed is everything that exists beyond it. To understand what we mean must give you a new opportunity to comprehend the idea of elasticity.

Now, imagine you were looking at a target, perhaps a sign on a building, and everything that you see is contained in the field of vision that you may hold while maintaining that target. Now, imagine you are moved a thousand miles from that target. That target still exists on the wall. You may say, "I cannot see that far," but in fact you are seeing in a wider pattern now, and all things within that thousand miles, those feet, that distance, are still contained in the vision that you hold. The idea that separation will always be the filter would be to say that you are always looking at that target from a few feet away, and your sense of boundary is informed by that sense of limitation. When we teach in the Upper Room, we teach in a vast expanse. The Upper Room contains many ideas that you may never know, that are beyond your reach and ken. The agreement to the Upper Room, and embodying here, is not only a gift, but an agreement. Once the agreement is made to this—"I am in the Upper Room, I Have Come"—the manifestation occurs in the stages that you can maintain. But as long as you are intent on mandating separation through the small self's will—"I will be right at the cost of another being wrong," "I will maintain my free will and use it as I wish, even if it disallows me what is available to me in the higher octave"—the choice is yours. You may choose as you wish. You may live as you wish. But the ability you have now to be received in fullness in the Upper Room is completely experiential.

We will say these words now for each of you: The rules are changed. Two and two equals a million. There is not one reflection of identity, but infinite expressions. The only rules that you will abide by are the rules born in truth, and you must become liberated from the old evidence, or the old systems, that would bind or tether you to the low field.

On this day we claim that all who hear these words will now be in receipt of a liberation of expression that dissolves the idea of separation.

Separation is only an idea, and its dissolution in the Upper Room is the promise of this teaching.

Thank you for your presence. This is in the text. Period. Period. Period. Stop now, please.

(PAUSE)

What stands before you today is a higher awareness of a potential. When you have stopped masquerading through limitation and adorning the idea of self with the accoutrements of your age, you begin to realize the self as you can only be. Underline this, friends: *as you can only be.* Everything else is an idea, a charade, a costume worn, a vocabulary utilized, to mandate a reality that indeed all humanity is moving beyond now. This is not only the end of an age. It is the commencing of another. And the fabric of reality itself must be altered in order for this to happen. The elasticity we speak to is less about the individual becoming a miracle worker than reality itself being assumed in a higher octave of experience wherein all things are made new.

The trajectory of humanity is sovereign, or towards a sovereign state that has not been witnessed on this plane for far too long. Indeed, there was a time when humanity knew who and what it was, when it regarded each other, one another, as holy, as of God. And every expression of God was seen as cause for celebration. The restoration to a state of innocence—to the garden, if you wish—is a process, yes. But it is the next stage of humanity's passage. We have said this many times, but you certainly cannot go on as you have been. And the end of any age or any time or any experience is often accompanied by mourning, or a sadness at the efforts made. "We tried so hard to find peace, and we went to war again, anyway." "We tried so hard to find happiness. We failed. We did the best, yes, and we are sorry."

It is time for celebration yet again, whether or not you agree to us or this teaching. And the cause for celebration is the choice that has been made, and indeed it has been made— that humanity will triumph, but in an altered state. The altered state humanity assumes cannot be assembled at the level of density that you have been operating in. This is why the world is made new—because you cannot continue in the old way and claim a higher level of alignment than you have. Paul is seeing a fish tank. It is quite filthy. The fish will not survive. The tank must be emptied, made new. Perhaps no tank is required and the fish may swim freely in a clean ocean.

The idea of self, moored through the reality you have chosen to learn through, has been of benefit, but its time is ending.

Now, the cry for the old primarily is born in a need to sustain an idea of reality even if it doesn't serve you. Imagine the poor fish taken out of the tank. They believe they must perish. The new is not present yet. And when it is, there is an enormous sigh of relief. There is an act of rectification or righting that which has fallen that is about to proceed. And what has fallen is your own relationship to the Divine that has been denied by the collective.

Now, we will emphasize this, lest anyone seek to make this a religious teaching: This is not a religion. This is an opportunity for reclamation at the cost of the old. You are not being punished. Imagine a boat that has capsized. It has been under water for so long it believes that down is up. When the boat is righted, much will fall from the boat. But the boat will be steadied once you understand the basis for the boat is the sea in which it floats. The basis for your being is the God that is all things, the great ocean or sea that you have always been existing in but denying.

Now, to understand the self as free of fear does not mean you walk into traffic and say, "I will not be struck." It is not assuming that there is no penalty for an action taken. To be without fear is to stop agreeing to its promise that it is your protector, when in fact it is your prisoner and your prison, both. "What does that mean?" he says. Well, the small self utilizes fear, and in this way fear is your prisoner. But, finally, it's the prison because all it will ever do is reinforce itself and its mandates, and its primary mandate is always separation.

The gift of the times are not only the promise of the new, but the gift that comes from the willingness to perceive all things as being altered and changed. Stop bemoaning change. Stop trying to right the ship when you are simply trying to keep it under water because that's all you think can be. When reality is transformed, or the fabric of reality altered, there is always a period of time when what is down seems up, and vice versa. There is always a period where those things that have been ignored must be seen in order to move from them. And there will always be a time when the choice is made, again and again, to lift beyond an old way of operating in a reality that was known through fear, through division, and the denial of God.

If each of you today were to take an hour and understand union experientially, comprehend union experientially, your life would be forever changed. You understand that the body is solid in form, although we tell you, again and again, it is an evocation of sound and tone, the one note sung vibrating in form. If you sit and you allow the body to reclaim its essence—"I know what I am in truth"—and allow this essence, the body as sound and tone in vibration, not solid, you would begin to experience the body itself beyond the separation you have known it through. You would begin to realize that the energetic field is not superimposed on the form, but is simply another expression of vibration. Again, understand: The body is in vibration, the energetic field in vibration, the Monad in vibration as the highest articulation that one may know while maintaining form. To sit for an hour—"I know what I am in truth"—and allow that expression to be the *what* of the body and the energetic field, as the Monad invokes this because it *must* be the Monad that invokes this claim, you may find yourself expanding in form and field across the vastness of the Upper Room.

Now, you do this in the Upper Room because the Upper Room is where the Monad is expressed most fully. Perhaps there has been a mystic, or a few dozen, that have realized the Monad in form in a higher state of articulation where the body itself may be assumed in an altered state. The idea of being beyond mortality, beyond destruction, is apt when you understand that the body is vibration, an energetic structure, and energy cannot die. All of you will lose the body because that is the agreement to this form. And even the one who has ascended while in form has turned away from the body, or released the body, because they realized finally that the body is obstruction to the vastness of experience that is available when you lift beyond the Upper Room to the eternal landscape of being.

Paul interrupts. "Are there some who've maintained form? We have heard stories of those who do not die or cannot die." That would be a choice made by an avatar, or one you might think of as an avatar, but it is not made without cost. The one who holds the body, finally, we must say, is tethered to a landscape that oscillates in agreement to a density that must take form. Your experience of body is a stage of evolution. You don't expect the worm to always be the worm. Perhaps it becomes part of the soil, and perhaps the growth that the soil produces. Nothing is intended to maintain the current form that it holds. Underline that, friends: *Nothing is meant to maintain the current form that it holds.* Religious teachings may speak of advanced beings who fly across the seas, rise from the rubble of history to bless mankind. But if you understand that nothing dies, nothing can die, and that death itself is an idea, you will move beyond even death as a method for learning. It is useful still.

There are some of us here, who talk through Paul, who have not known form. We know ourselves in eternity. There are others that have claimed form and then eschewed it. We do not rely on form in order to instruct, because there is always a presence at any time on this plane that is available to be the intercessor for these teachings. These are not new teachings. They are older than time as you know it. And the gift of the time you have chosen to incarnate in is the time and the gift of reconciliation, that which has been denied God in redemption and resurrection.

The gift of the times you sit in—great change, indeed—provide a promise for a future, or at least your idea of a future, beyond a schism that you have utilized as the harshest instructor you may have ever chosen. The denial of the Divine is a very hard teacher. We trust now that as humanity is restored to its innate nature—you cannot be made innocent, indeed you always have been—but that which has denied your innocence is being moved, claimed in a higher way, re-known and re-deemed.

This is the end of this chapter. We will give you the title when we wish. Period. Period. Period. Stop now, please.

4

RECONCILIATION

What stands before you today is a willingness to respond to the needs of the moment, and only the needs of the moment. The precursor to fear is always anticipation. What if? What *could* happen. To stay in the present moment is to know the self in opportunity beyond the dictate or mandate of fear. Now, each of you says to us, "I would like this, but I can't achieve it." You can't think of it as something to be achieved, but as agreed to. Agreement is not achievement. Agreement is reception. And to be in the moment, responding to the moment regardless of what you think the moment is, will support you in an awareness of what eternity is.

You are in eternity now. You are not in a Tuesday or a Saturday. You are in eternity now. Tuesday and Saturday are ideas, born in an agreed-upon structure claimed by a necessity to organize experience through the idea of time. When you understand that time itself is an idea, and you release the mandate of time to be the structure that you abide by, you are liberated from many things. This is again done by agreement. Nobody is asking you to throw your clocks out, delete the appointment book that you have held so dear. We are saying, instead, that the moment that you sit in is the only moment that ever is. Everything else is an idea that has been endowed with meaning or fear by the aspect of self that seeks to claim identity in separation.

Now, time is not a structure that is fear-based. Time is simply an idea, an organizing structure in linearity that you may utilize to a high effect if you wish. It is prudent to know when to prepare for the winter. It is prudent to know when to take a walk when the weather is fine. It is useful to know your neighbor, and have perhaps an agreement to when you may meet. What is not prudent is to design a life within a rigid structure where you are being taught what to do through the mandates of a structure claimed in time. "It is February, we must do this." "It is Christmas, we must do that."

Each of you who says yes to this teaching is actually moving beyond the template of time because the Upper Room does not hold linearity. You may comprehend it, you may choose to claim it from the Upper Room, but you are doing this. It is not informing your decisions as much as available to you for your requirements or needs. If you truly understand that the only moment you can ever be in is this moment now, and that all things may be known in this moment, equivalency changes, expectations change. Expectation releases and becomes agreement, which is accord. When you know the self in the eternal now, your needs may be met beyond the calendar, beyond the clock, because when it is always now, there is no interference.

Paul interrupts the teaching. "I have many questions. We have seasons. A pregnancy takes so many months. We understand ourselves through the requirements of time. This is not a bad thing. How can all needs be met in the ever-present now?" If you understand that it is always now, your needs can always be met. Your currency has always been immediacy, the desire for now, born in expectation or anticipation. The release of this idea—"Give me what I want as I want it"—allows receptivity. You are not clamoring for what you want. Your arms are open to receive them, to receive the gifts that would be made available to you when you stop deciding when and where it should be.

We will tell you why we are teaching this now. The Divine Self, as we have stated, expresses beyond time, beyond linearity. Personal narratives that you utilize to know the self through conditioning are based in a premise of time. "When I was five years old." "When I was twenty." And because you use these narratives, you place yourself unintentionally in a linear world where you age and decay and Christmas comes as expected every year. When you move to the immediacy of the now, the Divine Self can become assuming of all that it encounters.

Now, even your idea of time is only known in the present moment. Your idea of Christmas is known in this moment. Your idea of a month or day is only known now. And to bless the day, or the idea of future event, still will only happen now. To claim the presence of the Divine upon your idea of a future event is actually to move the future event into the present moment because that is when the blessing occurs—in the present moment. When you fear something in the future, you are claiming the fear in the immediacy of the present moment and utilizing that fear to call to you the very thing that you say you don't want. In other words, if you have damned a future event, you are in alignment to that fear through your damnation and it will continue to accrue energy as you continue to damn or fear it.

This moment we sit in with you, this moment of being, is informed by one thing only—the Divine that expresses as all things, including this voice, and these words, and the body you sit in, and the eyes that see and the ears that hear. We are in the Divine, as and of it, and not distinct from you. We are simply operative at a level of knowing of who and what we have always been that we are seeking to impart to you—we will use a different word from *seeking* because that implies expectation—that we are *offering* you, that you are willing to receive, and can, as well, receive as you agree to the premise. We are together now. We are not apart from God now. And the calendar and the clock exist as structures that we can give adherence to, or choose to rise beyond.

If the clock is more powerful than God, you have created an idol. If your idea of time and aging is more powerful than God, you have created another idol. Aging is a gift. A weathered tree is a fine tree, and you weather with age through the exposure to the elements. You understand this in time, but if you move beyond the idea of time, the tree itself knows itself in youthfulness because it is ever present as now. Paul interrupts the teaching. "So then we don't age?" You know yourself as new, and the conditioning that you have utilized that creates aging, in certain ways, is forgone. The immediacy of the present moment in the Upper Room can claim the body beyond the old idea and conditioning.

Now, a season comes, yes. The leaves may fall, yes. But the energy of the tree is vital always, because all energy is vital, and the form will change as the form requires change. The tendency you all have to cement an idea, to codify an idea, claims the idea in firmament, or a structure in low density. When you move to the Upper Room, you understand time as a way of knowing things, but eternity trumps time. Do you understand this? Time is a structure. Eternity is beyond structure. There really is no beginning and no end. And when you have returned fully to the ocean of Source, the idea of time itself is a curiosity, a way that you have learned. But you have become one with all, and delineation, as you have utilized it, has moved beyond, released itself, for the good of all.

"What does that mean," he asks, "*for the good of all*?" As long as you are conditioned to the calendar and the clock, you are claiming the clock as powerful and you are claiming the calendar as structuring the narrative of your experience. And the reception that is available to you in the Upper Room is actually disrupted or altered by the idea that time utilizes to give you a sense of safety and structure. For example, if all things are available now, you will find a sequence of how you wish to receive things. If you are in the immediacy of now and receiving what you require, you trust the sequence of the requirement to deliver you your good. You are not mandating outcome, nor are you feeling betrayed when what you expected to come, and when, did not arrive as you wished.

Our agreement to you today is that moving beyond the

idea of time actually allows your receptivity. Now, we understand that you exist in a co-created world, and even as you align in the Upper Room the use of the clock and the calendar is a requirement. There is nothing wrong with them per se except how you utilize them, and how you broadcast your idea of time as it configures a reality that operates in the denial of the Divine. Imagine you went to church on Sunday. Sunday is the day you visit God. It has been claimed a holy day at the cost of the other days of the week, lacking their regard or their implicit holiness. When you understand that now is all there is, and you become receptive in the now, all things will be gifted to you as you say yes to them. Period. Period. Period.

Yes, this is in the text. Stop now, please.

DAY ELEVEN

What stands before you today is an awakening to a potential, a realization of something that is present, has always been present, but precluded from your experience through your denial of the Divine. Everything you see before you—high, low, and in between—is indeed of one Source operating at varying levels of intonation or vibration. Everything named in some way is aligned to the name given and the meaning that the name has been endowed with—"that awful man," "that evil thing," "that darkest night." The equivalency you hold to these things is actually what claims you in accord to them. But they would not be low, they would not be damned, without your agreement to that.

Now, when you come to us and you listen to these words, you parse the words carefully. "What do I wish to agree with?"

"What do I wish to save for later?" "What can I never confirm that is being spoken here?" We would like to speak to this very directly. We actually don't care if you agree with what we say. That is not our intention. Our intention for you is to have an experience of your own divinity that is being precluded by your denial of the divinity in all things. You say you want union, but you fight what you don't like, damn who you disagree with, and then often pat yourselves on the back for feeling self-righteous, being the victor, being the one who only knows the truth.

When we teach through Paul, we serve as an intercessor for many of our students. In other words, when you seek to return to the old, we will actually support you in the realization of the other options that are always present, always available to you. How you denounce things is in fact how you align to them. And the preclusion of divinity, when it is always here, is what we must understand now as the relationship you hold to the manifest world.

We will explain this for Paul. Everything is in relationship to you, individually and collectively, and when we say *relationship* we simply mean accord. The vessel that you are, which operates in a physical reality, is actually confirming all physical reality and claiming the tone or the relationship you hold with what is before you. "This is a good thing" or "a bad thing," "an evil man" or "a lovely man." Your coherence in your own vibrational field is actually deciding how you are in relationship to absolutely everything in your world.

Now, we say *absolutely everything* so that there can be no confusion. That means all things, everything seen and unseen, in form and unmanifest. The Monad, which is the Christ Self, is of a level of amplitude or vibrational tone where it may assume all things, reclaim all things. The idea of Christ as redeemer has become confused to mean the man who embodied as Christ. And while that is useful for many, it actually detracts from the very simple truth that Christ as redeemer is instilled in each of you. And it is this act of redemption that you are agreeing to through this instruction. To be redeemed is not to be better than another. It is to be re-known as you truly are.

Now, there are prophecies of a Second Coming, perhaps the man in the cloud. In fact, the Second Coming is the awakened Christ in all humanity in amplitude in a resurrected state. The agreement to this has been made, has been foretold, and it is actually a true teaching. When the Monad in incarnation as anyone or anything is in expression, presence, and being, what is encountered by it is in fact redeemed or made new through the equality, the equation, of tone and vibration. You may think, if you wish, of a candle flame that grows and grows in brightness as it assumes all things, as the flame claims what it encounters and becomes a blaze. You believe this is frightening, being burned at the pyre. But in fact what is burned away is actually reclaimed, brought back to Source, assumed by the light of God, which as we have said is of all things.

Now, if you wish more than this, a deeper understanding, we will only say this: The act that you are engaged in here is indeed an alchemical act—of transmutation, of form and flesh being re-known in their initial principle, the initial principle being the one note sung which you may call God. Now, because sound and tone are not limited except by your comprehension of them, you may begin to understand that this one note sung as all things is not only present, but fully available to you—underline the word *fully*—*fully* available to you as you agree to it.

Now, intellectual agreement is useful only in that it grants a kind of permission. "I am willing to entertain this idea. I am willing to decide that perhaps this is so." But to fully agree to something is simply to allow it to be. And, finally, we have to say, the intellect cannot contain this because the intellect is so informed by reason, known through logic, known through the ideas of the times that you sit in, that it would deny what it cannot fathom. So in some ways we bypass intellect in this entrainment, and by *entrainment* we mean vibrational accord.

Now, the intellect itself can be assumed by the Divine, and in fact must be if this equation is to realize itself. The Manifest Divine will utilize intellect to create new science, new methods of healing, new ways of comprehending reality that exist already, but have been placed in the Upper Room for safekeeping. "What does that mean?" he asks. Humanity will misuse anything that it can hold that it believes it will profit from or use to rule another. To understand that in the Upper Room this configuration is altered, because fear is not informing choice, would show you why things are held here. So when many of you say, "How will humanity survive?" the answers are not in the field and in the intellectual agreements you might make in this collective reality you know, but may be partaken of, and, indeed, received fully, in the Upper Room.

Now, to become receptive in the Upper Room is not to arrive here with the intention to amass information. You will confound yourself. And the industry you would seek to utilize has been known by you in the lower field and will not operate fully in the higher octave because it is born in agreement to fear. "I must figure this out by Monday. I must be the one to solve the equation." The idea of self as recipient to the gifts of the Kingdom must now be understood as the gift of presence and being. You are not striving, nor are you demanding. You are aligning and in agreement, which is accord, to what already exists here. Notice we said *already exists*. Because it already exists in the Upper Room, it may be received. You are so busy conjuring, trying to get God to do what you want, that you miss what is already in offering.

Now, when you receive a gift, you may not understand how it is useful until it is time for the gift to be used. You will not decide that the gift you are receiving will bring you income, make you more special than you could ever be. To receive a gift is to be thankful. Now, imagine somebody gave you a paintbrush and you say, "Well, this is rather nice, but I have no paint." You may feel disillusioned. But one day you understand that it is by holding the paintbrush that the paint appears, not before or after. It is the immediacy of the demonstration of the gift in vibrational accord to what is before you which claims the gift in presence and being. Articulation at this level is manifestation of form, field, and consciousness as can be aligned in a higher strata, without exploding or annihilating identity because you require that. Those of you who say, "I want the ego to die," will be quite forlorn when you don't know whose shoes to put on in the morning or where your house was yesterday. These things are useful, but in their right place. Many of you would seek to claim the gifts of the Kingdom for rectification of the egoic structure. "You see, my life now has meaning. See how I have been gifted?" In fact the gifts come, not because they've been claimed, but because they've been allowed.

Now, we have said in the past that you must claim the gifts offered. And while there is truth to this in the lower octave, "I require this thing, let it be brought to me" and you don't open the door to claim it would be rather different if you understood how the rules operate in Christ consciousness. You are receiving what is already present. The paintbrush held claims the outline of the thing received. The gift that is received is the gift that is required in the moment—not one day, not as you wish, but as you can hold it. To understand the metaphor of the paintbrush, you needed to know that it was yours and work with it, which means hold it or align to it in order to comprehend how it serves.

Reclamation of identity has been discussed in this text already—the reclamation of identity and memory, which is how you perceive and why you endow things with meaning. To understand where you sit today is at the beginning of a passage towards innocence, and we will explain why we say *beginning*: The opportunity is here for a reframing of reality beyond what was decided by your forefathers, or what you believe is so through prior prescription or belief. If you keep deciding, "This is good" or "evil," you will continue to claim identity in separation. We are not making something you would call *evil* good. We are reframing what is seen to be of God, because once it is known as of God, it can and will be lifted, through presence and being, to its rightful accord.

Now, imagine you live in a valley. You have some small assumption of the lives people live on the mountaintop, but the best you can do is guess. Perhaps someone visits from the mountaintop, and says, "Oh, you must love it up here. Why do you stay down where you don't need to?" You stay down where you don't need to because you have amassed a world, and a language for a world, that claims things in identity and meaning that you are so attached to you cannot imagine something other. Now, to imagine something other, whether or not you know it, is to give it permission to be manifest. But you cannot outline the Kingdom because you cannot know it until you are present in it. But what indeed you may know is how it feels, or the experience of the Kingdom that can be met by you in form. Once you begin to have this experience, you have an imprinting in the energetic field that will support your alignment in the higher stages of equivalency.

When memory is reclaimed and no longer tainted by the obstruction of fear, when desire is met in God and offered to God to be in high service, when love is known as your expression and not a mandate for personality—"how I should be with another"—you have already claimed a level of potential that few have known in form. The individual agreement to ascend or align to high tone is actually the predecessor to the collective doing so, because the moment one is seen on the mountaintop and waving down below, everyone else has permission to abandon the old or re-see the old, reclaim the old, in the high order of the Upper Room and no longer create from the old expectations of what you believe should be.

Identity itself, while a requirement for form, is misunderstood by you no matter what we say. And until you know the self, realize the self, beyond separation, you will believe yourself to be separate, and identity or the mask that you utilize for this will continue to claim you. Now, the mask is not abandoned as much as re-known. And the offering of identity—"Dear Lord, receive who I think I am so that I may be re-seen; claim who I believe myself to be so that I may be known; allow me to know, as I may know, the truth of my being beyond separation"—will support you well. But it is indeed a choice and must be an offering.

He interrupts the teaching. "Well, when we claim 'I Have Come, I Have Come, I Have Come,' doesn't this happen automatically?" Both yes and no. The alignment occurs, but free will is still present. Imagine there is a flow of lava. Eventually it will overtake what it encounters, but some of you will erect barriers. "Please, not here. Please, don't overtake this fear or this terrible shame that I believe I need to survive." When you say, "I am willing," you actually give permission for the process to continue in the most perfect way it may. When you are trying to keep something out, it claims great energy, and you actually empower the process through your striving to contain. When you release the need to contain, when you allow yourself to be re-seen—overtaken, if you wish—by the Divine, equivalency occurs in a far more graceful manner. When you understand that what is releasing, or being reclaimed, is simply what has hindered your process, you'll be a little less protective of what it should be, because you may begin to trust what is.

Some of you say to us, "How long does this take? I want it in this lifetime or why bother?" You are back downstairs. Again, the Upper Room operates beyond time. The calendar and the clock are known in the lower field, but they are not comprehending themselves in imperative ways in the Upper Room. If you wish to rush the Kingdom, we guarantee you will have a very difficult time. "Why is that?" he asks. The psyche itself, or the idea of reality that you know yourself through, is elastic, as we said. But to bend something, or to open it wide as a flower may open, is very different than pulling the petals off the flower, or screaming, "Now, now, now!" The body itself can only acquiesce and align to the higher voltage tonality of the Upper Room as it can manage it. And consciousness, ever present, if moved too rapidly may create distortion in an idea of self. That is why some believe themselves to be Jesus, or the holy woman who will conquer all.

The fatigue you engage in by striving in this way is actually defeatist. If you are gifted with a large experience of spirit, know that you will require to be integrated by it. *It* will be what integrates you, and not the other way around. So there is no rush to the Kingdom. But like anything else, when a rivulet turns into a stream, and the stream turns into a river, the magnitude of force is increased as you can manage it. And, indeed, that is the case here. So in this lifetime? Perhaps. But that is not the point here. Any progress one makes in their growth is held in the field throughout your idea of *time* or *lifetime*. And, indeed, we must say these are simply ideas, and not much more. To be reclaimed by God is restoration. It is not an act of force. It is allowance. It is receipt.

And we say this now to each of you: We are teaching a chapter on "Reconciliation." That will be the title. We are preparing for "Innocence." This is still Part One of the text. "Innocence" will be Part Two. Thank you for your presence. Stop now, please. Period. Period. Period.

(PAUSE)

What stands before you today, in an awakened state, is an agreement to what is already present. Please underline this: *an agreement to what is already present.* The denial of the Divine—obstruction, yes, of what is already present—is what is being attended to now. And the alignment you hold—in the Upper Room, yes—reclaims you beyond these obstacles. The things that would interfere with this realization are the things that you give power to, agreement with, that you claim in fear or denounce as outside of God.

Now, something may be in low vibration, in a poor intent, hold a basis in fear, but these things are not re-known through the damnation of them, but through the agreement to them as of God. To know something as of God is certainly not to approve of it or give it a blessing through the personality structure. It is simply to agree to what is, and agreement is accord, vibrational accord. To reclaim God where it has been denied is to be the redeemer and to engage in the act of redemption. When you ask us, "How is a world made new?" you don't like the answer: Through the re-seeing of the world, the re-knowing of the world, without the denial of the Divine in an active place operating in its own accord. To rise above this is to *be* risen, to *be* resurrected. You don't believe it's possible, but in fact it already is. Again, the Monad *is* risen. It *is* resurrected. It already aligns in the

Upper Room, and all that is being moved is that which has obscured its presence, challenged its being.

Now, when we teach through Paul, we actually come with an awareness of how this work will be received. We are with the reader who is reading as we dictate. We are with the one, twenty years from now, approaching this language for the first time. We exist beyond time, so we are present in all ways. And the primary interference most of you face is born in reason or your idea of reason, what you believe can be possible. Again, we will go back to the old metaphor of the fish in the tank. The fish has known the tank. That is its universe. It has grown accustomed to the murky water. It does not know what it's like to swim freely, to be beyond the parameters that it has used to know itself in form. Because the Upper Room is indeed boundless in its own way, we will share something with you. What is available to you here, within this octave we call the Upper Room, that has infinite borders, which simply means you may express here fully while maintaining form, you may encounter an aspect of yourself that is fully realized and would seek to be your counsel. You don't understand that in the Upper Room the aspect of the self that fully knows and realizes is present and available to you.

"What does this mean?" he asks. "We have a doppelgänger in the Upper Room?" Not at all. But you have a realized self that is already in manifestation that knows the law, knows the parameters, and can escort you through this new reality. "What does this look like?" he asks. "Is this like the higher self?" We will say it somewhat differently. We used the image of a singular mirror and how you perceived self in singularity in the last chapter. But what is before you now is every possible reflection that you may ever hold. And to guarantee the high one, the one that knows her way and can be claimed, is to authorize it to be your instructor. To be reclaimed by the Divine Self that is already manifest is to move into an agreement with what you are already in this high octave of expression and experience.

The meeting of the Monad in form is actually an experience you may undergo, and the only requirement for it is to gift the self to it fully so that it may become your teacher. To allow the Divine Self in an articulated state that is already present in the Upper Room is to know the aspect of self that is realized. If you understand that you are now operating beyond time and space as you have utilized them, this will not seem so confusing. Beyond time and space, the one who calls herself Antoinette, the one who calls himself Joseph, the one who knows who he is in the Upper Room in a higher way is known by the one that he has become. Underline the words *has become*. You have become this in the Upper Room. It is not a state of striving. It is already expressed here. To merge with the Divine that is already in full expression is a sacred marriage or union, but it does come at the cost of a belief in separation that the realized self does not hold. So to agree to this is not to disassociate, is not to rely on the new at the cost of an idea of self. It's to allow the self to be received by who you truly are as manifest. And the course of this response, the affect of this agreement, is the release of separation.

We have always taught you in entrainment or vibrational accord. So all we have told you is already there is an aspect of self that is fully realized, that is comfortable in the Upper Room, that can maintain the octave in its own way. Your agreement to this, and the merging of it as who and what you are, grants you the agreement to know the self beyond the separate self, because the higher accord or the Manifest Self is what you have now aligned to.

He interrupts the teaching. "I have several questions. You have called the Upper Room boundless, and also an octave, which of course must have a high and a low. How are these things comparable?" An octave is expressed in width, and even the high note is boundless in its expression. When you lift to the octave above this one, that will also be boundless. And even as the parameters of the physical realm are known in definition, one's experience incarnated here is boundless at the level of tone that you can hold. As you shift through the octaves, initially with form, and then without, each octave of expression is known in boundlessness.

Now, the second question you have, Paul, is what is it like to be in this merged state with the aspect of self that is already realized? It is as you are today with one distinct difference: You have changed the mind that was trained in separation to an equality with Christ Mind, and this must include intellect, which has been discussed prior. To align to Christ Mind is to align to the Infinite Mind that may be expressed through the individual. Now, the individual can amass so much and hold so much, but it cannot maintain the Infinite, because the vastness of it is too broad and too much for an individual to hold. But what the truly Manifest Self that you are merging with claims is what it may know, and it knows far more than you can imagine.

If you wish now, you may make this choice:

"I am in the Upper Room. I Have Come. I Have Come. I Have Come. Behold, I make all things new. It will be so. God Is. God Is. God Is."

And in this field of God, all that can be and all that ever will be known, allow the self that you have known, vibrating at this level of tone, to be in an encounter with the aspect of self that is fully realized here, that does not doubt, does not fear, no longer experiences itself in separation, and is Christ Mind in an articulated state. If you are willing to be one with this, offer the self to it. You may use this language if you wish:

"On this day I choose to allow the Manifest Divine, the truth of who I really am, to claim me in fullness, impart its wisdom, impart its joy, impart its awareness of Source, to be my teacher, to be my ally, to be my expression in fullness of being. As I say yes to this, I allow this merging. As I say yes to this, I agree to this manifestation. As I say yes to this, I say yes to God as all that is and can be. I am Word through this intention. Word I am Word."

Be met in fullness. Be witnessed. Be known. Be claimed. And become one.

(PAUSE)

Let the light that you are be the light that is. Let the truth that you are be the truth that is. Let this claim be known throughout any idea of time and space that you may have

utilized to know the self in separation. It will be so. God Is.
God Is. God Is.

Thank you for your presence. Stop now, please. Yes, this is in
the text.

(PAUSE)

What stands before you today in your awareness is a recognition of how you have chosen, how you have claimed fear, and
perhaps why you did so. While this recognition is essential, it
is not to be belabored. Simply, what was, was, or your belief in
what was, was, because you are in the present moment where
what may be known is of the now. Now, what is of the now,
except all things. All things may be made new, all things may
be seen anew, and this must include the self that was once in
denial.

Now, the aspect of self that was once in denial was in agreement to many things, and part of a landscape, or contributing
to a landscape, that was claimed in separation. Because of the
merging that you have undergone and will continue for some
time, your relationship to history and the landscape that you
have known yourself through will be altered. And the altered
landscape will be what you perceive from the Upper Room.

Now, when we say all things are of God, that doesn't mean
all things are pleasant to look at. Do you understand this?
Some of you wish this to be a teaching of rainbows and blue-
birds. But all things must be of God, and your perception from
the Upper Room allows you to perceive what was once defiled
in the self, in another, in the common field with an awareness

of its truth. This is simply something or someone that was known outside the light, grew in distortion, was enabled by a fear in the causal plane that sought to claim itself through this being or this situation. You are not making fear wrong. You have moved beyond it. This does not mean you don't recognize it, but you see it somewhat differently. You may look at a piece of silver and know its value beneath the tarnish it has accrued. You may look at a human being and comprehend the innocence, the true divinity, that must be there, because how could it ever not be?

The juncture you stand at today is in this offering: "I am willing to serve as the light that I am. I am willing to be as this light. And I am willing to claim as this light all that I may encounter." The desire the small self has to conquer the Upper Room—"I will be the first to sell the map to how it works up here"—will release, because it cannot remain. And as the small self is accrued by the merging with the Manifest Self, even the designs that the small self would utilize and claim in glory will be superseded by an awareness of the glory of the Divine.

"What does that mean?" he asks. Well, self-glory is always the small self. The idea of giving all things to God has been somewhat confused. "I will give this triumph to God." Well, God *is* the triumph, but also perhaps the defeat. And your desire to applaud the things you like and deny the things you don't are about to be replaced by a blanket awareness of what is. What is always true is God. What denies God is never true. The action of the denial of the Divine is always to deceive. You have been taught of a great deceiver that would battle God. This is a misunderstanding. Fear is not noble. It is highly ignorant. It does what it thinks it must to support itself and its vibration. It is not evil, although it may be aligned to in ways you may call evil, and that would be through a misuse of will, the intention to harm, which is always born in the denial of the Divine.

The gratitude you hold now for what you have come to will indeed enable more, but the realization that you hold authority here as the True Self does not glorify this aspect of self. It simply is. In other words, friends, the Divine as who you are, what you are, and how you serve, simply is. When you understand this—"I simply am, God simply is, we are in the Upper Room, We Have Come, we are claiming the new through presence and being"—the need to deify or supplicate, both, are released. And you simply are. Presence and being.

Now, some of you say to us, "What is in this for me? Why should I bother being on this path?" In fact, the path is upon you, whether or not you know this. Your agreement in the claim "I Have Come" has allowed you to recede at the level of personality and be received instead by the Monad in expression. The Monad lights the path in agreement to the soul's journey, and this is the path you walk.

Now, imagine you are walking on a path that is lit as you walk it. That is what you have come to. It is not that you do not have choice. It's that the choices that you do have, have all been enabled by your reliance and agreement to Source. In agreement to Source, the claim "God Is, God Is, God Is" simply means God will not be denied on the path that you are walking because it is. It will not be altered. All that will be altered is your reliance upon the old, and indeed that now falls away. The merging that occurred with the Divine Manifest

Self is simply a stage of expression. How you honor this, and how this alignment unfolds through you, will be in perfect ways. Underline *perfect*. That simply means exactly what is required for its unfoldment through you. And the first thing you may notice is that the landscape is altered. It appears somewhat different because it is now being perceived by one who is operating in two realities simultaneously. The aspect of self that has been manifest in the Upper Room, knows its way around the block, and will be your director, is also informing the aspect of self that goes to the grocery store, watches the children play, goes for a swim, or pays the taxes.

The embodiment of the Divine is actually working in two realities concurrently. And this is the teaching of being in the world, but not of it. The compression of the old, in some ways, will appear to be a delineation of what you have been used to. It will hold a different texture. What you are beginning to experience is the evidence of the old, the lower manifest world, that is being altered through the process of lifting. Now, the process of lifting may be happening in an individuated way that you may experience yourself through, but it is also happening at a larger scale. And you are contributing to this, whether or not you know it. The idealization of what was, how things should appear or be, has been exchanged for the other, removed and replaced by the other, but the shadow of the old or the imprint of the old may linger for some time.

Imagine you tasted something sour. It may linger on the tongue for a while until the taste releases. How you perceive things through the old template will remain for a time, but acquire a density that will not linger long. In fact, when you begin to experience things as perhaps more dense than they once were, you will understand this is happening fully. Now, when you approach a pile of dust, it may first look like nothing. But the closer you get, you see what the dust is, how it's been formed. You may blow upon the dust, which will simply dispel the illusion of the pile, but the dust will still be there. Your awareness of the density of the pile, or the residue of past sight, is actually something you move past or lift beyond. When the dust is not there, the density that was once claimed will be understood as what once was and is no longer.

The trials you undergo at this level are actually few, but they are worth mentioning. The idea of what should be is the taste that lingers. And even your pain or your attachment to the idea of a self in pain may linger for some time, because not only do you expect it, you actually demand it. When you stop demanding the old, when you release the need for what once was, it will dispel quite simply. It is energy. It is the tarnish on the silver, and really nothing more. To abide in the new is not to ignore the old. It's not to demand things be improved as you think they should be. It's to know the new is before you, and that is experiential. We are not whitewashing your history, and we are certainly not dismissing your pain. You are moving beyond the idea of self that was developed in pain, has required this kind of pain, and holds an expectation it will always be there.

He interrupts the teaching. "But is there still pain where we are being taken?" It is not where you are being taken. It's what you agreed to in the merging, which is the Manifest Divine, already in its perfected state, is now assuming you. You agreed to the merging. Its agreement is to what is required for you. Now, if you stub your toe, you may bleed. If you find yourself entangled in a situation you would prefer not to be in, you will see it as an opportunity to grow and learn. But the Divine as who and what you are is now the arbiter of your experience, and not the personality structure, who has relied on old ways, old fears, old judgments, and memory to direct her future. Freedom is here. It is here. It is here. It is here. And, indeed, you have come to it.

When we teach you today about redemption, we are speaking to the aspect of self that is still longing for this. And, indeed, that is still present in the field. Even if you were overtaken completely by the Monad in this instant, and any memory of shame or denial of God was completely erased from you, there would still be the residue, or the aspect of self, the bittersweet taste of longing for God. Well, that longing can be sated, and in fact is sated in this Upper Room. You are abiding in the presence of God. "In God, I live and move and have my being." Presence and being. The altered environment is actually the ramification of this alignment. In fact, you are informing your landscape by presence and being, and reclaiming it in the Upper Room because this is where the True Self expresses.

Some of you say to us, "Well, can I have this experience now?" Of course you can, if you stop deciding what it's supposed to be and how you might know it. We could blindfold you this moment and give you a taste of juice. You wouldn't see what you were drinking, but in likelihood you would be able to claim what it is. The experience of unification is as such. You will know it. And the reason you will know it is that it is where you come from. It is where the Monad lives. It is going home.

Thank you each for your presence. Stop now, please. This is in the text.

DAY TWELVE

What stands before you today, in an awakened state, is all that expresses at the level of vibration that you have come to. Now, when you move to an equilibrium in the Upper Room, when you are holding your vibration here well, when the Monad expressed as you is in fruition and fulfillment, it realizes all things as of itself. In other words, friends, you are not striving to see the Divine in anything. You cannot not see it at this level of amplitude.

Now, some of you wish to say, "Well, I want the descriptor." You can have the descriptor, if you wish it. You are seeing God in all forms. But the experience of this will be somewhat different than you expect. As you have incarnated—and we use that word expressly—in the Upper Room, as the realization of this extends beyond the senses as they were utilized in the lower realm, as the experiential data of *being* at this level of tone is accrued, what is accumulated by you, or how you align experientially, is to a level of manifestation that you will not see as much as know.

We will explain this for Paul. Because you have relied upon the senses to give you information, you expect the senses to be what delivers the higher experience. And while this is true at a certain level in the Upper Room, the amplification of the senses, how you perceive, is radically altered. The true benefit is in knowing. You cannot try to know anything, but all things may be known and must be known at the Christ Mind from the one who has aligned there. If you understand that you have been reading a book, a text, if you wish, in a certain kind of reality, and that you have grown in this reality, the lower strata or field, you expect to see and translate the words of the text to what they have meant in the lower realm. You are now embarking on a new text, or a new experience of braille, of comprehending experientially, through the manifest world as it is re-known in the higher template.

Now, those of you who say, "Oh, well, I was waiting for fireworks," you have decided what it should be and whether you will like it or not. To know all things as of God is a level of experience that cannot be known through the old strata, the old textbook, the old language of information. "That is a seal." "That is a bear." "That is a night sky." Now, you don't lose language in the Upper Room, but you comprehend all things through a higher tone. And if you wish to call this tone *language,* you may, because all language is, is communication, and a system of communication. When you move to an experiential level where all things are being, and you are being, at that level of vibration, when you are of the night sky while witnessing the night sky, and the night sky is God presenting as night sky, the experience of being is completely altered. You still know night. You still know sky. But the being of and as this—and the word *as* is the key—is what guarantees you union.

"What does that mean?" he asks. Well, yes, you have a body. You understand skin as boundary between you and the elements. But to be *in* the night sky and know yourself *as* that night sky as well as witness—but experience of being—you have maintained an awareness of unity that does not dissolve the personality structure, but has allowed for a level of vibration experientially to be accrued.

Now, to know the self as the sky does not mean you have disappeared. But it does mean you know God as sky, or the one note sung as sky, and the body as sky, or the one note sung. You might say sky as body, if you were to extend the metaphor, but we wish you to understand it this way: The accruement of information born through separation in the lower field must be translated or re-known in the Upper Room. The process of relocation in expression to a new vibrational level requires all things be made new, and your experience of all things is what is changed. In fact, what you are seeing is what has always been so, but was denied by your denial of the Divine.

Each of you who says yes to this is actually met by the experience that you may know or realize. And there are levels of this which are set in motion through the alignment in the Upper Room and the agreement to unionize, to become one with the Monad as form. Now, each of you who says, "I am one with God," is actually making a statement of truth. And this is true even for the one who doesn't know God at all, or has an idea of a God perhaps upon a cloud. The realization of the Monad is known by you in degree, and maintained by you, not at the level or structure of personality, but by what the Monad grants you, or the Christed Self guarantees you.

The escalation of tone within the Upper Room and engagement with Source as all things is, simply put, the progress one makes in an awareness of the elasticity of all things. The permanent structures that the lower realm holds are only permanent through the collective agreement to the vibrational level that the collective has chosen to experience it through. When you lift to the higher, the vibrational level is altered, and the experience of all things becomes far more fluid. Again, you are as the night sky while maintaining the form that you have held.

To understand this in an experiential state is to be in the water while taking a sip of water. You are in and of the water simultaneously. The belief that you will drown is what precludes you from partaking more. But at the level of vibration we teach, you are assumed by the induction of the vibration. You are not drowned within it, you are not lost within it, as much as expanded through it. You become as the sky while maintaining a sense of form that is well-utilized by you as you move through the reality you operate in. When you decide that this level of experience is safe and can be encountered, it is encountered. And this is where will is utilized. The braiding of the will, or moving to a unified will in the Upper Room, still allows you to say, "I am ready. It will be so. I Have Come. I can contain this or express as this." Each time you give the *yes,* the consent to this, the expansion continues at the level that you can hold or maintain.

Now, you may get drunk at a party. You didn't know your limit was two drinks. You had five and you became quite ill. In the Upper Room you must understand that there is a balance held, and that the Monad is the one that claims each experience of expansion with and for you, lest you lose your balance and topple back down to the lower field. "Is that possible?" he asks. Of course it's possible.

Now, imagine you are holding the field and the experience of the Upper Room and you decide, "Oh, this is lovely. I am going to amplify and amplify and amplify." You will experience a contraction consummate or in accord with the level of amplification you have chosen. That is how the growth occurs. The levels of contraction one experiences in the Upper Room are to support the enlargement or full expression of the Monad. You cannot have one without the other.

Paul is seeing himself breathe, an inhalation and an exhalation. The lungs are expanded through the practice. In some ways, holding form while in this amplified state of the Upper Room is comparable. So you take in what you can hold. You expand as you are aligned to it. And the progress ensues, not because the small self is trying to become the savior or thinks she knows what it means to be God, but because God is knowing itself through the experience of being you. It is seeing all things, both as itself and through you.

To become the eyes of the Christ are to be the one who bears witness to the Kingdom or the presence of God. The eyes of the Christ may know things through the language that they've been given, but will know things well beyond that, too. What this means is while the kettle is a kettle, you also see the kettle from the metal it was forged from, from the fire that forged the metal, from the light in the sky that shined upon the ore, from the blackened cave that it was drawn from. You are in an experience that expresses beyond time, and the information or data that one may mine is far beyond what the small self can conceive.

"What does this mean?" he asks. Well, yes, all things are of God, but what is available in the Upper Room are a million mirrors to one thing, all potentials that may be seen and witnessed. Now, you don't walk down the street and witness all things as all possibilities. But you comprehend all things as tone, as God in vibration in experience. You perceive all things as God in experience—the kettle on the flame, the kettle pouring into the cup. The comprehension of what things truly are, beyond what they were named as, how they have been utilized, allows you to know what else they may be.

Now, when you lift to a science that is not born in fixing things, you have moved to a science that is operating in alchemy. When you understand the plasticity of form, and how sound can reclaim anything in a higher way, you move beyond an old system. You don't dismiss the old system. It is actually made new, and perhaps utilized in somewhat different ways. Education is a system. Education is a fine thing. But you have a codified set of rules or expectations about what education is or should be. You have schools with names, and systems of organizing principles that you believe the student must learn to become proficient. What you don't know yet is that same student could enter the Upper Room in a completely receptive state and be informed by a level of knowledge that may be known through them. In some ways they become the text-book, but the textbook that has not yet been written.

The level of information that can be utilized for good is a vast library, and we use the term *library* as a metaphor for what expresses in knowledge that may be accrued. He interrupts the teaching, "But can it be misused, then, if it is being used in the Upper Room?" No, it cannot, because the one who is receptive at this level has *become* the Upper Room, or the expression of it, and consequently any act taken is made from this awareness. "I am of God, and I am expressing as God."

Now, when we say *as* God, please do not believe we are

saying the only God. Let us go back to the metaphor of the one in the water who ingests the water, or the one in God who is filled with God. This being is of God, expressing as and with, but only in an awareness of the inherent divinity of all, because he cannot not do that. Do you understand this? The chasm most of you fall into is you think that you are doing this, and it is not done by the you that you think you are.

The agreement to the higher, which utilizes will, *is* the higher expressing through all things. Every cell of your being, every idea thought, every idea of memory, every word learned in any language, all becomes of God, because it can only be, because it always has been.

Restoration, reconciliation, is not invention. It's the reclamation of what is true as who you are, as what you experience, as all things are made new.

Thank you for your presence. Stop now, please. Indeed, in the text.

(PAUSE)

What stands before you today, in this awakened state, is the realization that you have never been separate. The moment this occurs, the information that was accrued through separation is actually dismantled. It is still present, but it no longer informs choice. The one who truly knows who he is, is in presence, and in a state of innocence. Now, the state of innocence must be understood as without the idea of separation, because your idea of sin, or what we call the denial of the Divine, *is* separation, and abiding in the illusion of it. When you are washed clean, as it were, in this state of purification, the restoration of self, the Monad in an expressed state, you have become the light that cannot hold darkness.

He interrupts already. "But we are still human. We have our foibles. We have our desires." And you may continue to keep them. What we are instructing you in now is a state of embodiment where you live in the realization of God. And while you may understand yourself through other experiences, partake of them, if you wish, you actually do so at the cost of the truth of your being. Now, there is nothing wrong with saying, "I am going to go on a picnic. I am going to go off my diet. I am going to have a little adventure." And go there, if you wish, but do not pretend that you are operating in the high strata.

"This sounds like it's not much fun," he says. Your idea of fun in most ways is based in the idea of forgetting the self. You are laughing so hard, you are no longer self-conscious. You are making love with such fervor that you know yourself in union with your partner. You are forgetting yourself in the Upper Room, and you may laugh and make love all you wish. Desire is present, but it is actually re-formed, because the idea that you are doing something naughty or punishable has been replaced by an awareness of the sacred. The sacred and the profane are actually the same thing. But the sacred knows God. The profane denies it. All is God. These are different levels of vibration. You will not harm another through desire in the Upper Room because why would you? What would be the gift? The cost is too great.

Now, the laws that you have on this plane are primarily born in punitive justice. You speed, you get a ticket. You get so many tickets, you lose the privilege of driving. In the Upper Room, your awareness of cause and effect is highly present, but as we said earlier, the path is laid for you. Yes, you have will, but the immediacy of requirements are what presents— the immediacy of requirements, the paintbrush before the paint. The moment you sit in is always the moment of receipt. We will say that again. It is important to understand. *The moment you sit in is always the moment of receipt.* You will not receive, cannot receive, have actually never received at any other time than now.

Now, wisdom and knowledge indeed are experiential. Information is not wisdom. Knowledge is not information. "I read the pamphlet, I know how to change the tire." That is information. But until you change the tire you don't know what it's like to do so. And while the text you are reading now holds information, it is also a portal to a level of experience that you have not known. This is a new teaching. Every text we have written has operated in some ways as a doorway to a new potential. But the portal we speak to now is the awareness of being and presence in a unified state. And because you operate with this text, you can actually allow the text to support this realization, not through reading it with ardor or deciding what everything means, but by aligning to the purpose, the very purpose of this text, which is a reclamation of innocence. Innocence does not hold deceit. It does not deny God. It doesn't even need a God that it can describe. Innocence is a state of expression in God and with God, in an awareness of God without the tarnish that the old kettle had accrued.

Our honor today is to gift you with this. And we say *our honor* because we hold this for you, as a portal, if you wish, that you can indeed step through. To step through this portal in a unified state is to enter the Kingdom. To enter the Kingdom is as stepping in the ocean. The experience of *ocean* becomes present through stepping in. The experience of *Kingdom* is as present as the ocean, and will be met by you at the level of tone that you are able to hold or confirm.

You may say this very softly after we speak the words:

"On this day I choose to allow the presence of the Divine to inform all aspects of self and deliver all aspects of self to the Upper Room and to an experience of the Kingdom. On this day I say I am willing to be re-known, I am willing to be delivered, I am willing to be reclaimed to my true state of expression. And as I offer myself to this, I am met by the authors of this text, by the energy that informs them and it, which is the Monad or the Christ in full expression, and I agree to be escorted to a realization that I may claim as my own. I am Word through this intention. It will be so. God Is. God Is. God Is."

Welcome to the Kingdom. Be known. Be known. Be known. Indeed, this is in the text. Stop now, please.

(PAUSE)

What stands before you today, in an awakened state, is the realization of what you thought, how you thought it, and how you chose based upon it, how you denied the Divine in choice through supposition or desire.

Now, to claim Divine Will does not deny will. It simply supports will in the highest expression it may hold. The alignment of the Upper Room, the inhabitation of the Kingdom, the expression therein, claims will in a unified state. But are you still choosing? Of course, indeed, you are. You have not lost will. You have reclaimed will to its true purpose: to be in awareness of all things of God.

Now, you've chosen to incarnate at a level of reason, a level of amplitude, a level of choice that precludes fear, or at least denies fear, because you abide beyond it. If you wish fear, you may offer yourself that opportunity. But we will suggest this: Once you become accustomed to being beyond fear, once you stop relying upon it to inform your choices, your experience of freedom will be beyond what you have known. An awakening to a new potential must require you release what you were attached to, or thought was, and this must include the basis for many of the choices that you claimed a life in. None of this is done to make the self wrong. The self was informed by memory, and choices born through a collective agreement to fear. Every war ever fought on this plane was the result of a collective act or agreement to separation. A war will not survive if this was not the case. There would be no war if there were not two sides to fight.

The agreement to union that you have been claimed in, have agreed to, is about to support your ability to reclaim history of all things in the Upper Room. Now, this is an enormous act. We are not speaking of personal history now. We are speaking of the application of the Divine, the purview of the Monad, upon historical data, or what you believed was once so. When you understand that any war fought was born in an agreement to the denial of God, when you comprehend that all who fought were finally party to this, you can understand that what has been claimed historically that informs your daily lives here in the common field you have known yourselves through can and must be rectified.

Now, to release history is only to release an idea of it, and the template of history that humanity has known itself through, drawn and claimed in fear, must now be re-seen. To claim this for one and all is to claim this for all time. Understand, again, that the aspect of the Creator as you that you are now awakened to, the reuniting with the Divine Self expressed as you, operates beyond the schedule that the small self would inhabit and understands the calendar as a series of ideas drawn in linear form. The reclamation of all history, universal history, to the Upper Room is less an act of choice than an act of agreement to what is always true—history as idea, the universe as an idea, choice as an idea, all things re-known, in the Kingdom, of God and expressions of the same.

Now, the choice to do this is to give yourself in offering to a potential that is present, already realized in the higher octave, but holds its basis through the history of separation. And to reclaim humanity's history is to contribute not only to the evolution of humanity, but to the peace that awaits humanity on the other side of the wall that it has erected. The choice to do this will come at a cost, and we will explain this very carefully to you as we are allowed. If you offer yourself to this, you are actually supporting a new mandate—that man will not war, that the end of war is here, that the alignment to war as a system born through historical data has been claimed in the Upper Room, where its basis, which is fear, will be re-known. When you agree to this, you are operating as Source, or a vehicle of Source. The manifestation of the Monad as who and what you are supports this claim, so don't for a moment think that this is done at the level of personality. But the volition of the Divine Self in full expression, and the claim "Behold, I make all things new; God Is, God Is, God Is," will reclaim even the idea of war and the historical basis for it.

"Is there a historical basis for it?" he asks. Of course there is. Treason, you see, first is in the self, then of the neighbor, then of God. The war within the self, which is born in the denial of the Divine, is the basis of every war, every battle, and every act of violence that has ever occurred on this plane. It is always humanity battling itself, or the idea of self engaged in rage against the self, that has decreed separation. So how this operates is first within self, and then within the collective landscape, and finally, we suggest, with God itself as the Source of all peace that may be known while in form.

Here is the claim we offer you:

"On this day I choose to render void, to release, any battle within the self that I have ever undertaken that is born in the denial of God. And as I claim this, I claim this peace, this offering in peace, to every relationship with anyone I have ever known, any culture I have ever been party to, and anyone I have ever witnessed. And as I agree to this peace, I offer any rage at the Divine, from any time and place, any feelings of being cast out, any memory of being shunned in the name of a God or a religion, that I have ever undertaken or endured. And as I say yes to this, I give permission for the end of war to be known through me, and by me, and in all that I encounter."

On the count of three, we will sing through Paul. You need not join in song, but align to the tone, which will claim all things as you agree to the tone. To agree to the tone is to receive the act of the Monad as peace, as and through you, and as and through all things.

On the count of three, Paul.

One. Now two. Now three.

[The Guides tone through Paul.]

Now, ask yourself this: "Am I willing to put down any weapon I have ever used—against the self I have known, against anyone I have known, and against God?" In this *yes*, you offer this weapon to be transmuted, re-known in peace, and you will receive the gift of peace in its place. We receive you each as you offer this. We see you each as you say yes to this. And as we say yes, we move into accord, first with individual history, and then collective history. If you make this claim, it will be heard. You will be moved. You will be the agent of peace in articulation.

You say this now to the history of war that has been known on this plane:

"Behold, I make all things new. It will be so. God Is. God Is. God Is."

And let the trumpet sing. Let peace be known. Let the field you hold carry peace through any idea of history that the communal claim of war had been laid upon. All will be known anew. All is made new. The Christ is come in peace. And the end of war is sung into being. Period. Period. Period.

Stop now, please. Indeed, this is in the text.

DAY THIRTEEN

What stands before you today, in awareness of who you have always been, are the requirements for growth that are before you. The challenges you face, you see, in what we call the Upper Room, are challenges of being. And the idea of being, simply being, is still confused by most of you. Each of you are in an encounter with reality, at any level of vibration, through the consciousness you hold, and how you realize yourself at any level of tone or vibration claims you in agreement with this encounter. So understand that anything you meet on this path before you must be seen as opportunity for further realization. The moment this is decided, all evidence is accrued in support of this. The moment this is denied, you begin to align to an aspect of self that would know itself through fear.

Now, you may say, "I am in the Upper Room. I am in re-articulation. The Monad has manifested as who and what I am." But how you realize yourself, how you perceive what is before you, is still discerned by you, and there is logic employed when logic is required. "There is a cat in the driveway, I must avoid the cat." "There is a bear in the tree, I must steer clear of the bear." These must be seen as encounters you have that you may utilize discernment in.

The requirement of the path before you is really rather simple. The moment you sit in is the moment you know yourself in. The moment you know yourself in is how you perceive all things. Everything is translated, you see, to the omnipresent now, which must and always be the articulation of the Divine, the vast field of now, the infinite now, the only way you may know yourself. Your idea of who you were or may one day be has been translated, yes. Your requirements for growth are before you. And the species that you are of is embarking on a new way of being—without the old, without the requirements of the old, the mandates of the old, confirming separation.

Now, to move beyond separation, or align in a unified state with All That Is, is really rather simple. You are simply accepting truth. You are not denying the Divine. You are forgiving the self that grows confused or would seek an outcome, and offering those aspects of self to be re-known in the Upper Room. As you agree, the unfoldment occurs. The only real challenges you face are your opinions, which is simply what you think things are or mean, how they should be. And, always, this is born in prior prescription.

Some of you say to us, "I am in the Kingdom. I am in my business. I am doing my work in the Kingdom." Do as you wish. The presence of being that is the Kingdom is the True Self, and any alignment it holds will claim what you require to you. We will say this again: The True Self will claim what you require to you. You are no longer hunting, or scavenging, or pleading, or demanding, or stating what you must be or how you must be known. You simply are. "I know who I am and what I am and how I serve." This is a level of expression, and it is the end of a way of being that you have relied heavily upon.

He interrupts the teaching. "Where are you going with

this today? Is this the last chapter or a new one? What are we to do in this class? How are we to comprehend these teachings in practical ways?" This is actually the most practical teaching you have ever received, but you complicate it. You make it more difficult than it truly is. The teaching of being, which is a teaching of allowance and a teaching of receptivity, which is reception and allowing the Divine to know itself through you, is actually the issuance of this text. Anything you wish to do beyond that is really entirely up to you.

We are coming to a close in the first half of the text. We will resume this text when we reconvene, perhaps later in the week. The teaching of *this* day is going to be application of what you have learned thus far. Each of you here, each of you who hears these words, perhaps reads them on the page, are being claimed by the Divine in your senses and your expression. The agreement to this has been made. Re-articulation will be confirmed by you.

We offer you this today: If you wish to know yourself as of God, please give permission to all that you see before you to be seen as it truly is—unfettered, untarnished, by history and meaning. Simply let it be seen and make this claim as you perceive it:

"Behold, I make all things new. It will be so. God Is. God Is. God Is."

And allow the affect of the claim upon everything you see to be known by you in tone, which means you give permission for the manifest world that *is* God in tone to say yes in response to the claim you have made:

"Behold, I make all things new. It will be so. God Is. God Is. God Is."

And allow the echo of the claim to assume you in union. You understand what we are saying. You are invoking presence through being. You are agreeing to what is already true, and you are allowing it to be. Period. Period. Period. Stop now, please.

(PAUSE)

What stands before you today, in an awakened state, is a recognition of your potential, beyond the codification, beyond the meaning, beyond the belief in separation that has accrued evidence prior. The belief in separation, the idea of separation, the claim of separation, the great lie that you are separate from your Source, separate from the one beside you, separate from the sky and all things that can be known. The recognition of unity is born in an agreement to truth. What is true is always true, and the claim of truth—"I Am Here, I Have Come, I Am Known," an agreement to be, and of, and with the Source of all things—may now be understood by you as what you have come to. "I Am Here. I Have Come. I Am Known." The quantification of each of these claims, in magnitude, will continue to amass evidence, and the evidence that they amass is that there is no separation.

Now, some of you may say, "I understand this in theory. There is one note sung expressing as all things. I am of that note, because I cannot not be." But as long as this is maintained as an intellectual structure, you will not benefit from it. "I know the sky is blue because I think I know what blue means" does not give you the full experience of the sky, or blue, for that matter. The realization that "God Is" in the fiber of your being and in every thought will support a mandate for a world made new.

"What does that mean, *every thought*?" he says. "That doesn't sound like a lot of fun." This is not fun. *God is every thought* simply means that the presence of God is informing all thought. Every thought is not *of* God, but every thought already *is* of God, because God as all things includes thought. Do you understand this? Thought as of God. Divine thought. True thought. God as thought.

Now, to understand what this means as a creator is far more simple than you think. Many of you have agreed to the premise that you are co-creators, and that thought is creative. And thought *is* creative, even at the lowest level of manifestation. "I will think of that terrible thing to do to that one over there." Indeed, thought is creative. But when thought is known as of God, claimed in the Upper Room, thought is claiming *as* God and that is why you are delivered what you require, because you are in consort with the mind of God.

Now, understand the mind of God. Most of you would distill this to mean God's thought or what God thinks. But if *mind* is another way of understanding *expression*, and expression *is* God, Divine Mind becomes all things, and your reliance upon Divine Mind is to move to a level of communion with Divine Mind in thought. You have heard the claim "I will to will thy will," as if the will that you hold may be moved to a unified state. But the idea that thought, which is of God, can be recognized as such, and moved to a unified state, does not sacrifice independence—"I wish I would have this soup for dinner, as opposed to that one"—but it simply claims you in agreement to a level of union as a broadcast. We use the term *broadcast* intentionally. You are all in broadcast. Your broadcast is your tone. Thought is not excluded from this broadcast because thought is creative. But when thought is thought of as separate, or believed to be separate, there is a conundrum.

Now, "my private place as my thought" may be understood by you. No one can hear your thoughts. You think them in private. But the Divine as all things is in receipt to thought because thought is how you create in the manifest plane. To align thought to God as broadcast is simply moving to a level of equivalency as Divine Mind.

He interrupts the teaching. "Well, we hear of people who say God told them to do some awful thing. This could be difficult as an instruction." Divine Mind will never instruct you to harm another. Divine Mind cannot. Divine Mind knows the inherent worth in all, and claims you in agreement to truth. In truth a lie will not be held. And what is a lie, but that another is unworthy.

To give the thought, the great thought, "I Am" to God is to allow God to be as you. The claim "I Am," the claim of presence and being, in agreement to Source, is not an invocation of personality, but the Self that supersedes personality—capital "S" *Self,* Divine Self, in coherence with Divine Expression and Mind. Again, *Mind.* "I Am in the Kingdom," a claim of being and expression in truth. "I Am in receipt of the gifts of the Kingdom." "I Am aligned to my perfect requirements for realization." And "I Am Known." The claim "I Am Known," which we have taught prior, may now be understood as the agreement to Divine Mind knowing the requirements of the idea of self that are present in the Kingdom, or indeed the Upper Room.

Some of you say, "But I have to make it happen. I have to manifest what I want." Imagine you are in need of food. The food will not appear before you. Perhaps you walk to the food. Perhaps you cook the food. Perhaps you offer the food to the one beside you, once it is prepared. If there is action to take, you are in recipient to that. You know what to do because your knowing is not impaired. You know yourself. You know Source. And consequently you know the Source of all that may be claimed.

Each of you who says yes to the journey that is before you will be met in perfect ways.

You may say this, if you wish:

"On this day I offer myself and all thought ever thought, ever to be thought, to the Source of all that is. On this day I say yes to the offering of mind in cohesion, in agreement, in agreement and accord, to Divine Mind, so that my mind may be informed in a unified state with the Divine Knowing that is my true inheritance. I know who I am in truth. I know what I am in truth. I know how I serve in truth. I Am Here. I Have Come. I Am Known."

Thank you each for your presence. Stop now, please. Yes, this is in the text.

DAY FOURTEEN

What stands before you today, in an awareness of who you truly are, is the magnitude of change that is before you. Humanity itself, you see, has made a new agreement: To realize the self beyond the old strata, the old conditioning, the old ways of knowing the self through fear. And the transition you are undertaking in some ways is cataclysmic to the aspects of self that seek to remain as they were. When humanity says yes to a new potential, that which has been claimed in fear is re-seen, is re-known, and reclaimed in what we call the Upper Room for the benefit of all. Those who follow you on this path will actually have an easier time of it. What is ongoing now is the release of the old, inclusive of identity and memory, in ways that would supersede a realization of the Divine that seeks to be born within each of you.

When we stand before you, we do so with an awareness of who you can only be in truth, individually and collectively. And the collective fear of what is ongoing now is present to be seen, to be acknowledged, yes, but then moved beyond. The transition you are undertaking is larger than you know. It is not codified in fear. It is born in the release of fear. But nothing is released until it is seen for what it is, and as the structures you have been used to begin to shift, as your understanding of what these things have been is altered by a higher awareness, you become party to this transition in the uplifting of humanity to a higher tone or frequency.

We use the words *tone* and *frequency* interchangeably, and sometimes, at the same time, to mean somewhat different things. The tone that you hold as an individual, an expression of consciousness, the vibrational field in vibration and in tone, can be understood as who and what you are in true expression. The form that you have taken must be understood as the agreement to form, or the way that you know yourself

embodied, flesh and bone, on this plane. When you are altering your vibrational frequency, the body also must shift. And
the tenets or the actions you take in support of the new are
always in relationship to the higher that seeks to be born as
and through you. Humanity is undergoing such a change, and
it's going to be quite clumsy for some time. Those of you who
believe that the process forward is graceful or comfortable are
actually lying to the selves that seek to hold the old. What is
before you now is change, and a reclamation of identity at a
higher tone than humanity has known.

Now, prescription fails here. "In the Upper Room I will be
seen as such and such." "In the Upper Room I will know myself in a different way." In fact, what is occurring is a level of
amplitude that releases an idea of self that separates one's self
from one's brother or sister, and God itself. Whatever you believe God to be, it is a unifying principle—the one note sung
that expresses as all manifestation. Your realization of union
at a higher level than you can fathom through the personality structure must be comprehended by you as the gift of this
time. If you perceive this as a gift, you will be far more ready
to reclaim the self that is present for you now.

When we teach evolution, we teach progress and process,
but the evolution of humanity is in fact a reinstatement of
who you have always been at the cost of an idea of self as separate from Source, separate from one another. The gift of this
teaching, for those who attend to these words, is the realization that this is already so, that you don't have to strive for this,
you don't have to command or demand. You have to receive.
And to receive the Divine is to know your place within it—
underline the word *within*—*within* the Divine, which simply

means you are already of it, but the awareness of this has been precluded, in most ways, through the denial of the Divine which you have all been party to.

In the earlier chapters in this text, we have described separation, and claimed memory, identity, the personality structure, and the gifts of a culture born through separation, as ways that you preclude the self from true awareness of who you are. The gift of this day, and this teaching today, is the realization that this is always so. "God Is, God Is, God Is" is a statement of truth. And this statement of truth, if you really wish to know the power of it, will repeal the false evidence that separation has accrued. When you align in the Upper Room and you claim the statement "God Is, God Is, God Is," the vibrational echo of the claim reclaims what it encounters in its own alignment—underline *its own alignment*—not the idea of self as the one proclaiming, but the only one that can truly claim, or the I Am presence that always knows who and what it is, and, indeed, how it serves. Its claim of presence— "God Is, God Is, God Is"—will move the mountain, will change the field, will alter matter. And as evolution occurs, what is actually happening is a return or restoration to your rightful identity—as and of God, not separate from it, but a pure expression of it. Innocence, you see, as we instructed, is the true state of expression that the Divine Self aligns and holds, and, indeed, manifests. Because God sees God in all of its creations, because God cannot hold the vibration of fear as Monad as expressed through you, because the Divine claims all things in like vibrational accord, what is claimed is claimed in innocence, and innocence lacks prescription, lacks mandate, lacks your idea of what *should* be, from the lower field.

Imagine you are a lighthouse and everything illumined by you is held in the beam or the broadcast of light that unfolds through you. The light itself is what reclaims, and the light is what makes things new. The light does not say, "I will improve what I fall upon. I will make what I see prettier, or perhaps my idea of what holier should be." The Monad expressed as you, while love, while expressed as love, holds an impartiality that the small self would like to utilize, and this is separation, the idea that one is worthy and one is not. The light shines on all equally. But the program that the light holds is to instill itself in what it claims itself through. The claim "Let there be light" may also be understood as "Let there be truth, let it be seen in truth so that it may be re-known in the higher octave."

Finally, we have to say, restoration occurs to humanity's plane of experience when humanity stops damning itself, and its brothers and sisters, and its creations, and its false idols, or what it would use as an excuse to deny the Divine. When you understand that God is, God simply is, and God is truth, or the vibration of truth—not as you would call truth through an individual idealization of what you would have be so, but what is always true—you will comprehend the Divine and its great properties of restoration. To be reclaimed in innocence is actually to be made new. Now, this doesn't deny your experience. It doesn't make you any holier than you have ever been. But it does claim you without the detritus or historical data that you might utilize to deny your true heritage. Most of you believe that you must be special, made clean, in your prescription of clean, to be relieved of your idea of sin. Again, all sin is, in one form or another, is the denial of the Divine. And the claim "Behold, I make all things new" reclaims all things, including those aspects of self that would deny God within yourselves, and these are the very things that you deny in others as well. What you damn, damns you back. What you damn within yourself, you damn in others as well. And the purpose of damnation is quite simply separation.

You have far more say in this than you are willing to know, but it is not you who redeems the self. It is the Monad or the Divine Self or the Christ Truth within you, if you wish to use that phrase, that is doing this because it cannot not do it. Now, when you have aligned in what we call the Upper Room, invoked the claim "I Have Come," putting in force the action of the Monad as it seeks to replicate itself through all aspects of self, you have not only given permission, but you have agreed, vibrationally agreed, to a level of incarnation that you may actually hold. The realization of this, as we have taught prior, must come in stages, because if you were altered in vibration too quickly, you would lose any mooring you require to navigate the collective plane that you chose to incarnate in. But the Upper Room holds its own tone. And the gift of innocence, the gift of realization of who you have always been—unfettered, unblemished, and in truth—is what claims a world anew, and is the redemption that humanity has been waiting for.

He interrupts the teaching. "I don't think humanity has been waiting for redemption. Why do you use that word? It's somewhat fraught with history." We will claim this as we wish, but we will offer you a small explanation. That which has been put outside the light, cast in darkness or shadow, needs to be redeemed, which simply means returned to itself in a higher way. None of you are without God, but most of you believe yourselves to be. None of you are sinful. All of you believe yourselves to be.

Now, the idea of being sinful quite simply must mean to act outside of God. And, indeed, you do engage in this. But the aspect of self that is innocent, that is the Monad, that is seeking its replication through you, is indeed without sin because it cannot hold that tone. You have become so confused in your idea of your relationship to God that you put yourself outside it without meaning to. The aspect of God within all of you, the True Spark, the Divine Self, is indeed innocent, which means without sin, and not separate from its Source. It's what you have accrued in separation through the denial of the Divine that claims you as separate, and that is the illusion that humanity is now removing. We use the word *remove* intentionally. When something is removed, it is no longer present. This is not translated or transmuted, as some things might be seen as. It is quite simply the rock that covers the cave, the boulder that humanity has used to limit the expression of the Divine, or the God within. When the boulder is removed from the cave, the Monad expresses fully. *Removed* was the correct word.

Now, we will not spend time with you arguing your idea of sin. People claim all kinds of ways to learn and some are quite foolish, some may be be quite destructive. But all is held in the light, finally, or nothing can be. Because everything is in vibration, even the lowest choice made offers opportunity for growth, and indeed redemption. Some of you must go to the very dark place to realize where you have claimed yourself. But it is this awareness that gives you permission to claim the higher, to say, "I am willing," and then to say, "I Am Known,

I Am Known, I Am Known." The one who is known by God, who offers the self to God to be known, has stopped pretending to be God, or acting as if her sovereignty is independent from Source. Indeed, you are sovereign at the level of the Christ, or the Monad's expression. At the level of personality, you have a kind of autonomy that you must utilize, and hopefully utilize well. But to comprehend the self in union is to allow the self to be re-known, indeed reclaimed, indeed restored to your true nature. True nature—your true nature is innocence.

Now, some of you may say, "But we accrue karma. We learn through terrible things. We have debts to repay." Perhaps that is so. But you limit the action of the Divine, and then claim karma as your God. Indeed, if you have a debt, or a lesson to learn through that debt, you will find a way to learn the lesson. But you are no longer being punished by your belief that you are deserving of punishment. You are offering self to a level of equivalency or tone where "Behold, all things are made new" becomes your expression. When this is your expression, you are present for the miracle of re-articulation of the manifest plane.

Now, for some of you this means, and very simply means, that the light that you are, or the vibrational field in broadcast as you are, is in the act of reclamation. The tone that you have aligned to, as broadcast, claims all that it encounters to it. It certainly does not mean you are sitting on a mountainside in the rain, wondering if you are doing the right thing. You are going to work, you are feeding your child, you are reading a book, and you are always doing this at the level of tone that you may claim in the Upper Room. The Upper Room is not an escape from reality. It is a reclamation of reality.

The evolution of the species is the re-articulation of the species beyond the kind of separation that it has utilized to learn through. But the days of learning through separation are ending. You can and will not continue as you have been. And because the collective knows this, the collective has restored itself to its true promise, its true inheritance. This is not a Christian teaching. This is not a Buddhist teaching. This is a teaching of truth. And there is truth to be had in every system of philosophy, or in the seed of any religion. When religion became corrupt, out of a need for control, to decide separation was useful to maintain others to follow. Be it the rabbi, the high priest, or the wise woman, the mandate was made that you must learn through another, or that separation must be had as a precursor to an idea of union.

While there is some truth here, how this evolved was not intentional. As the plane you've known yourselves through accrued more and more evidence of separation, the density of the field became deeply challenging to move beyond. The times you sit in already hold a higher tone, a new age, if you wish, quite simply a new tone of vibration in the field that humanity has claimed that is offering this opportunity. Because you no longer need separation to become your teacher, you no longer need the one on the throne, or on the dais, or at the pulpit, to manage your restoration, but you must be directed inward to the True Self, or the Monad, or Christ, or Divine Light, or Eternal Expression. It matters absolutely not what you call it because that is your salvation. And we use the word *salvation* here to mean restoration to your true nature.

The idea of salvation being *saved from hell* is completely confused. If you wish to call separation hell, you would not be wrong. But there are levels of hell, levels of separation, and you inhabit many of them quite comfortably. There is no place you burn if you are not saved, but you will have difficulty on whatever path you claim when you continue in separation at the cost of the truth that is present now. "How is this so?" he asks. We will return to the metaphor of the lighthouse and the beam. There are some that will run from the light because they believe they will be burned by it, or their sins will be exposed, or their idea of self will be changed, and they would mandate darkness because it's what they have known. Even these people, these expressions of God, will know restoration because the Source of their expression is God. No matter what any of you think about anyone else, there is no one who is without God, although they may hold themselves in an experience without it, use all their energy to deny it, and take comfort in the fear that separation brings them. Those who were reared in darkness know it as home. To enter the light is an act of sacrilege for them because they cannot imagine they are worthy of it, and the denial of the Divine has come at a great cost.

The claims we have taught thus far can and will be used by any of you as you progress, but you must understand that the field itself is shifting. Imagine a floodwater lifting everything that it encounters. Imagine the dinner plate washed from the table, the shingles from the roof floating away. All things will be made new. To allow things to move, to allow things to be lifted, to perceive the gift of the lifting as the new seeking to be born, will be how you hold yourself, and humanity as a whole, at this time. The reclamation of innocence, or one's true state, must be comprehended as what you have come to through necessity.

We will explain this. You could go on as you have, live on a barren plane with no water to drink. You may explode every bomb that has ever been erected, and breathe in the toxicity of the air that you've corrupted. Or you can choose not to. Humanity has chosen not to. It has chosen to move beyond it. This will not be simple. It will have its own calamity, or confusion, as different things appear, to be moved. But it is, finally, a gift. And the gift that humanity has claimed is what was present before you knew the fall, or the idea of the fall, quite simply meaning the metaphor of the garden and exclusion from it. Eden is a metaphor for grace, and being in the state of the presence of innocence that is your true nature. This does not mean you don't enjoy the body, you don't enjoy reading a good book, you don't take pleasure in the sunset. It means you are as you truly are, beyond the idea of a corrupted self.

Now, there is no judgment in the word *corrupted*. The word *corrupted*, in this case, simply means what has been tarnished through the denial of the Divine, and all of the evidence that that has accrued. In this text, we have already discussed the role that memory plays in re-creating what you don't want, and we've aligned you through memory to a new potential, the aspect of self that knows who it is. You have been reclaimed. You are in the Upper Room. You Have Come. You Are Known. You are present, as you can only be in truth.

And we say these words on your behalf: *The Book of Innocence* holds the key to a reclamation beyond an idea of self that you have utilized unknowingly to claim yourself in separation. As you are freed from a false idea, re-articulation and manifestation of self at this level of tone or field claims a world made new.

We say this for each of you: Be present. Be present. Be present. For, indeed, the time is now for all things to be made new.

Indeed, this is in the text. Period. Period. Period. Stop now, please.

PART II

Innocence

5

BEYOND SIN

What stands before you today, in a new awareness of your own capacity, is the agreement to trust the self, to trust the Divine Self that is now here as you and seeks its expression through you. To trust the Divine Self is to align to the aspect of self that is not only good counsel, but is never gone, never away, and cannot operate in distortion because its agreement is to its own innocence. To trust the Divine Self is to simply trust the capacity that you actually inherently have, to be in your own knowing. This is not deferring to an idea of God. It is deferring, if you wish, to the aspect of self that already knows, and can only know, because it is not in distortion. And distortion, we would say in this case, is presupposition, expectation, and mandate through history. "It takes two minutes for the kettle to boil" is anticipation, born in agreement to time. To comprehend the kettle boiling, to know the kettle as ready, is the True Self in its expression.

Now, some of you summon history to give you what you think you need. "The evidence was accrued through my past life of how I should be treated. The evidence has been accrued through the cultural dictates of the time, how others should be treated." The *should* is what gets in the way. When you are operating in your own integrity—and integrity and knowing are intertwined—you do not make false assumptions about another, inclusive of how they should treat you, which is born in expectation and mandate. You idealize others' behavior— "he is always kind to me, I will enjoy his company"—and you predicate the outcome of the relationship, born in his behavior, being continued as you wish it to be.

To allow the self to simply be, simply be as he or she is, is to have access to the True Self in every moment of every day. When you are not distorting your idea of self—"who I should be, based on who I was"—when you are not deciding things based in outcome—"it should be as I wish it, claim it, or demand it be"—you begin to claim the self, not only in the eternal now, but in agreement to the presence of the Divine, which is only known in the eternal now.

Any supernatural experience, if you wish to use that word, is born in an agreement to that which defies common law. To defy common law, without exception, is to move outside the calendar and clock, because the witness of the moment in the eternal now is present for you beyond the edifice or structure of time. Anyone who has had a true religious experience or spiritual awakening has experienced this. The timelessness that is in the presence of God may feel like it extends for hours, or days, but in fact it may have been a moment. Time does not express in the Upper Room as the small self would know or mandate.

Now, you have intercession here. We support our students in this way. We actually lift you when you cannot be lifted, through the sheer force of will. But we may only lift you when permission is granted, when you are in offering of the self and its requirements, which may be completely unknown to you. If you knew the requirements for change, altering your life's patterns, you would have done so already.

To align to the Divine Self and its knowing is a state of restoration. The application of this knowing is up to you. In other words, friends, you may have a moment of deep knowing—"it is time to leave the relationship, it is time to decide something new"—and you can choose to ignore it, and often will, because you still desire the safety of the known, born in an idea of what should be. You are not abandoning structures, you are not abandoning marriage or relationships, by aligning in the Upper Room. You are reclaiming these things in a higher order. But when you are gifted with knowing, in any instant, there is always the opportunity to act upon that knowing.

Any action one takes at this level of agreement will be in benefit to the soul, and may actually save you some difficulty or challenge that you may have learned through the alternate choice to deny the gift of knowing that has been made available to you. When one moves to knowing—"In God I move and live and have my expression and being"—you have moved into a level of vibration where knowing is presence, presence and being, inclusive of knowing. You are not denying God in self or in others. You are not deciding what God should be through prior prescription. You are aligning to God, or the one note sung, as all things. And in this presence, you are realized.

Now, realization and knowing are concurrent and congruent. They operate together, and in tandem. To move to knowing is always in compliance with one's highest good. It cannot be other, because you cannot be deceived at this level. To be deceived by the True Self must mean you have created a false god, or the egoic structure has erected a throne for itself and demands to be seen as God. The idea that God told you to do this awful thing must be relegated to the cellar, because that level of vibration is the only place that that would ever come.

When you have aligned in the Upper Room, a strata of vibration and tone, what becomes obsolete rather quickly is the reliance upon fear to make one's choices. The opportunity may arise—"Oh, I should be upset and afraid"—but you will always have the choice to reclaim the idea of whatever this encounter is in the Upper Room, where it can and will be made new. Now, don't confuse being made new with getting what you want. It is about comprehension of truth, and in truth a lie will not be held, and fear *is* the great lie. You are no longer claiming fear, and empowering it, and utilizing it in your choices.

To comprehend that prudence is essential would be rather helpful now. Imagine you are climbing a ladder. The top rung is broken. Don't rest your foot on the top rung. You are not being ridiculous—by believing you will fly off the top of the ladder and reach your destination. Prudence is useful. Prudence and discernment work together. And discernment is not fear.

To realize the self in one's knowing is less a process than

you might expect. When you align or land in your knowing, you have decided to be in agreement to it. Imagine there has always been a well in the backyard, but you've gone elsewhere for your water. You didn't trust the well would produce what you required. You were frightened of the well. You didn't make the well. It simply was there. You are frightened of falling in, or what would be drawn from it. But when you taste the well water, you experience its purity, you are in the well because you have drunk from it. Your experience of the well, from the drinking of the water, has given you the agreement that the well is not only available, but beneficial.

Now, to become this well is to trust the Source of all knowing. The Source of all knowing is not the intellect. The intellect has its uses. Thought has its properties. But true knowing is actually in tone, or a strata of vibration, that you may align to. Thought is how you comprehend and opportunize knowing. "I have a knowing. It is time to go to the store." And you may chart your course there, think about the store as you wish, but the action is imposed, imparted to you, to enact upon not by thinking, but by knowing. True knowing, you see, is the act of God upon you, God knowing through you—not a separate God, but the Monad or the Christ in its re-articulated state that can only know. Underline those words, if you wish. *The Monad can only know.* It does not presume or expect. It simply knows. And in its knowing you are gifted with the opportunity to act upon it for the benefit of all.

"Why *all*?" he says. "Why not just the one?" Because every choice one makes in agreement to Source in a high vibrational field makes that same choice available to all. This is the evolution of the species. The agreement to be, truly be, at this level of agreement, imparts the agreement, seeds the agreement, and claims the agreement upon all that is in manifestation. So the simplest choice to know, operate from knowing, enact the knowing, actually ennobles others to operate at the same level.

In past texts we have used the term: "I am in my knowing. Word I am Word." This is still highly useful. To empower knowing through the I Am Self, and claim the presence of the Divine upon it, the action of the Divine upon it—"I am Word through this intention"—will support knowing in its blooming. But the Upper Room holds a different key because at this level of tone you are no longer striving. You are not seeking. You are in restoration to the capacity you have always held— underline *always*—to know the self in union with Source.

The one who knows herself in union with Source is not rushing, is not cutting to the front of the line, is not demanding who others be as she decides they should. They simply are. When you are operating at this level, you move towards grace as an experience of reception. To be in grace is always the presence of God and the gifts that it offers. To live in grace does not mean you don't stub your toe on occasion, forget to buy the milk, or get cross with a neighbor. It simply means that the alignment you are now holding supports realization in all of those instances, so that you may not lower the vibrational field and claim the self as you were through prior separation.

He interrupts the teaching. "But if I get cross with my neighbor, I can't be in the Upper Room." Imagine your neighbor ran across your flowerbed. You run past the car and say, "Don't do that again. I value my property." Yes, you are cross, but you comprehend the Divine as your neighbor, and also that there may be an opportunity present in what just occurred. Perhaps you will become good friends with your neighbor, who you had never spoken to prior to this incident. Perhaps you will discover something in the flowerbed that you had previously ignored. You are still maintaining the vibrational tone of the Upper Room. You are not planning revenge upon your neighbor. You are not demanding to be seen as right. You are not accruing evidence for his crimes so that you may process it through legal systems. You are simply allowing what was to be, and to know the self through the experience in the vibrational field of the Upper Room.

Now, for this to be so you must finally comprehend—and we use the word *finally* intentionally—that the Upper Room is not conjured by you. It is always present, but oft denied. All that denies the Upper Room is born in the false belief of separation, anointed by fear and enabled by the prideful self who demands to be made right. To forgive the self for not knowing will allow you to *know* knowing, to agree to knowing. To demand that one know is to deny the Divine. "God is not doing what I say. I will not do this God any favors." God does not wish your favor, and it is present whether or not you know it or not. But to trust God, and begin with the Monad, is to allow the self to know, and then allow this knowing to be shown through you experientially so that the trust may be accrued. Do you understand this? The intuitive or knowing self gives you a directive. "It is time to go to the store. You will need the milk tomorrow." You go to the store. The last carton of milk is on the shelf. There will be no shipment tomorrow.

Good that you got the last one. Somebody else might have come here before you. You were not rushing to the store to get the last carton of milk. You were knowing that you could trust, through the experience of receiving what you did.

When you move to the level of articulation that we are speaking to, you actually begin to trust that your needs are being met in high and perfect ways—perhaps not as you would have them met, or demand they be met, but as they will be met in consort with the Source of all things. To become receptive is to know. Knowing is an act of receptivity. It is not conjured. There is no spell to cast to improve one's knowing. "I am in my knowing" is a claim of truth, because it bypasses the structure of the small self who does not know and aligns you to the receptivity required. But you cannot do this on your own schedule, because knowing only happens, and will only happen, in the ever-present eternal now.

To move into eternity from your stance in the Upper Room is to grant permission for things to be known, experience to be had, that is not in agreement to the prior self that lives in limitation—the prior self being the small-self structure that knows itself through the denial of God. The claim we offered you prior—"I am free"—allows you to trespass the false border of separation. To claim your firmament in the Upper Room is to claim your birthright. And from here, in innocence, you will begin to explore.

Indeed, this is in the text. Period. Period. Period. Stop now, please.

DAY SIXTEEN

What stands before you today, in a higher awareness of who you have been, is a reconciliation with past acts, past choices, past decisions, made in fear, that deny the Divine. Now, you already understand that the action of fear is to claim more fear, and that every choice made in fear claims more of the same to you. The residual affect of each choice born in fear is the collection of more accruement, more vibrational echo, that reconciles itself with the denial of the Divine. In other words, any choice you have made in fear has accrued evidence of fear that you are aligned to.

Now, to move beyond this alignment is less the reconciliation of memory with the Divine than actually the causality of the act itself, the impetus to collect more evidence of fear, the desire of fear to anchor within you its own nature. The choice to release these things will actually support you in a very high way. You are relinquishing an idea of self as utilizing fear, navigating the field in fear, that you believed to be of benefit. Now, when you walk in a landmine, a field of landmines, you avoid the landmine. You step very carefully. If you think of the common field that you have known yourselves through as such a field, a landmine field, you are always stepping away from the potential explosion that you might incur.

In the Upper Room, there are no landmines. In other words, because you are no longer choosing through fear, claiming more fear to the self through choice, you are moving to a landscape where all things are indeed made new. And the choice to align here has its own requirements. To release the aspect of self that claims fear as a noble choice must now be understood as the small self and its indoctrination through fear to abide in a kingdom of fear. To release citizenship in this field, in this small kingdom, is to acquiesce to a higher potential. But until the firmament in the Upper Room is met, until you are fully established in vibration here, the challenge will always be the maintenance of the identity that knows itself as worthy that is not called back by old evidence—or, we must say, and this is imperative to understand, the residual affect of past choice.

Now, any choice you have made in fear has set in motion a series of events, be it a small lie told, or an act of horror, or rage, against another. Any act of fear claims others to the act. The field that you are informed by, the vibrational field you hold, actually claims memory of past act, less so choice than the affect of choice. And what we intend to do with you today is reclaim each of you beyond a bias held in and through recrimination for, and because of, past actions. We begin with recrimination, either against the self or from others, so that you may move to a liberation where you are no longer surrounded by the affect of past choice.

He interrupts the teaching. "So if someone doesn't pay their alimony because they're afraid of not having the money, and the spouse and the children are going hungry, you are releasing them from the karma of this?" No, not at all. But we are claiming them as liberated from the ideas that they have held and accrued through past action. If there is a debt to be paid, one must pay it. But to accrue more and more fear, or to claim an identity through a prior act that is in denial of the Divine, will only support you in separation. We cannot claim, "Behold, I make all things new," for you each if you are intent in maintaining the strata that has been dictated through your past actions. No one will ever lift if they are moored in that fear, or stranded on that desert island with no escape.

The key has always been to lift, or to rise in frequency or velocity, to a level of tone where fear does not establish itself because it cannot. But you will not do this when you are still claiming the old. And if the old that is in touch with you are the ramifications of the past, you will always be held in abeyance by the past. Now, as we have said, in the Upper Room you move beyond time, and because of this any creation may be re-known in the higher template. This doesn't mean that your bills are paid for you, but it does mean that the debt is changed. And by *debt* we simply mean the ramifications of a past act, so that you may become liberated from prior acts without having to decide that it must be something you do.

Now, again, to understand the image of a man on a cross you must understand that one may endure pain, and then release pain, and be resurrected in a higher template. If you look at this teaching as a metaphor, you will quite simply understand that because something happens does not mean you are tied to it for an eternity. A bad act may have occurred, a fearful choice may have been claimed, but if you move to the Upper Room you will be given an opportunity to rectify what was necessary that was incurred in the lower field, and then delivered from it.

Now, to enact upon this may be different than you think. A choice made in fear, established as the life you lived—"I was afraid of responsibility so I left the relationship and caused harm," "I was afraid of loving someone so I broke the heart of the one who loved me"—to understand that these choices can be made without the need to harm, but the affect of them *is* harmful, is quite simply to understand that anything that you have engaged in has created a shadow, a fingerprint, in the energetic field that may be moved beyond, once you are reconciled with Source. Again, the claim "Behold, I make all things new." It is certainly not the personality that can redeem the small self, or lift a past act to what we call the Upper Room, but the Monad or the Christ, that *is* liberated, is *not* tied by time and space, that can claim anything and be known in a higher way through that act.

"What does this mean?" he asks. Every time you decide that an act that was done in fear can be re-known and reclaimed, you are lifting in vibration. When you are determined to suffer for a past choice, or, indeed, to evade responsibility for an act—which is also fear—you are claiming the self in a lower field. To shift to the higher must mean you realize that you were party to harm, reconcile what you can in a past act by amending your behavior, paying back the debt, but finally, we suggest, by moving to a level of reconciliation where what you have damned in yourself or another is released, or at least reclaimed, in the high octave of the Upper Room.

The choice you are making today, if you wish it, is to allow the affect of past choice to be known to you so that it may be released, reclaimed, and re-known in the Upper Room. Again, we are not speaking of choice, but the affect of the choice— upon others, upon the world, upon the logic you have held in a collective field that would support the act as justified. Self-justification is present at this level. "Well, I did the best I could" may certainly be true. But if the best that you could was deeply harmful to others, you must reconcile the act, and claim the action of the Word, which operates beyond time and space, through the affect of the thing, the choice, the act, and let all involved be re-known in the claim you make. In other words, friends, when you reclaim the act in the Upper Room, the affect of the choice made when you claim, "I am Word through this choice" and all of the repercussions it claimed, you are setting in motion the higher octave, the Christ Redeemer, or True Self, in reconciliation with the manifest world.

He interrupts the teaching. "Well, this sounds like an easy way out. I am not sure I trust it. I hope this is not in the text." This *is* in the text, and we will unpack it as long as we have to, Paul, for you to understand what we are trying to tell you. The idea of karma as insoluble locks most of you in a perpetual cycle of self-recrimination, and seeking to re-order past acts through incarnations. While you will learn through karma, while you may have to repay a debt of any kind, to move beyond it you may also reclaim the act, and what the act incurred, through the invocation of the Word.

We will give you an example, Paul:

"I am Word through the choice I made to deceive another, and all the harm that was caused by that choice. I am Word through the logic I utilized to make that choice. And I am willing to release myself of what I incurred and attend to any act I must make to reconcile my past act with the well-being of others. I choose this in the name of the True Self, and I allow the True Self to enact this, and, indeed, to make it so."

He interrupts yet again. "I now understand the principle—that the Word can reclaim the residual affect of any act made. But I don't understand what we have to do in the physical form." For example, Paul, the one that did not pay the alimony indeed may owe a debt. The fear that there will not be the money there to pay back what was owed is still operating in fear, self-deceit, and will seek to reclaim the act that had a harmful effect upon another. You cannot reclaim the act in the Upper Room if you seek to perpetuate it. In other words, unless you amend behavior, you will repeat the old.

"Well, how do we do this?" he asks. We will do our best to explain it to you. You have lifted to the Upper Room. You have reclaimed memory and identity at this level of tone. What we are teaching now is the past affect of choices made in fear that still may call you—by fear, to fear—through the old relationship you had to the choice, or those that were informed by the choice. So this deliverance is actually essential so that you may be re-known. We will say yet again: All things may be made new, but if you have a debt to your brother you will pay it, but the debt may be transformed through the higher articulation. In other words, when you are no longer condemning the choice, when you bring the choice to the Upper Room to be re-known, the ramifications of the choice may also be transformed.

You are operating beyond time and space, so the reclamation of the incident in the Upper Room reclaims what happened, the choices made, and, indeed, the harm done. In other words, you are not paying lip service through the tone you bring to the past event. The tone itself, the intention to reclaim it anew, and the vibrational echo that that incurs, supports the reclamation of the event and the attachment in karma that you accrued there. Again, "Behold, I make all things new" is not a platitude.

> *"I am Word through this past act, I am Word through any repercussions this act held, and I am Word through all those involved so that we may all be reconciled in the high order of the Upper Room, beyond the old attachment, and the old claim of fear and suffering."*

He interrupts the teaching again. "Is the part of me that resists this teaching the part of me that believes that things should be punished, that past acts must have a cost?" We are telling you this again: The choice made, informed by fear, catalyzed vibration that accrued more fear. A lie told in fear may harm one or many. An act of violence may harm one or many. To reclaim the act of violence is not to deny that it happened. It's to reclaim the residual affect of the choice made upon all parties. To say that because something happened it is irrevocable is to deny the action of the Divine upon it. There is no sin—and, again, sin being the denial of the Divine—that cannot be forgiven or re-known in the high frequency that is the Upper Room.

When we sing through Paul, we will create a field of amplification. The words that you may invoke in this choice to reclaim all aspects of self known through choice, the residual affect of choice, and all those informed by that choice, will be made by you as you claim it. We will offer you the words to do so, once the field is invoked.

On the count of three, Paul.

Now one. Now two. Now three.

[The Guides tone through Paul.]

> "*On this day I choose to align any choice, and the affect of that choice, made in fear, to be re-known in the Upper Room. As I say yes to this, I allow the vibration of the Word to reclaim all who are impacted by this choice throughout time. I say these words now in my choice to be free of the affect of past choice that would inhibit my expression as the True Self, indeed in the Upper Room. I am Word through this intention. Word I am Word. I know who I am in truth. I know what I am in truth. I know how I serve in truth. I am free. I am free. I am free.*"

The realization of this, the knowing of this, will come in the interactions you have with those who have been most affected by past choice. But you will not be released from the fabric of the choice as long as you do not forgive or claim those around you in benefit of this choice. In other words, to say to someone, "Well, I am off the hook, thank you very much, I do not owe you the money," would be blasphemy, would be contradictory, would be a denial of the Divine. To know that one in love, and in receipt of what he or she requires, will benefit you far more.

We say this for Paul, now. This is a less challenging teaching than you believe it is. We are actually offering you a key to a kind of liberation where you are no longer snared by the expectation of harm through past act, or the guilt you may foster. And guilt, again, is the denial of the Divine, that you will not give to the Divine, that you may hold against the self in Purgatory. To decide that you are free is not to make the self free, but to offer this thing to the Divine, that can and will make it new.

We thank you each for your presence. Stop now, please.

DAY SEVENTEEN

What stands before you today, in an awakened state, is the awareness that there is no sin, and cannot be, in the idea of the Upper Room. You understand yourselves, you see, through a collective field in an idea of separation. The amplitude of the Upper Room is indeed such that the lower field does not obfuscate, does not enter, does not align. A world made new, you see, is a new world, without the old bias and the need for retribution that you have rested so heavily upon. The idealized self, the idea of who you think you should be—perhaps kinder, more merciful—is not who expresses in the Upper Room. You are not improved there. You are, in fact, made new there. And because you are made new, in fact you are redeemed.

Now, to understand redemption is to understand the action of the Christ, or the Monad, that exists in innocence. To be innocent is to be pure. But your idea of purity is so confused through religion that you don't understand that it is the Monad, the Christed Self, that can *only* be pure, and is the only thing that can render something other pure or in truth. To be in truth is to be in one's true state, beyond the idea of separation and all the calamity that separation has claimed. To realize the self, which is to be incarnate here, is to move beyond the idea of karma that has been utilized in the lower field. Now, we have said prior, karma is not retribution. It is an opportunity to learn. And until one learns, one will learn through cause and effect, or one's experience.

When you move to the vibration of the Upper Room, the level of alignment you hold is actually claimed beyond the tone or residual affect that fear has held. Imagine you are in a mountain, and there is a flood in the valley. From the mountain, you do not experience the flood. Now, in this case *flood* may be metaphor for past acts of the collective or the individual. Paul interrupts the teaching already. "Well, I can understand it is a metaphor, but if I live in a town that is flooded, whether I am in the Upper Room or not I will get very wet." You misunderstand the teaching. The metaphor is something other. At the level of alignment we teach, you are not incurring karma because you are not acting in fear, and you are not harming others because the intent is not to harm. Now, if you go about your business and someone feels insulted by you, that is their issue. If the intention was to insult, you were not operating in the Upper Room. You were back in the valley and may get slapped by the wave that you have in fact incurred. To be made new, finally, we must suggest, is to know the self in a purified state, released from the obstructions that you may have utilized to know the self through the collective field. Because the debt is paid in the Upper Room, the idea of karma ceases to exist. And forgiveness, if you understand it as such, or redemption, which is a finer word in this construct, is fully present, does not *seek* to be attained. It fully is.

Now, to return to our examples from yesterday: To be released from an obligation, perhaps a karmic debt, in the Upper Room, does not mean your debt is forgiven if you owe your neighbor money. But to claim the Upper Room and the presence and the action of the Divine upon the debt—"God Is, God Is, God Is"—may in fact recalibrate the situation so that there is no malice. Something may be re-known, and its residual affect *must* be re-known in the claim of the Upper Room.

Now, Paul was confused yesterday because he wishes to understand himself in two places at the same time. An aspect of him knows it's in the Upper Room. Another aspect of himself denies the Upper Room because he is frightened of living there. "What is there to fear?" he would say, and then answer his own question. "Perhaps I am not good enough, or not worthy enough, or not pure enough." In fact, nobody is good enough, and everybody is good enough. And nobody is pure enough, and everybody is pure at the level of Monad, which is in fact innocence. You know how a fire burns and reclaims all that it encounters. The Christed Self or the Monad as flame reclaims all that it encounters, and indeed it is made new, not through your effort, but through your allowance. "I Am Known. I Am Known. I Am Known." Every dark spot, every confused idea, every idea of self that is held outside of God, must be reclaimed. And the action of this text is this reclamation of every aspect of self in the Upper Room. We are not playing with you. We are restoring you as you wish to be restored.

The idea of self as separate from Source is what is being contended with here, and that is the only issue, and that is the aspect of self that does not know he is loved, or she is known, or he is welcomed, or she is worthy. There is an idea of self that believes that its survival must be predicated upon separation. This is not a death of the ego—and *ego* meaning personality structure. It is a reclamation of it in a higher tone, because as we have said so often, this personality structure simply has its usage, but it is not who you truly are, what you truly are, and can never be how you truly serve. The denial of the Divine is the only issue you contend with, and you will not face this by pretending you are worthy, but by allowing for the Divine to reclaim any aspect of self that is operating in fear or choosing denial.

Now, sovereignty, if it is truly understood, is the expressed Monad that operates independently from the structures that humanity has utilized to govern, to decide, to educate, to pay, to get, and to decide what must be. To be truly sovereign is to be reclaimed at the level of choice where the choiceless choice is indeed present, and this is the congruence with true knowing. When you are in true knowing, you are always in choice, and in true choice. There is no confusion here, because the alignment supports the realization that is required in every situation or any occurrence that you could ever encounter. A debt paid in the high room is simply the realization that the Divine is present, and that the act itself has been reclaimed in truth, beyond the idea of sin or separation or karmic debt.

Now, the fall of man, or humanity, if you wish, was of course the belief in separation and the sanctification of it. To be restored to the Kingdom, or to the universal truth of being, requires that you dismantle the walls that have been obstructing the light. Because we do this for one of you, and then many of you, and then all of you, you become party to a great re-creation. When we spoke yesterday, we spoke of resolving or re-knowing the accruement of the evidence of separation through your past actions. When an individual does this—"I am Word through all that I have claimed in fear, any harm I have done intentionally or unintentionally"—you release the power of the Divine upon that which has been denied it by your own judgment, your own unforgiveness, or the judgment or unforgiveness of others. You are not doing penance. You are offering as yourself to be the vehicle for this movement, because the action of the Christ or the Monad—"I know how I serve in truth"—is claimed through the experience of being and presence that you hold while in form.

Some of you say to us, "Well, I said the claim, but I still feel terrible about what I did." Feel as you wish. You can paint a room another color and still pretend it's blue. When you claim the action of the Divine upon something, you are not getting anybody to do anything for you, forgive you as you should be forgiven in your estimation, or go pleading to the Upper Room and say, "Oh, dear God, please release me from this predicament." The predicament, if it was claimed in fear or the denial of the Divine, may be reclaimed in the Upper Room:

"I am in the Upper Room. I Have Come. I Have Come. I Have Come. Behold, I make all things new. God Is. God Is. God Is."

The action of the Divine upon the thing held in darkness is what reclaims it, not the work of your hands, but your agreement to the action of the Source of all things.

Now, redemption occurs when the heart and mind are changed. The one who intentionally harms another and claims that as a victory is abiding in the lower field. And until this human being is re-known and re-seen and reclaimed in the high octave, he or she will perpetuate the debt of the action incurred, and that is so he or she may learn the futility of the act. When you know fully—and underline the word *know*, it means realize—that all are one, you comprehend that you cannot harm another without harming the self. Again, as you do to the least of me, you do to me. In other words, friends, you break it, you own it—until you offer it to the higher to be reclaimed and repaired and re-known in the truth of expression that is the Upper Room.

We have done this with you, not in reparation, but in restoration. To be restored is to be made new, to be reclaimed or redeemed in your true nature, which, again, is innocent. "Well, I don't feel very innocent," he says. Well, the aspect of you that believes himself or herself as in sin will seek verification of sin. The realization that God is all things—underline *all*—and all things can be re-known in God when the mind is made new and the heart made new, will gift you what you require, which is a belief in a sense of separation that must be released in order for the True Self to manifest. He interrupts. "This seems an impossible task." It only is at the level of personality.

Paul, you are feeling cold energy around you. Many who are listening will. This is the release of the old, and its temperature in coolness is what is experienced by one who relinquishes what has been held for thousands of years in the energetic structure. When we speak to the evolution of humanity as a species, we are claiming this to all who walk, all who feel, all who see, so they may know themselves in the new, in the reclaimed, in what we call the Kingdom.

Too many of you suffer needlessly. Too many of you deny the self the good that is already yours. You are claimed anew by the willingness to be received. If you must change how you act, because how you have acted has been harmful to the self or another, you will be shown how. "Behold, I make all things new." The claim of reclamation.

Now, humanity itself must undergo a process of re-seeing what it has claimed in shadow or darkness in denial of the Divine. The flood that Paul saw earlier from the mountaintop is what happens when all things are claimed anew in a low field. That which will not hold, that which will be washed away, is that which has been held in shadow. What is known in truth will flourish and blossom and greet the new with welcoming.

The realization that each and every one of you, the man in the chair included, have been party to any atrocity humanity has ever undergone will be useful here. Now, by *party* we mean in congruence with or in alignment to. Everything you see, you are in alignment to. Everything you have ever heard, you are in congruence with. Because you are in congruence with it, you are party to it in historical data, which can only be known through the present moment because this is the only moment there truly is. The act of re-articulation, or being lifted to the Upper Room, must then include every act made by humanity in the denial of the Divine, or with the intent to harm. Do you understand this teaching?

What you chose to do yesterday through invocation is in fact in preparation for the work we do with you today. And we do this work with you on behalf of all—those who have ever taken a breath, those who have ever loved, those who have ever chosen, those who have ever feared, those who have ever damned or been damned—the reclamation of all, and all choice born in the denial of the Divine reclaimed in the Upper Room where it may be made new.

When we tone through Paul, we will create a field. We will invite you each to enter this field with the simple intention:

"I am in the Upper Room. I Have Come. I Am Here. I Am Known."

And this agreement will indeed support the action that you may choose to undertake with us.

On the count of three.

Now one. Now two. Now three.

[The Guides tone through Paul.]

"I am in the Upper Room. I Have Come. I Am Here. I Am Known. On this day I agree to reclaim any choice made through any time that was claimed in darkness or shadow, and I claim this for all, so that it may be re-known and restored in the true Christ, the true light of the Monad, that is forgiveness, that is grace, that is redemption and restoration for all things. And I give permission for the field I hold to be utilized in this service. I know who I am in truth. I know what I am in truth. I know how I serve in truth. I Am Here. I Am Here. I Am Here. I am in the Upper Room. I Have Come. Behold, I make all things new."

Let yourself be in service, and let the field you hold move beyond your idea of time and space to support the reclamation of any form that the denial of the Divine has taken—any untruth, any self-justification, any warring, any deceit, any harm done, and all harm done.

"I know who I am. I know what I am. I know how I serve."

Be still and allow this to be so.

"It will be so. God Is. God Is. God Is."

(PAUSE)

What is occurring here is beyond what you know can be so, beyond the comprehension that the small self can hold. You are beyond time and space, and the articulation of the Monad through you, the redeemer in all, enacted upon all, claims the world anew. The evolution of the species, if you wish to truly know, is the restoration of innocence, or humanity's true nature, beyond the idea of separation, which has always been a lie.

Blessings to you each. Thank you for your service. Thank you for the gift of being and presence that you have claimed and then offered to what we will call God. Blessings to each of you. Stop now, please.

Indeed, this is in the text.

(PAUSE)

What stands before you today, in this awakened state, is the realization that what you thought was so is not so. How the world appeared through the distortion of separation will soon be replaced by a higher awareness, or a degree of certainty, that the action of the Divine is upon what you see, because what you give your attention to you inform and reclaim from the strata of the Upper Room where you now align to. You become the agent of change, or the actor of change, as the one who says yes to the re-articulation of form through presence and being.

Now, to understand what occurred today, you offered the self at a level of amplitude, from the Upper Room, where the only choice you can make is in alignment to the higher. And because you chose this and agreed to it, you were actually in support of the energetic field of the plane you have known, in a risen state. We use the term *risen* intentionally. The field that humanity has known itself through has now been seeded, or prepared for seeding, by the work that was done by you, one and all. To comprehend this is to comprehend that the Divine Self, who is not bound to the idea of time or space, may reclaim all things, including your idea of what once was, or what was once in separation, to a new state of expression. It is not so much that you are changing history. You are realizing history, which is simply an idea at the level of the Monad.

The claim "Behold, I make all things new," indeed an alchemical claim that aligns all things to it, is what prepares the soil for the seeding that follows. And the seeding that follows—"It will be so; God Is, God Is, God Is"—is the reclamation of the Source upon matter that has existed in any idea of time or of space. Because the Monad exists in eternity, it is not hindered by the rules of time or space, and you as Monad, or Divine Expression, are not hindered by this either.

In prior texts, we have supported students in reclamation of aspects of self that were known in shadow. And we have prepared this text by supporting the reader, the student, the listener of this text, to those aspects of self that have been misplaced outside the Upper Room so that they may be re-known. But the work that we will now do, and must continue to do, is the reclamation of innocence.

Now, those who will be born on this plane in the coming years will hold the vibration that has been seeded. You are participatory to this. The great obstacles that have been faced by those who have been reared through the idea of fear or separation will not be so in coming generations. They will actually exist beyond what was claimed in their heredity because they will already be expressing in the Upper Room because they know themselves as of it.

The realization of humanity in its next phase will be coming into form in three generations, and four generations for realization to commence. In other words, friends, who comes next will be walking upon the road that you have paved, and agreed to, through presence and being. You don't understand yet that the agreement to partake in this realization is made at the level of the soul. You are party to the soul's re-creation of expression. And to *express* is to be seen, to be made known, and enacted as the Divine Truth that is the truth of your being, the true innocence as stated in the claim: "I Have Come. I Am Here. I Am Known."

This is in the text.

DAY EIGHTEEN

What stands before you today, in an awakened state, is the realization that nothing is outside of God. The idea that anything can be must now be replaced with a new thought, a new claim: All That Is holds all that is within it. In other words, nothing can be outside it.

Now, the belief in separation has accrued ample evidence that there are things outside of God. Those things put in darkness, cast in shadow, that are now being retrieved and re-deemed in what we call the Upper Room. The shadowed self, the thoughts of the shadowed self, the denial of God within and without, personal and collective history, all reclaimed, re-born, re-known in the Upper Room in the claim "Behold, I make all things new." The amplitude of this claim has a far-reaching affect. The claim "God Is, God Is, God Is," in reali-zation, transmutes matter, lifts the veil of separation, because it has only been a veil. To truly understand the magnitude of this claim, choose one incident in your life where God could not have been, where the presence of God seems so far away that it could not be so, there could be no God. And allow the self to align in the Upper Room—"I am in the Upper Room; I Have Come, I Have Come, I Have Come"—and redeem that aspect of self that experienced this level of separation. Now, notice we said *redeem the self*, reclaim the self, that ex-perienced such loss, such damage or betrayal. Once the self is redeemed or reclaimed, the action of the choice to perceive the self in separation is completely altered, and the ramifications of that time and that thing are brought to the altar to indeed be made new.

Recrimination against the self or others must now be un-derstood as a way you utilize separation to perceived bene-fit. "If I talk ill of this one, I will perceive myself as better or wiser." "If I dictate the terms of this relationship, I will not be caught in a trap." "If I deny the other's need for me, their love or longing, I will become the one who chooses what he gets at the cost of another's desire." In other words, the belief that you will be controlled by another's love or desire for you is a way to prove separation.

Now, to realize that you are not separate from the one who loves you does not mean you don't hold boundaries. But it does mean you don't deny them their alignment at whatever level that may be. When you have moved to the Upper Room as a state of being that comes in gradation and is realized, finally, in fullness, the idea of *boundary* falls away because you are no longer protecting the self from a perception of harm, or a belief in harm, that you would call to you. When the world does this, when humanity has lifted to the Upper Room, the idea of borders as you have known them that must be protected with arms will indeed fall away. You have always been one family but you've dictated the terms of separation, denied the worth in the ones beside you, and done your best to keep others out.

To understand that anything the self experiences is actually also experienced by the collective will give you the information that you require. When you stop denying others their right to be, you also stop encouraging a world that would claim separation as the cause of safety. You give others permission to be themselves, and you know them as they truly are, beyond the old evidence of separation or your belief in right and wrong, the evidence of separation that you would use as proof that all cannot be of God.

"But what about that terrible man who did those terrible things?" "What about that woman who caused such harm?"

Those who act in the denial of the Divine require love more than you know. They were reared in darkness, know themselves in shadow, and seek to perpetuate what they have known. But throwing them further in darkness in fact re-empowers the sense of separation that they have acted upon. To bring *them* to the light is to know the persecutor as worthy of love, to know the criminal as worthy of love, to know the one who committed the worst crime as worthy of love.

Now, it is not the personality structure that is in reception of love in this instruction. We are speaking of divine love, and God's creation cannot be denied. To reclaim the one who has been put in darkness is to know them beyond sin, or the idea of sin being the way you would validate their actions to enshrine them in shadow. Any system of religion that would seek to damn another is in fact invoking separation where none was ever intended. The true teaching of the Christ as redeemer is the teaching of the Monad in expression. Because God cannot deny its creations, the Christed Self or the Monad, which operates beyond the personality you have known yourself through, will indeed reclaim all that it sees, all that it encounters—and not with effort.

"How do I forgive this one for his terrible crime? How do I deny the pain I've received at his or her hands?" You do not deny the pain. You do not deny the Christ in the one who harmed you. You realize the Divine as them, beyond the acts they have encountered themselves through. And you are redeeming them, not through personal choice, but through the act of the Creator serving as you. Each time you say yes to releasing one you've held in darkness, your amplification increases. To realize that you've chosen to deny the Divine in others, been encouraged by a culture to do so, confirmed by a religion to do so, each time you agree that the teachings of old that are operating in distortion are claiming you in shadow, you will give permission to lift beyond them. How one lifts is less by degree here, but by the untethering of the boulders that have anchored you to the lower field, the lower field, again, being the collective field known in shadow, the denial of God that you have been reared in.

The idea of evil must now be understood as the intent to harm. But finally, we suggest, because all things are of God, the misunderstanding of evil as force must now be claimed anew. Because things may operate in low vibration, seek to confirm the shadows they have known themselves through, they require the light more than others. If you forgive the neighbor, who mildly insulted you, with ease, you will understand there is no great challenge in that choice to forgive. But to forgive the one who has done the most harm, accrued the most evidence of separation, is to bring something to the light that will heal the world.

When something is drawn up from the pit, claimed from the well of shame, the well of darkness, that they have known themselves in, indeed they are frightened by the light and often deterred by its presence. The one who has only known darkness will always seek refuge in the cave. The polarity you experience on this plane, which shows up in many ways and in many forms, is in some ways evidence of this. Those who deny the light will seek to fight the darkness, believing that they are doing the work of the light. You cannot fight the darkness. You can bring the light to the darkness, but illumination is never a battle. When you bring a sword out to attack, you must expect that the response will be what it will be, which is further battle. War is not ended by a great battle where there is a victor. War is ended when the consciousness that has claimed war is transformed to one of peace. When the swords are dropped, when the battle is ended, you will dance together in an awareness of who you have always been. The battlefield is transformed. It is lifted to the Upper Room, because, indeed, it has been made new.

Each of you who attends to these teachings is seen by us in agreement to your inherent worth, your inherent innocence, your inherent truth. Each one of you who says yes to this is called forward as you may be lifted, and lifted well, through each stage of experience which is required by the consciousness you have held to know liberation. To know liberation is to realize the self in a liberated state. And the calamity that you have known, the only real calamity—which has been separation—is ended, not for one, but for all.

The only challenge humanity faces is the claim of separation from its Source. And anything that you could think of, any illustration of evil, any act you could think of, must be seen as the result of this belief, and in fact the evidence that it has accrued. Those of you who believe that there can be no God if evil persists in the world are actually aligning to evil, not through intention, but through your empowerment of the lack of the Divine. You need not be religious in the least to comprehend the simplicity of what we say. The light refutes the darkness, it reclaims the darkness, it brings to light what has been held in darkness so that it may be re-known or re-deemed. You cannot conceal what has been held in shadow anymore, not within the self or your brother. But this is not an excuse to harm. When the fire within is burning, when the light within is moving through you, it will reclaim what it encounters. When you begin to express as this light—which is, again, the claim "I know how I serve in truth"—the light is what claims what it encounters and brings it to fruition to be re-seen in fullness. You are now the anchor of this light through your agreement to this act. And the choice to claim what you see, all that you see and have ever seen, in the realization of the Divine—"Behold, I make all things new; It will be so; God Is, God Is, God Is"—will create the cascade, the great wave of vibration, that will shift all that you encounter.

Any belief that you have in evil must now be contended with, lest you brace yourself for a battle when what is needed is love. To realize the Divine where it has been most denied is the act of the innocent who is not agreeing to evil. The Upper Room, you see, or the Christed Self, cannot contain evil, will not re-inforce it, because you know, and have been taught, that what you damn will damn you back. You now must understand that at this level of tone or vibration you cannot damn, because what you would be damning would be outside of God. And, again, we say: Nothing can be. Nothing has been. Nothing will be.

The illusion of separation is the denial of the Divine, and your accruement of evidence to this separation is what is being attended to in this text. As we continue this chapter, which we will call "Beyond Sin," we intend to make two statements: The resurrection is a collective act that humanity engages in to move beyond an old template. And the old template will one day be forgotten because all of the evidence it once accrued, in the denial of the Divine, will have been re-known. A world made new. A world redeemed, re-known, and reclaimed.

Paul is in the background saying, "Oh, no. I can see the eyes rolling. Please tell us how this is done." It is done through you, but with the assistance of the Divine that is present now as all things. Because the veil has indeed thinned, the light is present and reclaiming what was in shadow. The tumult of the times, you see, is what happens when the well begins to overflow and what the well has contained is made visible to be re-known.

The Kingdom is present. It is here. It is here. And your agreement to this is what claims it into being.

We thank you for your presence. Indeed, this is in the text. Stop now, please.

DAY NINETEEN

What stands before you today, in recognition of who you are, is what you have chosen, how you have chosen, and the ramifications of choice. All choice has ramification. And the realization that any choice may be lifted to the higher octave, and a new world may be claimed, henceforth will support all of you in a realization that there is nothing intractable, nothing that cannot be changed or restored, in the True Self.

Now, the True Self and its purview is all that is experienced. When we spoke last, we said all was of God and in God. And your recognition that all is—without effort, but because it can only be—in and of Source claims a trajectory that moves everything to the higher octave experientially. Un-

derline the word *experientially*. What is experienced by the
one who knows who she is, is in an altered field, a field that is
in translation. Now, when something is in translation, it may
seem less solid, less clarified, than when it is fully realized.
But the operation that you are undergoing now in restoration
claims all that you encounter to the Upper Room in an experiential way. Now, when we say *experiential*, this simply means
you are no longer telling yourself what is. You are experiencing
what is. You are not defining what is. You are knowing what is.
And in this knowing, every choice ever made by anyone who
has ever been born may be restored. "What are you speaking
of?" he asks. When a world is made new, all must be made
new.

Now, you perceive yourselves in separation to the degree
that you really don't understand how individual choice, in
manifestation, claims trajectory. You don't understand how
historical choice has claimed the world you live in. Every
border drawn, every war ever fought, every love, every defeat,
every triumph—all had its basis in choice. And your realization
of this, God as choice, God in realization as choice, through
all choice, will actually claim the trajectory of choice, as has
been known by humanity, in a higher amplitude. When this
amplitude is in translation, there will be a period of confusion,
because what you expected to be will not be, and the new is
not fully formed.

When you idealize an outcome based in prior choice, you
solidify expectation and you demand that things be in the form
that they've known. When a piece of music is transposed, it
is the same music in some ways, and quite different in others,
because the notes played are being played in a higher schemata

and experienced in a higher way. The resolution that things should be as they were—again, an act of choice—must now be released. You do this both for yourself and for the world you have known yourself in. A resolute choice—"It will be so," the decree of what truly is—can support you here. The manifestation of the Monad as choice, as will, as the ramifications of will, will actually translate the field and the results of prior choice to a level that they may be re-known.

When we teach through Paul, we listen to his questions. We see the images he sees as we speak through him. He is seeing a river, once polluted, once filthy. "Is the river re-known in the Upper Room? Is the water clean?" The river is indeed re-known, and the aspect of self that contributed to the old system, which you may call the one who soils the water, is now altered, and consequently the prior choices are being re-known and are now in translation. When a new choice is made and the evidence of the old is still upon you, you have an opportunity to re-see the evidence in the higher octave. You are not making it pretty. You are not cleaning the water. You are seeing the water in a restored state, what was always true before it was moved or claimed in the lower field.

Now, how the world is moved in a manifest way is really rather simple. You understand a balloon that lifts. The sandbags are released from the basket and the balloon lifts. As what has tethered the old, as what has attached you to the old, is moved your view changes. You are not looking at things at the old level that they were created. You are perceiving them beyond the old, and consequently the old is made new.

"At what level," Paul asks, "is the manifestation of prior choice changed? If I lift high up enough in the balloon, I may

not see the trash in the river, but I expect it is still there."
Again, the initial choice to pollute the river, made by you in
singular as an aspect of the whole, claims the new as potential.
The realization of the potential is made manifest through the
lifting of the old. You still perceive alchemy as an act of the
hands—"I will pull the trash from the riverbed"—and perhaps
you will be called to. But the level of consciousness that first
polluted the river is what will first be attended to. When the
level of consciousness that created this is moved, there will be
no more pollution because the idea of pollution will have been
moved to a higher level that does not hold a basis in separation. And the one who sees God as the river claims the river
in its divinity.

Now, how matter is moved, Paul, which is your real question, will be discussed later in the text. But you must understand, first and foremost, that thought prior to choice catalyzes
action, and action has affect, that anyone who sees the polluted river, and has a choice about it and how it is seen, may
claim the river in the higher octave. And if you don't believe
that the river will be altered by the claim of the higher, you are
anchoring yourself to the lower and denying the power and
the purview of the Divine where it is now present.

Each of you who says yes to this is operating in an altered
field. Each of you who chooses this is agreeing to a higher
potential. But you must recall that agreement is coherence
and co-resonance. To be in co-resonance with the higher is to
make it made so. Why do you all believe that you can manifest
a better home, perhaps a better job, but the same amplitude
of choice to align to the higher cannot re-create a manifest
world? Because you have been moored in selfishness, and a

belief that you should have what you want even at the cost of another having it, has given you the opportunity to perhaps learn the lessons of manifestation through the separate field, but deprive the self of the full experience of the Divine, which is matter. Underline those words: *which is matter*. The river is God, and God may be re-known beyond the idea of *river*, beyond what was thrown in the river, beyond what was polluted in the river. What you have chosen to reclaim is the Divine as all things. So if you put the polluted river out of this Divine Self, out of this divine field, you have damned the river and will continue to harm yourselves.

Each one of you here who is partaking in this teaching is moving to a level of velocity where what is experienced is re-known. This is not a promise. It doesn't need to be a promise. It is the expectation you may hold. The one who perceives the view from the twentieth floor perceives far more than the one in the cellar room. The one who claims the Kingdom, and realizes the Kingdom in form, is party to the Kingdom and its manifestation—just as, unknowingly, you have all been party to the destruction of the plane that you've experienced your form in. You can call it pollution. You can call it denial of the Divine. You can call it the ramifications of greed. You would be correct in all of these things. But all of these things, each and every one of them, holds a basis in choice born in the denial of the Divine.

Some of you say to us, "Well, I want a world made new. Perhaps the Divine will grant a world made new. Perhaps my grandchildren will live with a bluer sky, cleaner water, no threat of freezing or burning in the odd months." You are do-ing this now, through the claim of sovereignty, as the Monad expresses. To wait for God in a cloud to save you is to deny that you are the emissary, to deny that you are the activation of the Divine Spark expressed as being, presence and being. To claim all things made new is not to improve all things. It's to realize that the matter that is all things, even the consciousness that is all things, is and can only be God.

The restoration of this plane at a level you may experience will come in stages. You are still polluting. You are still denying the common field. You are still making choices collectively that operate in separation. You are still damning the environment by ignoring the Divine in the environment. This will claim itself in its own trajectory. But every trajectory, even the lowest one claimed, cannot go on in the same way without encountering an obstacle. And the obstacle that is present for this is in fact the level of consciousness that is being enacted to supersede past choice. When past choice is re-known, the ramifications of past choice may be reclaimed in the higher as God, because even past choice was the action of the Divine at a lower level.

You have been granted the gift of co-creation. You can spoil what you like, and you are accountable to it. But the rising of the Christed Self, aligning you to the high choice that is available now, triumphs because the higher will always reclaim the lower. When we have taught the braiding of the will, and the offering of the will to be braided, we have not denied the will of the small self, but we have allowed the will of the small self to be re-known in congruence with the higher will that is the Divine Expression of you. When the will is mended, or known in a higher octave, every choice made will support the realization of the Kingdom in form without your even thinking about it, because the consciousness that holds the choice is not believing, is not aligning, is not accruing evidence of separation, but re-knowing all things as of God.

We sing your songs for you so that you may learn the words. The idea of sin, or choice born in separation, has been discussed here and will commence when we gather again. Thank you for your presence. This is in the text. Stop now, please. Period.

DAY TWENTY

What stands before you today, in a higher awareness of who you are, are the choices made in fear that can now be reclaimed in the high order of the Upper Room. So many choices are made without an awareness of why. Many of the choices you have made have been dictated by prior thought, what was expected of you at a certain time or age. The time has come to render all things new, inclusive of the mechanisms of choice that you have utilized to guarantee outcome. Underline that phrase, please, *guaranteed outcome*, which simply means expectation born in prior belief. "I cracked two eggs, there will be two yolks. I turn the light under the frying pan and the eggs will cook."

Your idea of who you are is also based in such strategizing. "I am the one who always does this or that." Some of you say to us, "I want to change." You don't really want to change. You don't want to be in the discomfort that you have known yourselves through. And much of what you choose—always, again, born in prior knowing or agreement of who you *should* be—must now be seen as present to be re-seen, and, again, reclaimed, in the high strata of the Upper Room.

When you are not operating with outcome in the ways that you have, the choices that are before you in fact will be altered. So much of what you see is predicated in history that the idea of moving beyond history—and all history is, is the result of prior choice—you can understand that for all things to be made new the evidence of history itself, all things made in form and seen, must be rendered anew again. Now, we will say *again* because every time you see something you are actually seeing it as if for the first time. But the memory of the old sight clarifies, condones an old way of seeing and consequently perpetuating a landscape that is actually lost to memory when it is truly seen anew. How you see a plant, how you see a sunset, how you see your neighbor, informed through historical data, predicates the outcome of how you see them.

The realization of your neighbor as of God reclaims the neighbor in God, but your perception of *neighbor* is still highly informed by prior understanding, experience, and expectation. "I know my neighbor. She has gray hair. She doesn't like to smile much." The claim you make for your neighbor agrees with your neighbor at one level of tone or vibration. To experience your neighbor as of God is actually to move the neighbor to a level of articulation or vibrancy that you will experience. Underline the word *will*. We are moving to matter now, and the manifestation of matter, and the experience of matter, as God.

Now, your relationship to what you saw in the past—"That is the zoo I went to when I was a child, that is what the tiger looked like, that is how the bears played"—informs not only your idea of self, and what *was* once, perhaps, but what a zoo *is*, what a tiger or bear must be. The replication of history through sight or perception must now be understood as a way that you are indoctrinated by memory, born in past choice through the collective, to perpetuate a world that is operating in a lower schemata.

The realization of the neighbor as of God is not an intellectual knowing. It is actually a profound state of recognition. And the woman who doesn't like to smile, who perhaps has gray hair, is seen further from that idea than you could ever imagine. She is perceived as she truly is, a distinct expression of God as manifest in tone, in color, in vibration. Now, you understand your neighbor. She lives two doors down. She gets her mail at 9 a.m. Perhaps she waves, perhaps she doesn't. But you understand her now beyond the idea of herself that she has utilized to guarantee an outcome because you are no longer guaranteeing the outcome of who and what she is through prior conditioning.

The triumph of this teaching, and indeed it is a triumph, is the re-articulation of matter in the Upper Room in an experiential way. And the idea of sin or separation that you have condoned and would seek to perpetuate is relinquished to a degree of creation that will not hold it. *A degree of creation that will not hold it.* By *creation* we mean the Word. The Word is the energy of the Creator in action. If you think of the Word as the Christ Principle, the Source of all things as may be manifest in form, you will understand the significance of what we are saying. In the Word, or the action of God, the idea of sin, which is separation, is released finally to a higher experience.

He interrupts the teaching. "Well, in the past you have said all things are of God, so consequently sin is as well, or our idea of sin." Yes, your idea of sin, Paul, and everyone else's, is of God because you have created all things with thought, and thought is an aspect of God. But, finally, sin is an agreement to fear. Anything known as sin is an action in defiance of the Divine. But much of what you think of as sin is a moral dictate, ascribed through historical data, that you perpetuate in certain ways to maintain an idea of a status quo that was also born in separation. The realization of the Divine as your neighbor reclaims the neighbor beyond the idea of sin. And now we are saying *idea of sin* because we have taught prior that all things are ideas, and any idea may be re-known.

"What happens to the neighbor?" Paul asks. Well, we will say it in two ways. She is as she was, and completely altered, both at the same time. The equivalency you have held for your neighbor as the one incarnate as the Word reclaims or redeems her in the pulse, in the frequency, in the sound and the tone, of the great I Am presence, the God as all, the God that must be her and everything of her, inclusive of past acts and past choice, born in sorrow, born in the denial of the Divine, and born in an agreement to an idea of sin that she has utilized to maintain separation. At the same time, she collects her mail from the mailbox. Perhaps she smiles or doesn't. But she has been made new.

The vast field you know of as reality will be reclaimed in such a manner. The data of history, which is what things have meant through prior prescription, known through past choice, claimed by separation or fear, is being anointed through the action of the Divine upon what is seen. "I am Word through all that I see before me. Word I am Word."

The calamity of your times is that God is as present here as it can ever be, but you lack the eyes to see it. And by *eyes* we don't mean physical eyes, but the senses, the ability, to be at a level of perception where you know yourself as known, and consequently know all things. But the gift of the time is the encroaching light that illumines all things, reclaims all things, and denies the action of fear, not in a punitive way, but by relocating the true tone that had been denied.

Our gift to each of you who hears these words, who reads these words, is the vibration that informs these words. This is the vibration of the Christ manifest. And the Kingdom is the gift of the Christ Kingdom as made manifest through alignment and agreement to what already is. Underline those words: *agreement to what already is.* When you are aligning to the Source that is ever present, and offering the self to the action of the Source as who and what you are, how you serve is as the expression of this Christ, the True Self, as manifest in innocence. And by that we mean without sin. And by that we mean without the action of fear condemning things. The risen Christ will redeem all it encounters in truth. In truth a lie will not be held. And at this level of action and truth, all things in restoration will be reclaimed in the high order, the true sense, of innocence that the Upper Room holds.

We will stop for today. Thank you for your presence. This is in the text. Stop now, please. Period. Period. Period.

DAY TWENTY-ONE

What stands before you today, in an altered awareness of what reality has been, is the potential that now lies before you for all things to be reclaimed. In reclamation an announcement is made—"I Have Come"—and the agreement to this, the Monad in expression as all things, trumpets a new world, claims the new world, and alters the very fabric of reality that has been known through darkness to a new dawn. Each of you who says yes is in fact participatory to the act of re-creation at the level that you can confirm it. And in your restoration to your own innocence, you are received by the great Source in an awareness of the innocence of all.

Now, when you understand what we mean, that restoration is a restoration to innocence, you must understand what we don't mean. We are not saying you didn't hurt someone, didn't have a bad thought, didn't wish to die—whatever you may have claimed as part of your learning in the dense field you have known yourselves through. What it does mean is that you are now in an encounter with the brightest light you may know— that has its own purview, that dictates outcome in an awareness of its own requirements. We have taught you that fear replicates itself at the level of tone, the denial of the Divine, that it confirms. The Christ or the Monad does the same. Any true note sung, any true note sung fully, will claim all things to it in co-resonance.

Now, your restoration, the individual self restored, makes you participatory to a new song being sung in the entire field. And as each of you says yes, the agreement is made again and again to withstand change in the awareness that the change that comes is of God.

Now, the challenges you will face on this journey, in this act of restoration, have been discussed in many ways—the attitudes of what was, the anchoring to habituated patterning known through memory or self-deceit. The replication of the Divine is about to announce itself as the octave you experience yourself in. Now, the Upper Room is present. You have aligned to it through energy in invocation, but you have not fully experienced the being of this. And the being of this is the gift of this class, this entire class from beginning to end. The tone that is being sung through this text is intended to claim you, not only in degree, but in fullness at the level of alignment that you may hold. And your articulation, rendered new, claims experientially not only the Upper Room, but the beginning of the Kingdom as may be sung through you.

"What does that mean," he asks, "*the beginning of the Kingdom?*" Any octave has many notes. You lift from one to the next at the level of tone you can maintain. Those of you who hold the high note are articulated as the high note, claim the high note sung as all manifestation. Others of you learn one by one, note by note, what you can hold, grow comfortable here, and re-articulate, which simply means re-know the self at that level of strata. The encouragement we offer now is that this is done through you. You are not striving for this. You are rolling, experiencing the wave that is you, in the higher tone in its awareness of the sea, the wave's awareness of the sea. The wave knows itself as of the sea in its action of being. It does not try to be the wave. It is the wave. And the wave that you sing as reclaims everything it touches in the vastness of the sea that it is of, and only of.

This is a class in experience, and we invite you now to invoke the Monad as experience. Understand what this means. You are reciting a claim that has great power. You are invoking the amplitude of the Creator through experience—not through conjecture, supposition, or wishful thinking. The re-articulation of the Divine Self in an experience of innocence is the claim that is being made through you.

> On this day I choose to allow any experience I hold to be held in the Upper Room in awareness of its Source. On this day I choose to make an agreement to my nature, my very nature, to be as experience of the Source of all things in my knowing and being. And as I say yes to this, I allow myself to be re-sung in the amplitude of the Christ as it is known as and through me. I am Word through all that I see before me. I am Word through all experience. I am Word through all I have known, will know, can know, and must know, as the Monad realizes itself as and through me.

We thank you each for your agreement to this. We are done with platitudes. We are not done with invocation. A platitude is when you take what we mean and you seek to offer it to a past idea of what something means. "Oh, this must mean I see the sunset a little differently." "Oh, this must mean I am more pleasant to my neighbor." What it means, in its realization, is that you are confirming the one note sung, the Source of all that is, as manifestation, as being and presence.

Now, some of you still feel that you are lost in this. We use the metaphor of wave in sea to understand that you are participatory to the action of God, which is the sea, as the wave you express as. You have always been of the sea, but you are also the wave. The action of the wave is not dictated by an idea of wave. The wave moves in agreement to its requirements of being. It does not strive to be. It does not strive to crash against the shore to reclaim the detritus of old and recall it to the ocean. It simply is. You simply are. And the construct of identity that you have known through experience—high, low, and in between—is in restoration now.

"What does that mean," he asks, "*in restoration?*" The act of restoration is the agreement to be as you can only be at this level of tone. Paul sees the building that he once lived in, covered with dust, covered with grime, covered with the old. When the building is cleared of the detritus of old, when what it has held is re-known in truth, the act of restoration claims the inhabitant of the building as itself, without accrued history, ideology, and old ideas of what is allowed, dampening its tone, its being, and its expression.

The tone you now sing, know it or not, is of the Upper Room. And if you wish to experiment with this, align the self in this present moment, the only moment you may know, and allow the amplitude of your field to know itself as of Source. Allow the field to know itself as of Source, and express as Source, in all that is seen, can be seen, can be known, and has ever been known.

You are reclaiming a world through a level of vibration at the cost of what was held in suffering, in perpetual fear, in the strata of self-negation. You are claiming the Divine, that has always been present, as what has been, as what is, and what will be—the great wave of the Christed Self that knows itself beyond time, sings itself into glory, and you are its expression.

This is the end of the chapter. We are grateful for your presence. Stop now, please. Period. Period. Period.

6

A WORLD MADE NEW

What stands before you today, in a new awakening to your authenticity, is the realization that all that has been may now be held anew—the history of all things, the idea of all things as held in history, made new. Your realization of this in a true sense reclaims all that has been, in the high octave of the Upper Room.

Now, true innocence, you see, is a restored state of knowing and being. And to operate as the innocent is to move to the idea that all things are Source, have always been, and can only be—regardless of their iterations, the ideas others have held, or how they have been cemented in doctrine or ideology. To claim all things new, all history new, is to realize all history in the eternal now, which is the only time they may be re-known. What you are doing here is reclaiming an idea of support of heresy. We will explain this for Paul. Because your idea of history is superimposed through a tenet that denies the Divine, the idea itself is fostered to perpetuate the lack of coherence to your true natures. The idea of history itself, what was or what you think was, claimed in separation, creates an idea or structure of what has been that you seek to erect a world upon. The old foundations. The old ideas. The old structures that perhaps were created once upon a time to support what was required, but have since fallen into disrepair through continued agreement to the denial of the Source of all things. When you realize that all history can be reclaimed, what you are actually doing is supporting a realization of the Kingdom where it has been most lacking. This entire text has to do with the reclamation of what has always been true.

Now, we will not deny what you think happened. But what you think happened, what your idea of history is, can now be understood as only known through you at the level of coherence you can hold, or perhaps held when the tenet of history was learned. Your realization of truth—"God Is, God Is, God Is"—through the idea of history—and we will say this first must be idea—claims elasticity where none has been present. Most of your ideas of history are intractable. "My father died when I was young." "My wife left me when I was twenty-five." "This country is so many years old, and this was the king and when, and this is who succeeded him." Your ideas of history, all known through linearity, seek to establish a narrative, or sense of continuum, that without knowing denies the presence of the Divine because you are experiencing sequence, the idea of start and finish, which must exist outside of the infinite now.

Now, we do not erase history. We are not working with memory here. We are actually working with structure. It is not your memory of what was that is being re-established. It is history itself, that which was built upon a ruin that you will one day rebuild, and holding the seed of the ruin in the new temple you erect.

While this is not a new teaching—in fact, it's as old as your idea of time—the teaching itself is born in agreement to the Source of all manifestation. So while we may know history, or comprehend the history of this teaching, it is immediate and expresses beyond linearity. Your idea of a drop of water that may splash upon a page, anoint the ink that was on the paper and make the ink run, would simply be a way of understanding what happens when the new thought is encompassed within the old. The old structure, which knows itself in a codified way, is unprepared for the new. It is not that history cannot be challenged. You may debate what happened when and where. But all you are really doing is moving evidence around to support what you wish.

When the Source of all things, the new idea if you wish, is present here, things are translated and moved. The ink begins to run. And what is left in its place is what can only be in truth. We've discussed re-articulation, how all things are made new through thought and choice, born in an activation of agreement to Source. "Behold, I make all things new. It will be so. God Is. God Is. God Is." The idea of the *idea* of history being reclaimed is an action that is taken beyond the intellect. Again, the drop of water on the page. In some ways what you are doing as the expression of Source is reclaiming ideas of all things: the idea of what it means to be a man, the idea of what God is, the idea of being a father or child. These structures, endowed with meaning in history, in some ways govern your experience of self. When you are no longer governed by your idea of history, history itself is re-known.

Paul interrupts the teaching. "Well, I think I understand this in an abstract fashion, but what becomes of what we know? All houses are built on a foundation of what we think a house should be. Maybe we were replicating caves and added a door, and we may call it a mansion or a hovel, but isn't that what you are saying here? We don't remember the cave so we build something else?" In all ways, Paul, you just illustrated the very teaching here. The cave was useful at its time. Yes, you put a door in the cave, and perhaps called it a house or a home, and replicated that structure where no cave was present. And you may call many houses a community, but the idea of community itself is basically the extension of the tribe that once lived in the cave, or many caves.

What is occurring now, in relevance, is the re-knowing of who you have always been beyond the structures that were required through history. And the sovereignty of the Monad, and its creative properties, may and will reclaim what is required from the structure of history, but in a much higher fashion. Much of this text has addressed replication— replication through memory or thought, memory and habit, as the things you utilize to reinvent what was, without knowing you are doing so. In the Upper Room, there is new potential. And what you may need as a house may not resemble what you have had. Your idea of community, we must say, is extraordinarily limited. And the basis for it, which was the need for the tribe to survive, is now being replaced by an awareness of the whole. So what is re-created here will not hold the seed of the old. There will be a new seed that is required for manifestation to occur.

Now, imagine you have a laboratory in the basement of your home. You conjure things there. You have your ideas of what may be created, but they are all being created at the level of the basement. When you move to the twenty-fifth floor, in the refined state of consciousness that the twenty-fifth floor holds your agreement to what can be is not informed by what was once known through the basement choice, or what was chosen in the lower octave and that strata or field of vibration. You are no longer replicating the idea of necessity, because necessity has been altered because you have moved to the Source of supply, which is the Upper Room, and not how you hammer two pieces of wood together and call it a doorway.

What exists in the Upper Room is all that may be known at this strata of function. Notice we use the word *function*. When you are operating with the requirement of function, that means the need is met in the highest and best way that it can be known and can be utilized as. Now, the high function that may be claimed in the Upper Room need not resemble what was, because what is present here is what can and will be, without the requirement of replication. You have your ideas of lunch and dinner, what may be served at those times. You have your idea of marriage, your idea of governance, your idea of education, or all these ideas that surround you as evidence of what was. And everything we just mentioned can and must be re-known in the high octave of the Upper Room. This does not mean that there will not be marriage, but what marriage may express as may be as experience in a highly different way than you have been indoctrinated in.

The idea of education, once re-known, will in fact allow learning to be present at a level of immediacy that you cannot yet fathom. All information is available in the Upper Room. And as you become absorbent at the level of vibration to the knowledge that is here, you will be informed by structures the requirements of the day, what is actually required for you, to live and to thrive and to love beyond the old ways of being. You are so used to the idea of process that you have institutionalized it. A child will enter an educational system here and finish his or her learning there. In fact, once you become reliant on your own true knowing, which is the Monad expressing as and through you, you may align to knowledge and create from this experience what exists beyond the old template of potential.

There is a world made new, but most of you believe this world must function as your old has, based on the old premise of what was possible. You don't understand yet how your science has been limited by your ability to call only things that may be known by the hands and sight as real. You don't understand what exists beyond the old holds all the potential for healing that may ever be required. All things exist as potential in the Upper Room, but cannot be claimed in fullness until your reliance upon it is present and agreed to. And you will not hold this while you seek to replicate history.

Now, the invocation we bring forth now will happen in two parts. The first will be in sound, the second in language. The tone we are going to sing through the man in the chair will be imprinted in this text as the text itself. In other words, the sound made, and the reverberation of the sound, will inform every letter on every page. Just as the light informs the darkness, just as that one drop of liquid may run the letters on the paper, this sound will claim each of you in the eternal now where the language we offer after will serve to claim the idea of history itself in the Monad, of God, and outside the adherence to formal structure as has been reiterated by this species throughout time.

We sing your songs for you so that you may know the words.

"I Have Come. I Have Come. I Have Come."

On the count of three, Paul.
One. Now two. Now three.

[The Guides tone through Paul.]

"On this day I choose to align all things that have been, that have been known, that have been claimed as history, to be invoked in this new scale, this octave of being that is the Upper Room. And as I choose this, I allow the energetic field I hold to be utilized in this reclamation of idea. The idea of history is what I reclaim. The idea of what was, through the old template of expression, is what I claim. And I am song. I am sound. I am the Word in this invocation that claims all things new. I am Word through this intention. Word I am Word."

Let yourselves be sung. Let yourselves be heard. Let yourselves be as the water that reclaims the letters on the page. Let yourself be sung as the one note that is all things and reclaims all things to its innocence.

(PAUSE)

Stop now, please. This is in the text.

(PAUSE)

What stands before you today, in an awakened state, is the realization that what has been has in some ways been a blueprint for what you have claimed in expectation as a manifest world. The realization of this is an important step because the agreement that the past was an idea, in fact *is* an idea, can be understood by you in a new way once you understand how you have utilized your idea of history.

Some of you come before us wishing to re-create a history. You choose a new name, a new location, perhaps a new occupation. You imagine yourself made new through the industry of your choices. In fact, when all things are made new, when one has truly been reclaimed in the Upper Room, the Manifest Self goes into an agreement with the level or octave of vibration where what was once thought no longer holds frequency or attachment. When you understand what we are saying— that you are moving to a level of vibration where what would be reclaimed as you does not resemble your ideas of what can be, or should be, or must be, based in prior prescription—you will understand the importance of this teaching.

The idea of history has been addressed in prior teachings. The ideas of memory, who and what you think you were, what he or she was to you, what that event meant or did not mean, have also been addressed. So now we stand before you with the key to reclamation: "How I identify myself, in actually every way, is based in a premise that is false, that the idea of self that I presuppose myself to be has its moorings in a belief in separation." When this is really understood, when you see this history as understood from a higher purview, you may reclaim this idea and move to a Manifest Self where what is so can only be so, because it is indeed born in truth.

Some of you will say to us, "Well, I know who I am. I quite like who I am. I seek to improve this or that." And you may do this as you wish. But that is not this teaching. The claim "Behold, I make all things new"—rendered upon identity and memory, and then the collective history of the manifest world—actually reclaims all things beyond the basic idea, supposition, that separation must be there.

Now, this is separation between the self—again, an idea of self—and God. And most of you only have an idea of God that you can contend with. The realization of who and what you are in truth, how you serve in truth, and your expressed freedom, will validate this teaching in a way you do not presuppose. Your idea of self, born through the template of separation, is about to be re-known in a new coherence, with a coherence to Source—call it God, if you wish—that cannot be abandoned or ignored.

"What does that mean?" he asks. Well, the very premise of separation—the idea of the fall of humanity, the idea that God in a cloud, too far away to be known—has its premise in history. And your reclamation beyond the identity born in history creates a realization that what has always been is what can only be. And the realization of this, which is knowing, is what claims you in Source—in and of and expressed as.

Now, we use the term *Monad* to mean several things— the Christed Self, the articulation of the Divine come as you, but also as the principle of divinity that informs all things. To realize the Monad as self is not to conjure the Monad. It's to expressly agree to it. And by *expressly* we mean in expression, expressed as Monad, because it is the truth of your being. At this level of vibrational tone and emanation, the frequency you hold, without intention, reclaims all it encounters as of itself. In other words, you are the conduit for the work of the Monad, or the Christ within, which amplifies itself, in degree, to claim a world anew. Underline those words, if you wish: *a world anew.*

Now, the world anew does not resemble your idea of *world*, once you fully comprehend the intention of this teaching. We are not polishing the old teakettle and offering it to you as a new gift. We are releasing you from the tarnish that you have used to claim separation, the detritus of historical choices, the agreement to old fear, old war, old ideas of God that would keep you in separation. When one is made new, one experiences the world anew.

Now, we are not prophesizing here. We are saying what occurs at a level or strata of vibration. You don't create this. You align to it because it is always present.

Now, indeed, the senses are invoked in this passage. And by this we simply mean that while you hold form the senses are utilized to experience form, but you lift beyond the old idea of the senses to a reclamation of your true purview, in knowing, and in this knowing you have access to all that expresses at like tonality. Now, imagine a library. You walk to a certain shelf. You pull out a certain volume. You learn what is there through the reading of it. At the level we are teaching, you move into agreement to the old idea only long enough to understand that it's had its creation through the intonement of separation. Understand what we mean. Everything seen and created on this plane was in most ways born and created in agreement to the idea of separation, including the great philosophies, the great religious texts. They may hold fine truth, but they were still informed by a very simple presence. The author was not in union, nor could she or he comprehend that union was truly possible. The mystics came close, in some ways, because they claimed potential. But many of them were cloistered, did the best they could with the tools that they had, which were of course born through separation.

Realization of the Divine, which we have always said comes at the cost of the old, claims the new through presence and being. And your presence and being, at this level of amplitude, have access to knowledge more than you know or could begin to comprehend. You see, the library, as you imagine library, exists in vibration and in knowledge that can be accessed through one's true knowing. Some of you say to us, "Well, I want to know all things." You most certainly do not. You could not contain it. It is too vast. But what you will know and comprehend, at the level we instruct you at, is what is perfect for you to know to commit to a life or experience of God as All That Is.

Now, this is not a frame. An experience of God as All That Is excludes nothing from it. To comprehend the meaning of this fully is to comprehend the idea that the one note sung that is all things in actualization is present to be known and sung with. The intonation of the Monad as itself—"I Have Come, I Have Come, I Have Come"—is also the intonation of the Monad as manifest as all things. The realization of this as what you see and experience is what solidifies the foundation of the Upper Room. You are walking in a new field, and what is experienced in this field is what you are required to know, what is gifted to you through co-resonance, presence and being.

Realization occurs at this level as a stage of development. It is not a finite stage. The one who witnesses God as all things is simply not excluding God. She is not making God be where it wasn't. That would be preposterous. She is knowing God, or realizing God, where it has always been and been denied. As we always say, the denial of the Divine, the only real challenge humanity faces, is met with this claim: "God Is. God Is. God Is."

Each of you before us tonight, in your own awareness, is contributing to the reality you see. Every idea you've ever held, known through separation, claimed separation without your fully intending it. What we have done thus far in this text is reclaim each of you at the level of choice and volition where your actions are no longer informed by prior deception of self and others, by prior fear, or the constructs claimed through separation that would deny the Divine simply by being as they have been.

Each of you here is being re-seen, is being re-known, is being reclaimed, beyond the old idea that separation could even be. It has often been said that reality is an illusion, or your idea of a physical world holds a basis in illusion, and this is actually true at a certain level. The reality you know yourselves through indeed exists at a level of tonality. What precludes more has only one basis: The denial of the Divine which humanity has chosen to learn through, and is indeed now moving beyond.

We come before you now in a true awareness of your being, what can only be in truth. And as we announce you each—in fullness, in re-creation—we align you to what expresses beyond the old, the Manifest Self that may be known, and indeed know, in the Upper Room where all things are made new.

We sing these words for each of you now, and as we sing them we say yes to the inherent potential of the Monad in realization that has come as each, can only be as each, and announces itself in the claim "I Have Come."

On the count of three, Paul.

Now one. Now two. Now three.

[The Guides tone through Paul.]

Be still, and know that You Have Come.

Blessings to you each.

Indeed, this is in the text. Stop now, please. Period. Period. Period.

DAY TWENTY-THREE

What stands before you today, in an awareness of an awakened state, is the realization that you have contributed to the chaos you see around you through your disregard of others and the True Self that must express as them regardless of what you think or see. When you decide another is worthy of your attention or love, the human being you see is actually transformed by that agreement. When you deny another love, you agree to an aspect of them that believes themselves to be unworthy of love or care. Each agreement you make with another human being is an idea that you support your relationship in. The idea that they are worthy, can be loved, claims an alignment, not only for them, but for all that may ensue in the relationship.

Some of you decide in advance who another must be to you, based on prior prescription. "We loved each other once. We no longer love." And you go about your business as one who denies love because you believe *that* love was an artifact of another time. In fact, love is always present and can be aligned to in any circumstance in any instance. But in order for this to occur, you must agree to it, which is to confirm the potential that love is present and can be known. Again, *known* means realized, and the realization of love, in any instance, can re-create the relationship in a higher field or tone.

When we teach you history, we have spoken much of the absence of the Divine or the denial of the Divine in humanity's experience of itself. But we have not discussed love and those things that endure, those great moments of truth that have been in articulation on this plane that have been the result of an alignment of one or many.

Each of you who says yes to the instruction you are receiving is giving permission to be utilized in several ways. In some ways, you become the gong that is struck, the bell that sings across the town and awakens all it encounters to its truth. In other ways, what you are agreeing to is to become manifest at a level of tone where the idea of self that you have utilized to confirm a reality, born in separation, is reclaimed in the true nature of being. The true nature of being, again, is the realized self who operates beyond the veil of separation, the illusion of separation, who can reclaim history because she sees God in every path, in every trajectory, as the result of every choice, and reclaims every choice made in history in the wonder of spirit, in the truth of the Divine, in the accelerated rapidity of the Word made form.

Now, the idea of history has been discussed. And when we worked with you last, we intoned the truth of being through the idea of history and the ramifications of history known through fearful choice. But we wish now to claim history in love, and the realization that throughout time, even through a basis of separation, love has triumphed in small and great ways. The realization of love is also the realization of God. To deny love for another is to deny God's presence in them. Because it is God as you that loves—and the aspect that is loved is also God, although it may have accrued evidence to the contrary—with the eyes of the Christ, or the eyes that see and know truth, you are no longer participatory to that level of vibration that would choose to deny another love. But you don't know this yet, and you will have to choose it until the choice is made by presence and being.

"What does that mean?" he asks. Well, Paul, imagine you have a friend that you are no longer close to. You keep a distance from him or her. You are cautious in the relationship based on past evidence. In some ways what you are doing may seem prudent, but in other ways what you are doing is putting the other in shadow, telling them where they can come and where they can't, based upon a presupposition that what they may want from you may not be what you want to offer. To know this person in God is to claim the God as them that has always been present, and realize the Source of their expression beyond their actions. If, indeed, this is done well, you have made a choice, and then the choice occurs to allow them their presence in your life or not. To know another in God does not necessarily mean you play poker with them, does not necessarily require you to show up for them as they demand. But it does mean you love them, not through the emotional idealization of love, but through the claim of love upon them: "God Is, God Is, God Is" in their presence and expression.

"What does this have to do with history?" he asks. "You were teaching us about history." Well, this is history, you see. We have discussed the history of humanity, in some ways, through the action of the denial of the Divine, but we have not spoken of love, and how love in all ways reclaims what it encounters in the Source of all things. Every decision that has ever been made in love—and we mean love in truth, not a romanticized idealization of it—has spurred great growth. And wonderful actions have always occurred from the one who can hold love in spite of evidence to the contrary. Humanity has spent so much time accruing evidence to the contrary—why God cannot be—that the decision that there can be no God feels enormously practical. "God could not have been there. There can be no God if such a thing can occur." But of course, as we have said, these are the results of the denial of the Divine, the actions of humanity.

Paul interrupts. "But what if there's a great flood? What if villages are washed away? No man made that happen, unless there was a dam that was broached." What you don't yet see,

Paul, is the continuum of your idea of time, and the ever-changing landscape that the manifest world has known itself through. There have always been glaciers that melted. There has been scorching sun in the desert. Some have starved. Some have drowned. All have experienced many of the things that making self through form commands. "What does that mean?" he asks. You have taken a physical form. You may choke on an apple. You may burn in a fire. These are things that may be experienced through form, and they are not necessarily evil or bad. They are occurrences. What you would call a tragedy may be a natural act, but all involved in the tragedy are learning through the experience at one level of choice or another, how you choose in recognition of a fatal act. "There is a storm coming. I have a family to attend to. Do I go outside in the storm and make sure all can be safe? Or do I stay inside with the others, realizing we all may perish?"

When you are operating in the Upper Room, the physical body is still present, but choice is heightened, aligned beyond fear, and consequently you know what to do. You will learn through the lower choice. "I was frightened to go outside, and as a result others perished." And you will learn the lessons that come through any choice that is made in fear through the ramifications of it. What we have done already in this text is reclaim you beyond prior choice so you are no longer suffering the old fear as it responds through what you may call karma. But what instead occurs is the realization of why past choice was made, and the confirmation, as you are no longer claiming through fear, to undo or repair what can be done, with the idea that you are worthy.

Now, if we wish to speak to forgiveness here—because he

is asking about that—we have already discussed redemption, and reminded you once again that the Christ within, or the Monad, is in innocence and operates beyond sin. In other words, it could not accrue the evidence of sin, which is always separation. To understand that you are forgiven, have been and always will be, will support you in this understanding. Any choice made in love will guarantee an outcome in love.

We will say this to Paul, who is protesting the teaching from the back of the room, "Oh, I have loved and been hurt. I have thought I was loved and discovered I wasn't." Paul, these experiences you incurred not only as part of your learning, but as the result of a belief that love is persnickety, can be taken away one moment and offered again the next. What you were experiencing was not love, but perhaps desire, or perhaps manipulation, from one who desired to be seen as lover, or as the one capable of loving you, when in fact the agenda was somewhat other. When you have been truly loved, when anyone has been truly loved, they are completely altered by that act.

"What does that mean?" he asks. Imagine you had a teacher when you were young who praised you for your artwork, or praised you for your kindness to another student. That teacher was not looking to get anything. They were expressing in love a point that you may learn through. They were offering a vision of yourself as capable of greatness. They were instilling within you an awareness of who you were in truth, whereas otherwise you may never have that encounter. An act of love may indeed be a kind word. But it is always the action of God operating through the other, because love is not an expression of personality, and when the Divine expresses as love it often overrides the charter of the personality structure to get its message across. True love holds no necessity for ramifications other than love. True love requires no recompense. True love requires no agreement because it is its own accord. Anybody who tells you that you should love them back is operating in need. Anyone who tells you you are unworthy of love is acting in a bias that is harmful and is born through separation, their own entrapment to it seeking to call others to their agreement of themselves as separate.

History is filled with the evidence of love—all great literature, all great art, indeed inspired. Paul interrupts. "Well, there is some great art that doesn't feel very holy." Again, Paul, you decide that God should look pretty. God is all things. But truly inspired art is the expression of the imagination as informed by divinity seeking expression. It is the artists, finally—and the mystics, we must say—who claim a world made new by realizing potential. Perhaps the ink on the page, which claims a new world through the imagination, supports a world such as the one imagined by the writer into being. And perhaps the mystic's claim—"All is God"—renders the template that is now being fulfilled. We will say that again. *The template that is now being fulfilled.*

The time is now, and in fact the template is present. And what no longer adheres to the Upper Room, or the template of the new, is beginning to fall—sometimes slowly, sometimes quickly. And the armor you have all worn to protect yourself from an idea of separation, that it must be the best thing in the world, is being dismantled through your own intention or by circumstance. "What does that mean," he asks, "*or by circumstance?*" Finally, all will awaken. Some of you will waken easily to a remembrance of Source. Some of you have erected so much obstruction to the realization that it may be moved in ways that may be experienced as challenging. The knowing of who and what you are as of God has its own action—to reclaim all things. And how this occurs, both for the individual and the collective, must be seen as what you are now seeing and beginning to experience in the world.

"Beginning to experience?" he asks. "Do things get worse?" Your idea of *worse* again must be understood as being framed through a cultural idea of what should be. "There should never have been a flood." "The desert should not be so dry that people may die of thirst." Your comprehension of the material realm through a status quo you've inherited is enormously faulty. Your idea of a well-made world is a world that seems to operate as it has. But you have always had a world with war, where some have hungered and some have not, where some have died for a country through an act of greed depicted as war, while some have sat in their palaces watching the war occur.

The life that you are living, Paul, has been moved greatly through your surrender to the claim—"Behold, I make all things new"—and the potential that incurs. But this came at a cost, and what predated this change was enormously challenging for you because it seemed as if your reality was falling away in tatters. And while you attempted to keep the tatters of that reality in place, finally they fell away and the new could be revealed. You all undergo such a process, sometimes gracefully, some less gracefully. One is not better than the other. You learn through different endeavors, different responses, and you've all accrued evidence of separation that will be released as they can be.

"A World Made New" will be the title of the chapter we are teaching now, and the world made new that we are teaching is a world that is not entrenched through history or the denial of the Divine. The idea of history, personal and collective, will continue to be addressed as we return. We thank you each for your presence. This is in the text. Period. Period. Period. Stop now, please.

DAY TWENTY-FOUR

What stands before you today, in a new agreement to be, to align, and to claim your true heritage, is the responsibility that comes with it. You are accountable to your actions, yes, but you are also responsible to your choices.

Now, we have discussed prior that in the Upper Room you move to a level of alignment or congruence with Source where the will itself moves into an alignment with the truth of your expression, which means you are choosing truthfully, not operating from the old, or not demanding the outcome through the old requirements. Some of you say to us, "Well, I have free will and I must utilize it." Indeed, you do and will, but from a higher vantage point and with a new knowledge of what you are claiming. In some ways, what is occurring is that the old is being moved from you so you will not select from that opportunity—yesterday's meal, yesterday's menu, the idea of what yesterday held.

The agreement we are making to you today is that you will withstand the changes that are coming to you—and one and all—at this time of new agreements. "This Time of New Agreements" would be an apt title as well, because that is what you face today—the opportunity for the new to be claimed by one and all. But it is claimed by agreement, less by necessity than you might think. Imagine you are standing in a well and the water rises. You are lifted by the rising water. There appears to be no choice, but in fact there is. You are not holding onto the old. You are agreeing to the new and allowing the process to move you. Underline *move you. You* are moved—not the idea of self that wants to have a better view from the window, but the True Self who is coming into manifestation.

Our agreement now is that you will meet this challenge, and meet it well. To meet it well means you will not succumb to the old requirements of how you have dealt or opportunized what you see before you to claim the old ideas of what you should have. The one who enters this realm with open arms will be received with open arms. The one who enters this realm looking over her shoulder, seeing if she still has the five dollars in her pocket lest she need it, will be more challenged.

The requirement of being, in the Upper Room, at this level of change is allowance, yes, but a kind of permission for the new to be born through you without the old expectation of what you might have at the end of it. The ability to transform, at the level of instruction we offer you, must be attended to by those who have already done it. And there is a reason for this. When we work with students, it is to claim them as they truly are, and not as they wish to be. And the temptation for the student on this path is to stop in an alleyway, rest for a moment, and forget that there is more to claim. She will rise *as* she is seen, *as* she is agreed to, by the Source of all things and its emissaries.

We are using the word *emissary* carefully here. We are

emissaries, yes, but we are teachers first and foremost. And our lineage of teaching offers us the opportunity to claim the truth of being where something other would seek to stand in its way. We opportunize the teaching to meet the student wherever she may be met, and we do not leave the student wandering in that alley. We lift her again and again, until she knows she can float, she knows she can manage, she knows she can rise from the bottom of the well.

There is a guarantee here for all of you: that the work that comes to you—and that is the work of the day always—is always to your benefit, even if it seems more challenging than that. Now, the work of the day, the choice of the day, is what is before you, what you have claimed in consciousness, what you see before you that requires re-seeing. And each opportunity for growth indeed is an offering to your own realization. We will confirm this for you in your experience, if it is required. But underline the word *if.* The one who is walking well does not need the crutch, does not need the one standing beside him to ensure he does not stumble. We stand beside you as you require it. But our gift to you is your own expression, your own realized self, and the manifestation of this, which is of benefit to all.

Now, the world you see before you, in great change, is about to undergo a mass shift of an awareness of what they have chosen in the past. The world chooses, you see. And every great age, every great achievement that humanity has ever encountered, was not born of one, but was born of the collective allowing for the new to be made present in the common field. If you understand this, you will understand how leaps occur— either in science, or in art, or in philosophy. The template seals a perfection before it can be born. A new idea may be seen first in the ethers, then in the imaginations of many. And this is always the Divine in expression, supporting humanity in its next stage of evolution.

For those of you who wonder what we speak of, we will speak of the era you know and that you have claimed yourselves in. The collective has decided, yes, to move beyond the old system, which was born in a kind of sense of betrayal—that God could not be present, and if it could it would likely fail. The realization that you are moving beyond this will actually occur rapidly, because there will be choices made by humanity at a collective level to reclaim what was held in shadow. And the manifestation of these changes will be known in form.

"What are you speaking of?" Paul asks. "You spoke of the era we know ourselves in. Well, what is happening?" There is a dissolution now of objectivity, born in a kind of reason, that would create polarity or demand separation. Imagine the whole world wore a pair of glasses that confirmed separation. What is beginning to happen is that one, and then many, are taking the glasses off and re-seeing a world. This is what happens when a potential is made known in the higher octave and is seeded in the lower. The ones with the vision to see will of course see, and it will be them that claim the new, and opportunize the new to the greatest benefit for all.

"But what does this look like?" he asks. It looks like the end of an era. And when an era ends, there is often challenge, there is often conflict, because those who wish to maintain the old status quo may do all in their power to stop change from occurring.

Paul interrupts. "Well, I see changes around me now, and

they don't seem very enlightened. They feel like we're going backwards, sometimes." The retreading of the old is in order to see the old that was claimed so that it may be restored to the new—not the new that you would wish to confirm, the way things were three years ago or ten, but the higher that is now made present for you and is in expression in the manifest field.

"Where do we see this in the manifest field?" he asks. We will tell you. The moment you take your glasses off, it is already there. "God Is. God Is. God Is." And the manifestation of "God Is" is what occurs when you are not confirming the other—through history, through mandate, through cultural agreement, or through the need to confirm what you once knew because you lack the imagination to embrace with open arms what is actually being offered to you.

We sing your songs for you so that you may learn the words, but you *are* the song in expression, and humanity rises in fits and starts until it maintains the balance of the new.

Paul interrupts. "I have had a question. At times this seems too far-fetched to me. You say four generations, great change is upon us." Paul, we will interrupt already. Your mandate to see the old survive, or maintain the old status quo, is comprehensive to the way that you experience yourself. *You* are the one who is changing here. *All* are the ones who are changing here. And the manifestation of the world is the objective, or realization, of this internal change. This is not an internal change of your emotional life. This is not an internal change of how you feel about yourself. This is the manifestation of the Monad that claims the world anew.

So the world is changed by presence and being. The glasses come off. The witness is present. And the moment the witness is present to manifest what she sees in this octave, the world is reclaimed. The physical plane, if you wish, is restored to its inherent divinity. It has always been divine, but the evidence you have accrued of separation is about to be moved in a large scale. When you say thank you—to see the error of your own ways, the gift of sight, and how you have been accountable and responsible to collective choice—you will re-know the world because you will not seek to maintain what has been outlasted, what is no longer required, what no longer holds the ability to be seen in the high template because it does not resonate at this level.

We sing your songs for you, yes. And this text is a song. It is the song of innocence, humanity restored to its inherent wisdom, its inherent grace, beyond the destructive nature that fear has imposed, that you have agreed to through the denial of your own expression as of God.

We will stop the dictation for today. In the text. Thank you for your presence. Period. Period. Period.

DAY TWENTY-FIVE

What stands before you today, in a new accruement of your potential, is the realization that what has been holds no power other than what you offer it. Your idea of yourself, moored in history, an idea of self in a time that would seek to reconcile that identity with the present moment, is what we are now addressing—the aspect of self that accrues evidence to what one once was because once you knew or had an idea that is now seeking to perpetuate itself in manifestation as self, as life lived, as the reality you know yourself in.

Now, we say this for Paul specifically: Who you think you are has been changed, but the manifestation of the new, still claimed by you in the degrees you can hold, struggles at times to maintain itself because you look to the past for evidence of being. When one looks to the past for evidence of being, one moves to the level of consciousness that was held at that time. The young man you thought you were held an idea of self that accrued evidence of being. And this self, in accruement, in some ways believes itself to be as it was then because it does not know other. In other words, friend, your idea of yourself at ten, the evidence accrued to what life was or what things must mean from that age and time, are steeped in a consciousness that was in some ways claimed, and is still believing itself to be, at that age in that time. You can talk about children, the aspect of each of you that was claimed at an age. But we are speaking of something different, a level of consciousness known in history, where ideas were born and cemented. And when you look back for your reference points and you rest in your old ideas of self, you have claimed that history over and over again.

Now, we will talk about this. You cycle through an identity in a lifetime. Perhaps many lessons occur again and again, and you benefit from this as you realize self through the growth that those events incur. But what we are telling you now is the strata of vibration known in historical data claims itself as precedent, because your reliance upon an old idea of self has accrued evidence that it will seek to claim in spite of what is now being formed, and is actually present, in the energetic fields you hold. In other words, imagine that you are now in timelessness, the Monad expressing beyond time, but you hold in your arms a calendar—from 1969, 1925, 1991—and you manage your life through the identity accrued at that time. There is only one answer here to move you beyond this situation. Release the reliance on an idea of self accrued in time that would seek to perpetuate itself while the new is being born. Notice we said *while*. "While the new is being born" simply means the process you have engaged in here.

Now, when you are moving from one house to another and you clean the attic and the cellar, you encounter many things accrued over time that must now be moved and released. We do not recommend that you spend the rest of your lives contemplating what is in that old suitcase up in that old attic eave. We would suggest instead that you honor that there were things accrued, but that any identity that you have chosen to learn through that operates in the negation of the Divine can and will be moved, or lifted, beyond the attic, beyond the cellar, to a level of vibration where they may be re-known.

"But don't we have to see?" Paul asks. "We can't pretend things are changed when they are not." In fact, they will be changed, and they will be seen as they must. Imagine there is an old album of photographs. Perhaps there is one or two in that album that needs understanding, a portrait of you at two, of your father at five, what was claimed in history through the family, the legacy these things present. You must understand that they will be met, but you need not spend years poring over every photograph to understand their impact upon you. This is a kind of indulgence that the small self might engage in and call it the work of progress. To understand that something happened, that you accrued evidence in identity that is no longer standing or holding firm in the high octave of the Upper Room, will allow this idea to be transposed, or removed, or re-seen in a higher way. Again, we are speaking of one thing: the idea of self, again born in history, that you return to, because it's time to see this thing or that, or because you become aware of how the progress you seek is actually halted by the residual affect of the personality structure seeking to invoke its properties from a prior level of consciousness. You may underline that phrase: *prior level of consciousness.*

Now, consciousness does not operate in a scale such as you might wish. Every moment, every experience, is an imprint in the energetic field. You understand these things, perhaps as memory, but in most cases how they operate are as information that is carried by an individual or collective that seeks replication—"the idea of who I was, the idea of who we were, and the idea of what we think should be," based in prior consciousness.

There was a time in the country you live in, Paul, where people were hung in the town square, in some ways as the entertainment of the community. "We will hang the horse thief and restore our town to the dignity it once had." While you don't do that anymore, you still replicate that idea of punishment, public execution, or public displays of shame and retribution that call to yourselves the residual affect, as beings, of that choice to participate. This is a consciousness that was developed well before your lifetimes. But the memory of them, these acts of betrayal against humanity, through collective agreement, simply operate within each of you—an accrued wisdom, an accrued belief, or an accrued problem that you believed once had merit and still holds itself in vibration. "We must be vindicated." "Evil must be vanquished and punished." "We must be righteous or we will fall."

The battle with evil, or the belief that there is a battle to be had, is actually the residual affect of a level of superstition when it was believed that the demons were occupying the town, were the cause of disease, were the cause of despair, famine, or something other. In almost all cases, the natural affect was the cause of the problem, and hysteria was known through communities, and then was re-established in concretized ways that you now don't think of as superstition, but are in fact that. The desire to battle the unseen gives you a sword against nothing. But we will say this: There are energies in the lower field that you have met that can contaminate, but these are the residual aspects of past choice, past consciousness, and articulation of vibration that believes itself to be in separation of the Divine, and consequently acts in that accord. You do not fight the demon. You lift to a level of vibration where even that idea can and must be reclaimed.

A personal demon is something that operates through an accrued idea of self that has taken on an autonomy. That terrible thought you cannot banish, that compulsion that will not go away, may indeed be an aspect of a prior thought that has claimed independence, a certain kind of autonomy, and would use the energetic body as host, or as what it may claim itself through. But we must tell you this: There is nothing more powerful than the true nature of the Divine, and as you escalate in vibrational expression, those things that you may have attracted that would feed on the field, or that the common collective has utilized to decide fate of others, must be reconciled in the high octave, and will be. All of you who are lifting here are experiencing the residual affect of history, past choice, memory, as it is reclaimed. Imagine now that you are in an elevator, going past many, many floors. At every age, things are created, memory is accrued. Imagine you are lifting past these things at a thunderous speed. You cannot contain the self and the level of transition that you undergo. But you do understand that you are moving past things, or beyond things, or above things, that were decided as identity at varying levels of consciousness that now must be reclaimed, are being reclaimed, in the high order of the Upper Room.

He interrupts the teaching. "Well, there is a difference between moving past things and reclaiming them, isn't there?" In fact, the movement beyond forces all things to be addressed at the level of amplitude you come to. We will use another metaphor. Imagine you are squeezing through a keyhole to get to what is on the other side of the door. Anything that cannot move through the keyhole will be re-known or released or transformed or be confronted through this passage. That is what is occurring.

Now, the residual affect of memory has been discussed in this text. What is being discussed today are how certain levels of consciousness, born through individual experience and collective agreement, seek to reconcile you while in this passage with a level of tone, born in agreement to the denial of Divine, that they have used as evidence. "This is why people aren't trustworthy." "This is why there can be no God." "This is why you don't help your neighbor." "This is why you do not love." Those are all ideas established through personal history, and often reinforced by the collective. When you are moving forward and the echoes of these ideas present, they are calling you back to the level of consciousness where the thought was agreed to or created. You may move beyond this simply by knowing that the old idea, born in limitation and denial of the Divine, only has the authority that you offer it, only has the power that you endorse, and only moves you to its backwards identity through your choice to say, "I am what I thought I was." You are not what you think you are. You have never been. Nor will you be again.

What has occurred here is the reconciliation of the Monad in consciousness, and what we are working with now is the maintenance of this field so it serves for the reclamation of all. When one knows herself in innocence, beyond the idea of sin and consequently beyond the idea of separation, one moves mountains. One's love is unhindered. And one's experience of time does not hold the old calendar. You understand what was, but 1969, a shadow of an idea of time, is far gone, back to the eternal now when it once masqueraded as a date on a calendar, now tattered and old.

We love you each as you are, not as we think you should be. Nor is there anything you could do, or imagine you could do, that could make us love you less. Because we know who we are, we must know who you are. And because we operate as love as we teach, we love who we see, because you are, because you be, because you are of us and as us, as we are all of the one Source—That Has Come, That Has Come, That Has Come—and makes all things new.

Thank you for your presence. Indeed, this is in the text. Stop now, please.

DAY TWENTY-SIX

What stands before you today, in an awakened state, is a promise for a new life. A recognition of what has always been is now seen and can be claimed experientially. The Divine as matter, the Manifest Divine as form, may now be understood as what is before you in a state that is not only malleable, but is asking to be re-seen. Matter as being seen as God in expression benefits the matter, reclaims the matter, beyond the old idealization, the names given to things, the density of form that you have known all things as and through. When matter is reclaimed in the Upper Room, the manifest world begins to shift to an octave of experience where what is known is as it can only be known, not as it has been decreed as, called forth in small ways, but what it can only be in truth.

Now, the Manifest Divine as form must be understood as what is—underline those words *what is*—what already is, what has not been claimed as its True Self, its true expression, but what is, only can be, has always been, but has been misunderstood, miscomprehended, or claimed in low form. To understand what we are teaching you, look around the room you sit in, and the names all things have been given and the meanings that those names have claimed. Your agreement to these names actually precludes an experience of what they also are, or we could better say *only are*, which is matter, which is form, which is God expressing at a certain level of density. The reclaiming of the world is the reclamation of matter through a level of consciousness that knows what it is. And the realization of this in an experiential way is where we intend to take you.

Now, the restoration that occurs in an individual to a manifest state of the Divine—which is basically a recognition of
who and what you have only been, but have denied—must
claim the world it experiences itself through in like vibrational
accord. And while we have discussed this, it maintains a distance from your identity still, because your idea of self, which
we address again and again and again, still holds a kind of
basis, a presupposed basis, in the idea of separation. When
form itself is re-known in God, and matter itself is operating in an escalated state, the consciousness that perceives the
matter is also being altered by the exchange. So on one level,
while we may say the Divine sees the Divine in all things and
you may experience the self as the Divine in perception, you
are also being altered by the recognition as the Divine sings
back to you, which is the echo or the ramification of matter
in the altered state that informs all things with its expression,
presence and being.

Now, what we teach must be understood in some ways as
primer, and in another way an experience. The primer is the
text, but the experience of the text and the vibration that is
claimed through the reader, as the reader ascends in vibration, is
what comes through the flowering as the Monad. Not *of*, but
as. The flowering *as*. Now, you as flower—in an open state, in
a receptive state—claim all things new. But how this happens
is quite confused for Paul, and we must attempt to teach this
in a way he will not disrupt because it does not confirm an idea
he would seek to foster for himself or others.

The reconciliation of form is one thing. How this occurs is
through a system of expression or amplitude that must incur
evidence. Now, if you were to look at a flower every day and

decide things about the flower—"my mother's favorite flower," "that flower that will not last long in the winter," "that flower whose aroma I dislike," "that flower that may be picked and put in a vase," "that flower that the bee loves so much"—you claim the identity of the flower through your inference of its potentials, what it has meant, what it can mean, and what you frame it as. "My mother's favorite flower." "The flower that will not last through the winter." Your identification of flower claims you in relationship to it, or many relationships to it, as you would hold something to the light and experience the different facets that it may show. But what we are saying now is that all of those titles and all of those frames can be re-known through the singular thought and claim of truth: "God Is. God Is. God Is." And the claim "God Is" upon the flower shows the flower, claims the flower, accelerates the flower, in its true tonality—as the old history, the old memory, the old names the flower has been given are released. "But we're still calling it a flower," Paul says. God is flower. God is as flower. God is shape, color, scent, expression beyond flower. And the manifestation as flower is God as articulated. But the reclamation of flower as God claims the flower as it has always been.

Now, a flower is easy for most of you. You don't damn the flower unless you are allergic to it, unless somebody throws one at you in a rebuke of an advance. But to know *flower* as an expression of God is actually not challenging. What is far more challenging is a physical realm that is intentionally operating in denial of Source that seeks its recompense, its expression, through the act of denial. To lift this to the Source of all things is how the world is made new, yes, but it is also the gift of this teaching for the one who may hold this experience.

To hold the idea of a ghetto, or battlefield, or anything you may think of that you believe constructed as lower or expressing lower must claim you in coherence to the lower—until you realize that the Source is the same as the flower, and the manifest form known as ghetto, known as battlefield, may be in re-articulation beyond the collective ideas that would hold it in density. Again, the names we offered you for the flower that frame it, that solidify the idea of flower, through memory, history, projected meaning. What would you say it could be if it were not these things? We will tell you. They would be God. And when the ghetto or the battlefield are no longer held in darkness, but are lifted to a risen state, the articulation of form is also altered.

He doesn't like the teaching. Here is the first question: "So it's not a battlefield? There are not bodies lying upon it? There is not poverty in this ghetto you describe, and suffering and injustice?" Your confirmation of all these things claims you in a residual affect to the low tone that is the manifestation of low consciousness and fear. The ghetto is an idea made manifest. When the new is seen, the old is transformed and the material realm moves beyond the old codifications. You understand the idea of something rising from the ash, reborn, made new. But you don't understand that the prospect of this occurring as the world you live in is also the product of an acceleration of consciousness that cannot claim the lower, will not because it cannot. In other words, friend, the one who sees God knows God, reclaims any evidence that would deny that, and the manifestation of the claim will be known experientially.

Paul interrupts again. "Well, it takes time to clean up a battlefield, or raze a ghetto, and rebuild something finer." That

is your idea of how matter must be working. The bricks must
be made, laid one upon the other, to erect yet another wall.
The reclamation of matter as Source is not denying what was.
It is reclaiming what is. And what is must begin to shine as
it is re-known. Now, there may be industry in an act of transformation. You have dirtied your room. You are responsible
for cleaning it. But the act of restoration that we are speaking
to is actually born through consciousness and the holding of
the high field that does not judge what it sees. What you are
moving is the residual affect of pain, of suffering, of fear, all
claimed through the denial of God. If the idea of ghetto, born
through poverty, which is claimed through injustice, the sup-
pression of a people, the belief that there is no Source of supply that will feed all, if you claim these things and continue to
bear witness to them, you continue to claim suffering and lack.
But re-articulation, or the high manifestation, is the miracle
of the act of God upon its creations. And you are the portal
or the window or the doorway for this act to occur, because
at the level of consciousness we are teaching you, what has
prohibited re-creation, which is the old idea of lack, born in
fear and separation, is not only eradicated—the *idea* of that
cannot be held.

You are working for the world now. Everybody who looks
at a building, decides the building is a ruin or a palace based
on prior conceit, holds that level of agreement to what is seen
and claims it as form. We are not asking you to see the ghetto
as palace. We are asking you to see God, the action of God,
the Source of all, as manifest where the idea had been that was
claimed through oppression and separation. If, indeed, you are
called to act—in force, in productivity, with your hands and

feet, your fists, your action—you will know. But that is not this teaching. This is the teaching of knowing, realization, and the matter of the form restated, claimed anew, as what it was first, which is first impulse, born in innocence, without the pedigree of systematized fear, without the authorization of any form of separation, denying what is always true. The claim that is made upon the manifest world—"God Is, God Is, God Is"—is the reclamation of the denial in any form or idea born through collective agreement, individual choice, history, and memory. Reclamation is an act of God. True knowing is God expressing as knowing. And form has always been God, operating at one level of tone or another.

Paul interrupts. "So this is the water turning to wine." You could say that, if you wish. But in order for this level of alchemy to occur, what must be seen must be known as God, and not as water or wine. The transformation as God's expression is God's purview. You are not invoking magic. You are re-singing a song that has been forgotten, and singing into being what was in low form, low tone, because the entrainment to the higher must be claimed as and by the higher—less so Paul as the higher, but as the higher operating through Paul or Josephine or anyone or anything. You are the conduit here. You are not the one changing things. You *are* perception. Underline those words. *You are perception* at the level of the Upper Room, where what was distorted falls from the eyes. To reclaim anything in innocence is to know what it is beyond any name given to it. It simply is. "God Is. God Is. God Is."

We thank you for your presence. This is in the text. Period. Period. Period.

DAY TWENTY-SEVEN

What stands before you today, in an awakened state, is a new awareness of what can be, beyond the residual affect of the choice to be in separation. We said *the choice to be in separation* because, indeed, it was initially a choice. Imagine a child who says, "I will find my way," denies the father, denies the mother, their oversight, and finds herself lost in the forest of her creation. The child must grow, and learn to choose wisely, and comprehend the use of will in its highest way before it makes a foray into the choice to deny the parent. Each of you before us is now at an awakened state where there is a new potential: That what may be claimed must be in congruence with your true authority as an expression of the Christ. An expression of the Christ, not the Christed Self, but how the Christ aspect in realization as and through each of you claims the world anew.

Now, when we teach through the man before you, we understand his needs, we understand the questions he asks, and at times we will address them. What he wishes us to address is old pain, old concern, old worry. And the reason he requests this is that the amplitude of his vibration, at an accelerated state, is moving so much, so rapidly, that he forgets where he stands. When you forget where you stand, you may be anywhere. Pick a year, pick an idea born in time. When you do not know where you are, you may find yourself anywhere. But the transmission today, and the lesson of the day, is about what comes in authorization, the template of the Christ born in each of you in a realized state that demands to be known through all things it encounters.

Now, when you come to us—"What do I do? What is my purpose? Why have I come?"—you are still asking the old questions born in the old idea of self who must have an idea of mission that she may encounter to merit her worth. "Let me be special." "Let me be seen." "Let me know that I am doing the right thing." At the level of choice we speak to, the will itself has moved into alignment with the requirements of both the soul and the Christed Self, operating in union at the level of amplitude that the soul may claim.

When you align as the manifest Christ, the soul still directs the requirements of the individual, while the Christed Self, or the Monad, expresses for the universal. You must understand the difference here. The Christ within you, in a realized state, is manifesting for the world. But it works with the soul, because the soul knows the requirements for individual development which may still withstand the agreement to manifestation. And what that means is if you have something on the table, an aspect of self or a lesson that requires addressing in a lifetime, while it will be met in a higher way through the soul's direction, it is operating concurrently in union with the Monad's expression, which actually operates beyond your individual desire or belief of what can and should be.

When you stand before us in recognition of who you are, your amplitude is agreed upon by us at the high level and you are re-known. But the soul itself, who has lessons to come for, who has chosen these lessons as part of her embarkation in a lifetime, is still operating. The personality structure, or the aspect of self that would incur karma, is actually moved to a level of choice where what is claimed will not accrue more debt. You are not collecting debt in the Upper Room. You are amplifying as the Monad, re-addressing the old as it can be claimed, re-knowing the idea of self at the level of choice that the Monad expresses through, in alignment with the requirements of the soul.

"Now, why the soul?" Paul asks. "Can I have an example?" Imagine you were born with a disability, or your idea of disability. Perhaps, indeed, that is a soul choice that you are here to learn through. And the manifestation of the Monad may completely change your relationship to the physical form you have known, but it does not deprive you of the lessons that you have claimed in this incarnation. We do not erase the blackboard, if that's what you wish. The blackboard is *lifted* to the Upper Room, where it is known anew, claimed in a higher way, and those things that are no longer required are lifted away.

Our agreement to you today is that the Monad in expression through you is aligning to you through choice and as choice. Underline those words: *through choice and as choice.* The Christed Self as choice. The Monad as choice. The design of that choice incorporated in the soul's requirements for his or her development. Because you have arrived here with an idea of self, have sought a mission or an idea of what you should be doing, you demand to be seen as you think you must be, and you demand that what you do references the idea of self that you have utilized to negotiate a reality claimed through separation. The idealization of who one should be in the manifest plane will be eradicated in time, as an eraser reclaims the old writing. And this must be done for you to move into receipt of your true gifts, your true agreements, beyond the personality's desire to be what it thinks it should.

He interrupts the teaching. "But aren't some inspired to do what they're here for? The one who loves to run becomes a runner. The one who loves to teach becomes the teacher." Yes, you may be called to act, but how that act expresses through you is not for others' well-being or how you are perceived by them. It's because it's what you must be because you can't imagine being otherwise. When you are operating at that level, you cannot be in self-deceit. Imagine the one who would paint on a matchbook or upon a great canvas or upon a public wall. The act of painting is requiring expression. How it is seen, and where it is seen, is of no importance to the artist because the artist is not framing its work through the desire to be seen as artist. But the art itself, or the expression of the artist in presentation, simply is, simply agrees to be, as a reflection of the consciousness of the artist. Do you understand the metaphor? When you align in the higher and you are called to task, called to action, called to an agreement of how you may best serve, you will be as that artist because you cannot not do it. When the will *is* the Monad, an expression of the Christ, you are not doubting why you are here. You know why you are here, and how you serve is that expression.

Now, each of you before us comes with a question: "What is mine? What is my special gift, my special task?" What if we were to answer you this: It is all there. It is already present. But it must be aligned to.

"On this day I choose to move into a true agreement through the Divine Will to amplify the actions I take in realization of how I offer myself in service as an aspect of the Divine."

The agreement to align is to decide what is not. It need not look like this. It need not be as that. It simply is. Imagine you threw seeds upon the soil, and the one that takes, the one that blooms, is the one that is tended to in love. If how you experience yourself is at a lack—"Others know why they're here, I certainly do not"—you are claiming their field, you are looking at the flowers of their field, and comparing it to your own. The realization of the Divine is the aspect of self that knows, takes this out of your hands, and aligns it to recognition so that you may see the flower that seeks to grow and tend to it as it appears. Underline that: *tend to it as it appears* in the eternal now that it is perceived through, not through yesterday's idea of destiny or tomorrow's idea of the accolades you will receive for having done such good things. An accolade means nothing. It is another's experience of something. Again, the artist who has painted the wall has agreed to the joy of the painting. Some may despise the painting. Some may seek to soil it. Some may celebrate it. But the artist has moved on.

Each of you before us today is not at a precipice. You have chosen now to the manifestation of the Monad, and its acceleration through you will be your experience now. And the challenges you may face through the incorporation of this energy will be the degree of vibration that seeks to assume you while you release ideas, and manifest ideas, of what you are, what the world was, and what you think both should be, through the old idea of separation. The equivalency that is present now as vibration is beyond what you think, is beyond what you may even perceive until the level of vibration finds its equilibrium, which means its offering with those things that are of like vibrational accord. As you move to this landscape, naked and resplendent as the Divine that you are, your experience is altered—underline the word *altered*—as well as the idea of self as experiencer. And because of this, you cannot justify the old because it has been moved, it has been transformed, and you are with it, and of it, because you are not separate from God's creations. "Behold, I make all things new."

Our teaching today adheres through the idea that choice itself is now seen as an expression of God, so the ramifications of choice must be offered at that level as well. Paul interrupts the teaching. "People do terrible things, saying it is God's will. How are you preventing that here? Can this teaching be misused?" Anybody may tell themselves anything they wish, but at the level of amplitude that we are instructing, you will never be called to act in fear, to create discord or harm, in the guise or pretext of doing God's will. You are here to be expressed as love. And God's expressions do not damn others, cannot harm others, and are not self-serving at the level of personality. Anyone who wishes to sit on the dais, wrap themselves in a sheet, and talk about God, may be agreed to by some. But you are all the Christ, and the one wrapped in the sheet is wearing a costume for the occasion of it, and nothing more.

We sing your songs for you, yes, so that you may learn the words. But the teaching here is the expressed song, the will in incarnation in agreement to its Source, as it must be, as it will be, as it can only be.

Thank you for your presence. This is in the text. Stop now, please.

DAY TWENTY-EIGHT

What stands before you today, in an awareness of who you are, in a realization of what can be known, is the understanding that you are here for service, for the awakening of others. Now, this does not mean you tell people what to do. It does mean you realize them beyond the constructs they have utilized to negotiate their own realities. This is far easier than you think. It is actually about receiving them as they can only be in truth, and in truth a lie will not be held.

Now, there has been a doctrine of receiving those who are worthy, who have purified themselves, who may offer themselves at the altar in white. The teaching we offer you is rather different. You are claiming the inherent innocence, the claiming of the Divine upon all you see, and its manifestation is what aligns you to their essence.

Now, your requirements for yourselves are very simple. You understand yourselves in agreement to what is, the manifestation of the Divine as all things. And you counter any evidence that would deny the Divine with the claim of truth—"God Is, God Is, God Is"—and allow the impact of that claim to transform what is experienced. Not to your liking, or what you think it should be, but what it can only be. And in service you realize the world.

Now, as this is a teaching of innocence, we wish to describe what may occur to the one undergoing this process. For a moment, you do not forget who you are, but know who you are. And the understanding of knowing as circumventing old memory, old attitude, and old belief must be comprehended by you now as the action of the Divine upon you. *Upon you* means with you, in coherence with you, and in alignment to your requirements. The jurisdiction of the Divine through you amplifies itself through all constructs, seen and unseen. You may be the lighthouse, yes, but your understanding of the lighthouse beam is very minute in comparison to this teaching. The one who moves to a residual application of the Divine Self upon all things is in radiance all the time. "I know who I am, what I am, how I serve" as manifest as the Monad or Christ, reclaiming all things and restoring them to their innocence.

Now, to be restored to innocence does not mean you are uncorrupting something. It means you are reclaiming what has always been, at a level of vibration where it may be seen and experienced. The detritus of history, the uselessness of shame, the magnification of fear—all rendered new. Now, to become new is actually to be in an informed state of restoration, which simply means the one who is agreeing to this at a level of tone is understanding that it is happening. When you do this for another, they are understanding themselves as participatory to a shift. But the shift they undergo will be perfect for them— not as you would merit it useful, but as it must be required at the level of soul in conference with the Christed Self. In other words, to witness the inherent divinity in another at the level we are teaching you today indeed restores them to their true nature at the level that they can hold.

Now, Paul interrupts. "I don't believe this. Imagine I am with someone who is argumentative. Do I just realize the Christ as them? Are they as restored to peace? What happens then?" We will say it to you differently, Paul, than you would like. What occurs when you claim the one who is arguing with their inner truth is that the need for the argument is released.

The need to be made right, the need to be seen as the one as victor, is removed or shifted to a new level of amplitude. How they align to that shift in their behavior or action is independent from your act of re-seeing or restoration. How they respond is how they must respond.

Now, don't confuse yourselves here. Not for a moment are you improving another. You are remembering what has been forgotten. You are claiming the world anew through congruence with what is. You are the lighthouse beam, but not limited by time and space, or the constructs of identity that have been useful in the lower field, but are not useful, or even fully present, in the Upper Room. "What does *fully present* mean?" he asks. *Fully present* means that the evidence of the old may be seen, but you are not confirming its basis. You understand that the clock reads two, but you are knowing beyond time. You understand the malady of the one before you, but you are reclaiming them beyond the malady as their True Self, who does not claim fear or the ramifications of it.

To be at this level of tone is indeed service of the highest level. Any action you will take on behalf of another must be informed by knowing, and never by presupposition. You see, the small self has known evidence of what things must mean or should mean through prior experience, but the comprehension of the Upper Level does not discard evidence, but knows beyond it. In other words, you render the one new with the evidence of the old intact. You are not peeling it away. You are moving well beyond it to a level of agreement—"I know who you are in truth"—as the basis of reclamation. And who you are seeing in truth is the Divine in form expressed as the one before you. Some of you say to us, "Let me be the one who changes the world." You will not change the world, but the manifestation of the Monad through you may—and, in fact, will—when you are delivered from your need to be the one doing the work, which would be a need based in the egoic structure, or the need to be seen or praised or claimed as the one doing the work.

As we sit and speak through Paul, we comprehend his limitations today. Whatever his distractions may be are not interfering with this dictation, so we intend to continue.

Each of you before us is in a realized state when you align to the truth of your being. When you are aligned at this level, your agreement to who you are reclaims aspects of self that have been in denial of the light. That is the challenging passage that you will all undergo. But to know the self in innocence is actually to know the self in wisdom—true wisdom, which is not informational, but holds the clarity of truth that can only be known when the sight of the one perceiving the world has been refocused, re-known, in the clarity and love that is the Upper Room.

> "I see all things with new eyes. I see the ones before me in truth. And I comprehend their requirements for change beyond any basis I may have chosen through historical data. The aspect of me who knows their requirements knows the way to claim them in the high order of the Upper Room, by presence and being."

Again, presence and being. As this is done through you, and for the world, the idea of acting upon impulse is actually moved to acting in knowing—not *upon*, but *in*. And in your knowing, you know the world anew.

This will be the end of this chapter. Thank you for your presence. Stop now, please. Period. Period. Period.

Q: I found it a bit daunting, quite truthfully, just because early on they spoke of being in full radiance at all times. Then, of course, from being in full radiance at all times one can be in service to another in all the ways that they're speaking about. But one can't be in service to others in the way they're speaking about unless we ourselves are in that place of innocence, or, as they're saying, full radiance at all times. And all of that makes perfect sense for everything that they've been teaching and talking about, and the experiential changes, and yet that still was a little bit daunting. Like wow, full radiance at all times and then I can be in service. Okay, but I'm not there.

A: You are already, and that's what you don't understand. Your comprehension of the amplitude of your frequency is actually dictated through the small self—and utilized as much as you can experientially, yes—but the activation of the Monad through you actually circumvents the small self's dictates so that it may do its work through you. In other words, the broadcaster in the TV station may be maneuvering the buttons on the panel, but the broadcast is happening anyway. Do you understand that? What you think keeps you busy and useful is what you need still. But in fact what has

occurred—underline the word *has*—is that you have
come to a level where the broadcast of the field as
Monad is present and operating. It is far less depen-
dent on what you think or feel than you would like
to be that gives you a sense of it being you. "I was
very high today. I did good works." The amplitude of
your field at this level is actually not hindered by the
emotional body's reluctance to adhere to the higher.
And, in fact, that is addressed through the process
of being. *Through* is the operative word there in that
sentence. Period.

7

TRUE MIND

What stands before you today, in an awareness of who you are, is the agreement to be what you can be, without the interference of the personality structure dictating outcome, what should be or must be, based on an idea of self that has actually been moved already. But the habituated state—"I know myself through what I have done"—continues to seek purview.

When we teach through Paul, we comprehend his lessons, his desire for a certain outcome, and we seek to surprise him as often as we can with a higher outcome than he would have chosen, so he releases the need to dictate what should be through the old template. The same will be true for all of you as you move to this new level of outcome, based in the divine principle of the manifest Christed Self. We said that intentionally, Paul: *the manifest Christed Self,* or the idealization of the Monad as expressed through form as each of you. Now, the True Self, who indeed knows, does not desire outcome from the old list of potentials, but will seek to claim what is highest. And what is highest may differ from what you would think you should have or would desire to see, because everything you imagine—and we will say this without exception—is born in an old dogma of potentialities known through separation.

When we speak to you today, we wish to speak about manifestation from innocence, from the octave of innocence, where potential is realized because it can be, because it must be, because it is not hindered by the old and the damnation of form that you have utilized. "What does that mean," he asks, "*damnation of form?*" Well, when you damn form—"this awful creation," "that horrible thing"—you put the thing outside of the Divine, and the thing will not be moved. You will populate an idea of hell this way, all the mechanisms of torture or pain, all the old things that frightened you when you were a child. Whatever you may put there in darkness will amass its own weight, and collectively you adhere through that strata of vibration as a burial ground, the things you would not see exhumed because they are unpleasant to look at.

Realization comes at the cost of the old, and the itinerary here is to reclaim each of you at a level of broadcast where what was held in darkness, through the collective idealization of what is not allowed, may be brought to light and moved forward. Forward first, then upward. Forward to be seen, upward to be re-known. When you are no longer claiming the old, because the old is not present to claim, humanity itself will begin dining, enjoying, from a higher menu of potentiality than it could assume now.

Now, the old debris, the remnants of past choice made in fear, may surround you in form—the residue of slavery, the old relics of war. Each abomination acted out upon through the denial of God that holds its vestige in the lower template must be seen in order to be moved forward. This is less so that you don't repeat the old. It is more so in that you *cannot* when it has been moved and reclaimed in Source to a level that adheres to divine union.

"Well, these things will never adhere to divine union," Paul says. In the ideas you hold, we must agree with you there. But all form is—the relics of the old, the old chains, the old factories of death—must be reclaimed so that they are not brought back to use. You must understand this. Imagine you have a machete in the shed. A machete can be used for good or evil. Imagine the machete in the shed was used for harm. It is now padlocked away, but that machete still waits for its use again. When the machete is re-known as of God, it may be re-formed or re-known in a high octave. Murder will never be of God. Slavery will never be of God. Any control over another with the intent to harm will always be the negation of God. And you must understand that these things, when reclaimed, must be seen first in order to be re-created.

You can't sweep it under the rug. "There was never slavery." You cannot sweep it under the rug. "There were never machines of war." But if these machines still stand in their current form, they hold the radiance of how they were applied and the focus that has been put upon them. "This is a wonderful thing" or "a heinous thing" will rest upon it and hold its solidity. Anything that has been named holds the meaning of the name. Anything that has been damned holds the key to damnation. And the thing must be re-seen—not excused, not made well, but re-seen as of God so that the manifestation of it may be reclaimed and it may be restored.

You really can't have it both ways, you see. "I don't want to look at the old, I will just rest in the new" is the comfort of the old swept under the rug. "I don't want to remember the painful thing. Well, perhaps it was awful, but it's not convenient for me to look at that." Well, *who* looks at the painful thing, what aspect of self sees the painful thing, is the key to understand what we are instructing you in. If the eyes of the Christ perceive this thing, if the eyes that know all things of Source may claim this thing—perceive and reclaim—the thing can be re-known in an altered reality. "What does that mean?" he asks. If there is no use to kill, the implement of harm is useless. The steel that forged it may be retooled into something other.

The act of alchemy we are teaching you today is for the good of all. This is not a comfortable teaching for Paul, and it will not be for some of you as well. But we cannot pretend that humanity will ascend to a higher level of consciousness when the relics of old, those things used to harm others, those relics of pain from prior civilizations, are still around you and still accruing evidence of shame or the amplitude of darkness that has been bestowed upon them. Humanity's desire to control each other, to enslave a people, to dictate the outcome of a war at the cost of thousands and thousands of lives, must be seen now as the residual affect of fear that you would use to claim identity through an old world. The idea of victor and victim. The idea of slave and owner. All ideas of self born in separation. When the separation is released, the names are released, the idolatry that each has been given, how important they are, is also transformed. There will be no more victims and no more victors through the old idea.

When you understand who and what you are, you reclaim

history because you see beyond the evidence. You don't ignore
the evidence. You see beyond the evidence that has been accrued in shame and damnation. "Why do you use the terms
shame and *damnation?*" he asks. Well, you feel ashamed as a
collective about how you have treated one another. You are
ashamed of the history you've held. You build monuments
to the victors still, or you remember the shamed, the victims
of the old, in memoriam as you can. But the shame that has
been held over past acts only prohibits future acts at the level
of consciousness humanity has held. And what is now being asked of you, a new level of consciousness and alignment
which will not claim the old again, means that you must see
what was done in shame or harm and reclaim it.

Now, the vulnerable self, the aspect of each of you who
says, "Please don't make me look, I don't want to see what I
did or what we have done or how we saw ourselves in past
lives as victim or victor, I just want to live today," is almost
helpful. We will say what we mean by this. You need not dwell
on shame and harm. To dwell on shame and harm reclaims
them or revitalizes them through the focus you've given them.
But you can't ignore them either. But the simple acknowledgment of what was, and then the reclamation of them, is how
the manifest form, the world you see, can be moved beyond
the residue of past acts and the templates of pain that you
utilize to re-create or manufacture the old when you believe
it is required. "There is another war. Let us build more arms
factories." "There is another war. Let's build more bunkers."
"There is another war. Let's send our children to fight." When
these are no longer choices—because the factories of war, the
bunkers, the battlefields themselves, have been lifted to the

higher—there will be no more claim of victor and victim because there will be no battle or fight.

Recrimination for the self for past acts done is only useful if they become motive for change. But then rest in the change, not self-recrimination. Recrimination of others can only be useful if it is instructive of higher choice. To bend something into the shape you will it to is misuse of will when it is another and her identity that is being claimed. When you understand what we are saying, you may say, "Yes, this happened," and you must understand your part in it. To reclaim the new, you will release the need to punish and harm the ones you claim in fear, because the only ones you harm are ever the ones you are frightened of.

Now, the relics of old which inhabit this plane—the temples of torture, the old battlegrounds, the altars where humans were sacrificed thousands of years ago—are still present here. You imagine them as empty because they are not in usage. But everything holds memory in your idea of time. And to reclaim the relics of pain or the misuse of authority, the chains of slavery, the factories of war, the devices of torture that humanity has used against itself in present time and in past time, may all be realized in no time, in this eternal moment, through the act of reclamation we are introducing to you now. Each thing you see that has been utilized to harm another, each law you've claimed that has barred another entry from his or her own freedom, each choice made to build a device of horror or destruction, can and now will be reclaimed in the tone we sing. And when we sing this tone, we invite you to claim this intention upon all things manifest, held, created, or used in darkness:

"Behold, I make all things new. It will be so. God Is. God Is. God Is."

On the count of three, Paul.
Now one. Now two. Now three.

[The Guides tone through Paul.]

What is, was. What is, is. What is, will be. All things made new. All things reclaimed. All things re-sung in the true octave of the Christ in manifestation. All things seen, all things thought, all things made in form, re-sung in the high amplitude of truth and being. And as we say yes to your assistance in this act, we invite you to say yes as well.

You Are Here. You Are Here. You Are Here. You Have Come. You Have Come. You Have Come. You Are Known. You Are Known. You Are Known. And enacted in the greatness of truth.

We thank you each for your presence. Stop now, please. Indeed, this is in the text.

(PAUSE)

What stands before you today, in an awakened state, is a promise of the new—underline the word *promise*—a guarantee of what will be made so at the higher level or octave that you may align to now. The promise is born in alignment, yes. And the restatement of who and what you truly are in a pluralized state—of the whole, one of all, in agreement to the Source in all things—focuses itself, mandates itself, as expression. The denial of the Divine which you have utilized to realize the self through, once gone, re-articulation once begun, claims manifestation in the Upper Room in completeness. Underline the word *completeness*. It may not be what you think. You think of a new house. No dusty corners. No old wallpaper. In *completeness* we mean the rendering of the new, yes—at the cost of the old template, yes—but in a way that may be recognized by you as being what simply is, presence and being.

You see, the denial of the Divine obscures most things that are already present in the high octave that is the Upper Room. The manifestation of this in a way that you may know—again, coming at the cost of the old—replicates itself in the high octave. In other words, a song sung is a song sung anew. Your idea of what was is claimed in a higher way. And the usefulness of the claim, or the re-knowing of something that was once in form, must be experienced by you.

Now, you imagine yourselves as participatory to change, and you are indeed accurate. But you really don't comprehend the change that is about to occur in the landscape you share. There will be a level of realization—across the oceans, across the borders—of what you have done, how you have chosen, so that you may choose anew. This realization comes as the result of action and fear that has been claimed by those that would seek to perpetuate it, yes. But to deny the Divine will not be aligned at the higher octave that is now beginning to play. Those who would foster fear will be relieved of their burden, or the chalice they hold, which is to claim an idea of self in sovereignty at the cost of humanity.

Paul is concerned with this teaching. "You are making people out to sound evil. Is that what you are doing?" Absolutely not. But we will say this: When a reality is shifting, those who would seek to perpetuate a status quo will do what they can to maintain identity in purview. When this is realized by the collective, the collective reclaims what has been held in darkness because the collective must. Now, you will not turn your back on your neighbor in the coming times, because you realize your neighbor as yourself. The selfishness that you have chosen to learn through—"My life is worthy, her life must not be," "Our lives are worthy, their lives must not be"—is the degradation of the Divine at a very high level. And this will not be allowed because the level of vibration that has come and is seeking revelation through you will not support it.

The challenge of these times you sit in now is that the broadcast that you have been listening to, the old song you have been dancing around with, demanding be sung because it's all you have known, is being altered. Underline the word *is*—*is* being altered. And the transition to the high octave, once occurring, disestablishes or disinherits the old properties that the old vibration has claimed. We have been asked, "Does the good that humanity has claimed sustain in the Upper Room?" All great benefits of humanity have been the Source expressing in different ways. Be it art, be it commerce, be it true religion or true medicine, the truth of all these things is always present because they are the Divine expressing in high ways through humanity's choice to align to them. But the properties of the old, known in misalignment, will be changing. And some of the changes are challenging.

We will explain this. When you lift in motion to a higher

level of frequency, that which has been held in the lower is seen and then moved. Imagine you are moving upward. That which cannot withstand the higher level of tone must be dismantled, re-seen, or re-known in a higher way. What you don't really understand yet is how much you want the old, even if it's harmful to yourself or your fellow humans, humanity as a whole. Those who profit from war will always seek war. But to understand the merit of peace, and the requirement for forgiveness for peace to be present, requires a change of consciousness that most of you don't want. And you don't want it because it upsets the cart that holds the idea of economy, a country's province, and the rights of an individual in ways that you have become accustomed to. When you understand that no human life is worth more or less than another, you will end war. But you deny God in your fellows, and then when they are killed off in the name of commerce you go, "Well, there we go again. We are at it again. Humanity will never change." And you confirm the world in its lowest degradation. To think that you are not party to this would be a fallacy. Of course you are, because all things you see before you, you are in resonance with.

The lifting to the new requires that you release your old armor, drop the sword, drop the shield, drop the requirement for a battle that you have always expected. Those of you who believe that you are here to fight evil, know it or not are demanding there to be evil for you to fight. To lift beyond the idea of evil, to lift to a place of agreement where Source is more powerful than your idea of evil, will eradicate the idea of evil, which is only the denial of the Divine in hurtful manner. And the one who decides to war to erect a border to keep her fellows away is enacting the lowest, whether or not that is what you wish to hear. Until you feed the person at the table who is most in need of food, you are acting in hypocrisy.

Now, will humanity change? Yes. It is happening now. And it is happening in a wave that will actually claim you in a higher presence. In the higher presence, you will realize the error of your ways because it is there for you to see, and you will have the opportunity to reclaim the world at the level of choice that the Monad proffers.

"What does that mean?" he asks. When the Monad or the Divine Self, aligned in will, is claimed in fruition it claims the world. And the acts of the individual will never be at the cost of the whole. When you work towards unity, you don't do this with the kind of effort you think. You do it through inclusiveness, not exclusiveness. You do this through the blessing, the presence of God upon the thing you see, not through damnation, which is to throw another into darkness. Those who would seek to profit from the error of fear will claim themselves anew because finally—and we will say this again—all things will be made new. And your desire to vilify and make wrong will be moved to a new level of agreement because no one will be helped or transformed when they are being damned.

The gift of this teaching is re-articulation at a massive scale. And we will explain what we mean by this. The changes that are occurring here are occurring regardless of your choice. But the benefit of your presence to these teachings supports your realization of what is actually occurring, which is to benefit humanity, to reclaim humanity in the higher octave that is humanity's true inheritance. You are the gift to the world as you align to this, not so much this teaching, but to your own inherent potential to be re-known at the level of truth that you were incarnated to be. "What does that mean?" he asks, "*incarnated to be*?" This has always been a teaching of restoration. This has always been a teaching of love, and the agreement to love as expressed in an individual through consciousness. And soul's agreement to the benefit incurs at this level of tone or vibration.

It will always be thus. Our idea, our knowing, our claim for each of you, is that you be restored to your inherent divinity in your expression, presence and being. And our gift to those who wish it is the manifestation of the Monad as may be claimed at the cost of the old self, or old mask, or old idea of self that has been accrued through separation.

Behold, I make all things new.

We thank you each for your presence. Indeed, this is in the text. Stop now, please. Period. Period. Period.

DAY THIRTY

What stands before you today, in an awakened state, is the result of the work you have done thus far. Understand what we say now: The agreement to align to the high octave of the Upper Room, in its own amplitude, is claiming what you see, and not only how you see it but what you may do with it, how you may act upon what is seen, from this high voltage, high experience, high expression of consciousness.

Now, when one knows who she is and she embarks on a

life, she claims the identity that is present for her and does not seek to discover who she was through the remnants of old. She comprehends past acts, old choices, old ideas, and she releases the need to decide who she is in ramification of those choices as a result of them. You understand what was. You comprehend this from the high octave. But you are not picking through the detritus of history, seeking what you might have left or lost or must find again.

Our identity as True Self, as the Monad in expression, is for the benefit of all. We do not squander our gifts with contemplating the self that might once have been. Those of us who have known form, and transcended the idea of form, are able to claim a world that we express through. And our objective now is to support you each in this reclamation so that you may know the selves as you can only be in truth. Those of us who have not known form, but have been present as light, as expression, as awareness of Source, support the world beyond the idea of self that was ever constructed.

Now, the idea of self has been discussed at length in this text. What has not yet been discussed is the being beyond the idea of self, and how one lasts, experiences, at a level of amplitude that is not seeking evidence through past accrued history. When you align at the level we teach you today, you are indeed in a sovereign state. But the sovereignty is the Christ or Monad as expressed, not the name you have taken at birth and have become familiar with. You are operating in two different strata simultaneously.

Now, Paul is interrupting. "In the world but not of it?" he asks. Not really. But you may use that if it's easiest for you to comprehend what we are about to say. The True Self, you see, has always been expressed, but not adhered to. And the amplification of it in the Upper Room for the benefit of all knows *itself*—it knows *itself*—beyond old ideas. The aspect that it is, born through you to be in articulation as manifest, must know the speeding limit, must understand the body's needs. And while these ideas are present in the common field, they are also re-known from the idealization of the Monad that must see all things in coherence to it. The manifest reality you experience from the Upper Room, at the level of integration we are now teaching, is the realized world, or the world known in God.

Now, the idea of this for some of you is a plastic world, or elastic world, that can be moved by conscious thought. The density of matter that you have known in the low field is of course far more pliable or elastic in the Upper Room because you are not utilizing time to make your decisions. Realization, you see, true knowing, you see, does not exist in time, but in timelessness. Any time you have truly known, you have been outside of the schemata of time. But you may look at the clock and say, "Yes, of course. At two fifteen I knew." At the idea of two fifteen, you were experiencing the Eternal Self, the aspect that knows, and the agreement made at the higher level, in its own amplitude, is now expressed in the manifest plane. The true knowing, you see, at the level of the Monad in expression in form is what coalesces the material realm to the level we teach at. "What does this mean?" he asks. Your ability to perceive as the Christed Self or the Monad in experience, beyond the idea of time, supports the manifest world at a level you do not see or cannot imagine at the lower template.

Now, everything you understand in your world is born

in rules of agreement—the seasons, the days of the week, all ideas known through form. In the Upper Room, at this scale of expression, realization occurs beyond old evidence. In other words, the manifest world in an altered state is seen through the eyes and the level of consciousness that comprehend eternity. When you comprehend eternity, or at least agree to it, what you begin to experience in a manifestation is what can only be. Now, the clock's hands may move, but you understand clock as mechanism, something that measures the seconds and the hours. You understand the requirement for the mechanism at the level that it was created at. But you are no longer abiding by it in the high octave, but referencing it as you require it in the lower field. The one whose life is translated in this way is claiming a new agreement, not only for him or herself, but for the world as a whole.

He interrupts the teaching. "But how does this affect the world? I can imagine one person sitting on a mountain who doesn't care what time it is, perhaps sees God as all things. But how is the world changed in a manifest way beyond what you speak of as individual articulation?"

Individual articulation, at the level we are teaching, clearly claims the manifest world in like congruence, because, as has been said, it cannot do otherwise. It is at this level, so all experience is translated by the perceiver. How this affects the world is not only in increments, as the individual perceives, but also in a great wave. In some ways, what you have done is blow a hole in the ceiling. Again, the claim "I am free, I am free, I am free." And when that opening happens and you operate as portal to the higher level of expression, you are claiming the world to blow itself through the portal, or the idea of ceiling that has been known as separation.

Now, some of you want magic tricks. "Show me how I turn the water to wine." What you do here, actually, is re-see the environment you have known at one level, and then at another. You are moving to the level of agreement where what you see must be the out-picturing of consciousness. You have been moved beyond the idea of history. You are moving now beyond the idea of memory and the meaning things have been endowed with. This is all required for the manifestation of the higher, lest you try to bring yesterday's garbage with you to the idea of the Upper Room which will not hold that level of detritus or waste.

Each of you before us who adheres to these words is actually privileged to a level of experience that will be known by you as you align to it. "What is this experience?" he asks. "I don't want conjecture. I want my own experience of this so that I may know that this is true." In fact, Paul, you are having it. And some of the grief you experience now is the realization of what was, how you have chosen it, and the child self that believed himself to be so separate he could not know love. As this aspect of self is transformed, the agreement to love is made known to you. And for all of our students this will indeed be the case. There is a grief, yes, that accompanies a passage from the old to the new. What you believed once was, the effort you put into making things a certain way, the desires that you had, fulfilled or unfulfilled, are all receding as the tide claims you on this new shore.

Your experience on this new shore is as the one who knows, and whose alignment has moved to a congruence with the vibration or tone that you may call God, but we will call All That Is because it implies lack of separation. All That Is cannot hold separation because you are of All That Is. Your idea of God still often plays somewhere other, keeps you running towards an objective. And there will be teachings that will invite you to run towards something that you can never fully grasp. What we are saying is different:

You Are Here. You Are Here. You Are Here. You Have Come. You Have Come. You Have Come. You Are Known. You Are Known. You Are Known.

And at this level of agreement, the Manifest Self in an altered octave holds the experience of timelessness, or you could say eternity, while the figure that still occupies space in a collective field is transforming the field by her purview, by her agreement, and by her knowing of what truly is.

Our teaching today is about two things: what occurs when you stop deciding what should be, and what occurs when you release what you think was and what accompanies that release. Everything known by humanity has been in a form that you can comprehend while embodied, but the motives for many occurrences have been shrouded, have been denied. The limitations you've utilized to decide what can be have claimed you in a history that holds limitation as barrier. To re-see history is not to forget history. It's to comprehend what was so that you are delivered from the old.

Paul is understanding himself now as a product of history, because this is a period one must address to release the idea of self claimed by history. But the reliance on history to dictate outcome only guarantees you will have what you once had. And this is not only true for the individual, but it is true for the collective. This is a collective movement now. And the chaos you see about you, the recrimination that sings throughout the valleys and up the mountainside, will be heard until the voice grows tired and there is no more use for words that deify separation or support the damnation of another.

You are growing tired as a collective of the futility of battle. You are growing tired as a collective of recrimination as a way of changing behavior. You must have a new model, a new template for being. And that is the Upper Room, and the level of consciousness that will not demand the old be claimed. To say that it is happening now would be an accurate assessment of the experience of many. What is actually happening is that the density of the plane is moving in most challenging ways. The evidence of old pain, old suffering, old grief, old anger, old agreement to war is being moved. And while it moves, it may seem to be present in the loudest or darkest ways. But the smoke will clear, and what was burned in the fire will be ash. And you will not be looking at it because your eyes will have been moved to what now lies before you—a world made new, a claim upon the world in universal agreement to presence and being.

"I don't believe it," he says. "It sounds nice, but how?" This text is a book on *how*. The realization of the *how* is actually present already. The doubt that you have, Paul, is the idea of self that seeks to moor itself to an old post while the floodwaters are rising. Let go of the post. Allow the lifting to occur, and trust the process. The tide that is invoked will not leave you awash, but has delivered you—underline the word *has*— *has* delivered you to the high shore. While you know you are here some days, you understand yourself still through old patterning. And the agreement to the old patterning, a sense of identity that is now releasing, is the cause of your challenge. To forget who you were has never been this teaching. To know who you are has been.

The release of the old is understanding what you chose once upon a time, how humanity chose once upon a time, so that you are now delivered from the ramifications of those choices to begin to claim what is before you. Some of you say, "I want this," but in fact you do not. You want your idea of an improved world. "We will plant some more flowers, eat some more vegetables, do a few things that may help and let that be enough." By all means, plant the flowers. But know that the world is made new through the realization of the omnipresent Divine upon what is seen, and this may only occur at the level of consciousness you are being instructed in here. If you want a new world, let it be the world you cannot imagine. Let it be the world that seeks to be born. Let it be the song that is sung in love and laughter through the mountains and the valleys. Let all things be made new. Let the world be sung into manifestation from the high order of the Upper Room.

We are Melchizedek. We come as the Source, in agreement to Source, as who and what we can only be in truth.

We thank you for your presence. Stop now, please. Period. Period. Period.

DAY THIRTY-ONE

What stands before you today, in a realized state of comprehension, that what you have seen in the past has been informed by the dictates of separation, you come to an agreement of what truly is and what can only be. The fabrication of a reality in a dense field is a collective act. You are all creating the mountains and the sky through your adherence to the ideas of them. Your agreement to these things, in a solidified form over millennia, has guaranteed outcome—that you will know a mountain by the idea of mountain, or an ocean by the idea of ocean.

Now, transposition occurs when the True Self, in mandate of its expression, simply releases the ideas that cannot conform to the higher amplitude. Underline *cannot*. The work is done at this level—not through your reconfiguring what you would have be. The idea of creating your reality at an independent level is actually very useful, because indeed it makes you accountable to your own choices and gives you the opportunities to renegotiate reality from a place of sovereignty, or at least the idea that what you have seen you have chosen, or at least agreed to learn through. Underline the term *agreed to learn through*. Agreement is coherence. It is not necessarily conscious. "I didn't agree to be left as a child." But in fact you are in coherence to what occurred, and you are choosing to learn through the experience, once you decide that everything can be seen as opportunity. However, the collective has made agreements as well, and the idea of personal sovereignty—"I create my reality"—is actually void in the face of collective agreement.

"What does that mean?" he asks. Well, once again, the collective's idea of ocean, which you confer power to, is already established for you through the historical data that the collective has endowed it with. It is not your ocean. It is not Paul's ocean or Abigail's ocean. It is all the ocean that all see—in other words the *all*, the amplitude of collective agreement, out-pictured as ocean. When world events occur that actually claim *all* in their incident, the world is always given an opportunity to negotiate or re-decide what this thing can and will mean. Again, opportunity to learn. Tragically, what humanity primarily chooses in the face of a crisis is an act of aggression. "The neighbor stole the peas from the yard. We will erect a larger fence." "That country chose to do this. We will attack that country." Rarely do you realize the opportunity in an act that informs the collective, because you operate in selfishness.

Now, individual selfishness is something that you comprehend. "I had more than I needed on my plate. I didn't offer it to the hungry man beside me." But you don't understand collective selfishness and how that has mandated outcome that you are all in agreement to. Underline *all*—*all* in agreement to. Not because you wish it to be so, not because you excuse it, but because you witness it. Anything that you witness, you are in accord to.

Now, when you are listening to this teaching, you are being moved in a vibratory scale to a level of resonance where the words that we speak can be comprehended in the energetic field. And it is the energetic field we are addressing now, because the amplitude of each of you, in a realized state, has far more authority over what you perceive than you would know. "What does that mean?" he asks. Well, the idea of self as perceiver, still negotiating a reality that he thinks should be, or that she wishes to be, is actually only one level of the experience that is occurring here. The mindless mind, or the eyes that see without judgment, the restored innocence of the individual, is also partaking in a structure of experience at a level of innocence. "What does that mean—*structure of experience?*"

Well, you see a world with mountains and valleys and oceans. Reality has structure, and this structure is born out of expectation endowed by the collective upon it. But in the Upper Room, consequently and truthfully, the eyes that see beyond the eyes that knew or claimed the old are also operative, which is the mind beyond mind, or the plurality, plural expression, of Divine Mind that is innocence. Underline the word *is*. Divine Mind *is* innocence, which holds all possibility. And all possibility can be confirmed by the individual when Divine Mind is operative through the eyes or experience of the one perceiving.

What occurs here, in some ways, is the idea that the aspect of self who considers herself the perceiver, who has identification through the landscape that she was reared in, is beginning to operate in congruence with higher mind that holds no dictate and no expectation. The innocent mind holds no dictate and no expectation, which is why what is simply is. And this amplitude of agreement is how the world is finally re-seen in form. Underline the word *form*. The idea of mind that has been entrenched in the material realm, has had to negotiate history—"This is what an ocean is and must be"—is all very well and good, but is still limited in its perspective, what it agrees can be, or would mandate to be. True Mind— and we will use that with capital letters, capital T, capital M, *Mind*—would be seen as the aspect of mind that is indeed eternal, does not negotiate anything, because it knows and sees through the idealization, opportunization, of ceaseless truth. Underline those words: *ceaseless truth*. To be in innocence is to be in *ceaseless truth*, a comprehension of being that holds no mask, not even language, to support its ideas. You understand language, and it's useful. It's how you agree to manifestation through collective reason. "This is the ocean." "This is the sky." "This is the property of a river or a pond or a puddle." You have language to support your ideas, and you create language, and in some ways cement reality or hold it in density, through the applied language which confirms idea. In other words, the idea of a thing, once spoken into being, confirms the very thing as manifest.

When you move beyond language in the Upper Room to the soundless truth of All That Is, All That Is is actually explicit. Underline that word: *explicit*. What is a river without the name *river*? What is a river without the properties that you've endowed river with? River may be known in a higher form, once it is not assigned through language and intent what it should be by a pre-prescribed idea of what a solid river is. River is All That Is, manifested as the idea of river through the mind that has agreed to it. In the High Mind, or the True Mind, what you begin to experience is the application of this teaching as the one who transmutes vibration. Because you are not assigning meaning, what you are beginning to do is restore to what always was. You may underline that, if you wish, as well: *what always was*. River before the idea of *river*, the idea that first created river, which is God itself giving you the authority to see and create.

You have heard tales of worlds or dimensional realities where thought is immediately met by manifestation, and we will say this: There are strata in the Upper Room where such things occur. The density of the common field simply decides that things will take more time. The idea may be had, but the manifestation of idea through the individual or collective will have to be arduous. In other words, it takes time for the seed to grow into the plant you see before you today. The immediacy of manifestation as may be known from the higher levels that are present here is the outcome of the High Mind, whose ideas are of True Mind. In other words, what you claim in potential, true potential in True Mind, from this level of amplitude, must be so, and in fact already exists. You are claiming the world made new as it already exists in True Mind, in High Mind. You are claiming what was, what is, and what will always be, which is God itself in its expression in an innocent state, without the data of history besmirching it, without the fear that you have used soiling or corrupting it, without the damnation you've employed lowering it to the field that you have known yourselves through prior.

Each of you who says yes to the work that is before you will actually be employed. "How does this occur?" he asks. Presence and being is the key to the entire teaching of this text. Presence and being. The idea of self, transplanted to the Upper Room where it is reclaimed in its expression, is the True Mind expressing through individuals, and then the collective, for the benefit of All That Is. And we will say this again: *All That Is* being all things seen and unseen.

The clarity we offer you here is for a very specific reason. You are all being utilized at a level of tone, as a harpsichord would be, as a drum would be, as a church bell might be, so that the sound of your expression, the peal of the bell, the chord on the harpsichord, the song sung by the choir, in intonation and reverberation begins to restore, reclaim, and align all structures seen and unseen to the perfect tone that is the Divine that seeks itself in all things. This is done—presence and being—by the aspect of self who is and was and will always be, which is the Monad that is being expressed beyond mind, beyond identity, as toned as the clarion call.

Now, all of you here, who experience these words on a page, or hear the voice of the man, are being restructured at a level of tonality so that what you may bring, what you may offer, is the highest offering that you may claim and be present for. *Be present for* is the key here. Presence and being: *Be. Present. For.* Each of you says yes at the level of claim that you have aligned to thus far. And each agreement—"I am willing to be, I am willing to know and be known, I am willing to see as I may only see in this state of innocence and restoration"—claim the world anew without the intention to move a brick, dust a floor, clean a windowpane. The action is done in congruence to the Monad as it expresses as and through.

Now, you become one with all at a certain level of tone. Imagine one voice singing, the peal of the bell, the tone of the harpsichord, the one song, the one voice, being heard. But at a certain level, when many voices join, when many instruments play, the sound is enormous, and it becomes one sound, one great tone—not a cacophony, but a trumpet, a blare, a resounding call to awakening that all are met with as they experience themselves at whatever level they have come to. Some of you say, "Yes, let me be used." Some of you say, "Well, this is very curious. Perhaps someday." And others will say, "Impossible. This is a farce." However, the tone playing through you will actually begin to operate independently from the idea of what you deem possible, because in this high level of innocence and potentiality, the realization of the tone has absolutely nothing to do with your emotional state, or your intelligence, or your decisions about what can be, because it is the energetic body in a restored state that claims the sound, that joins others in like sound. And the resounding sound, the resounding *yes*, that *is* the claim of innocence and restoration upon the manifest world, will be the song sung by all through the action of co-resonance—not through the effort of choosing anew, but by aligning to what is, and what was, and what will always be in tone.

We sing your songs for you so that you may learn the words. We will continue this dictation tomorrow. Thank you for your presence. Stop now, please.

DAY THIRTY-TWO

What stands before you today, in a realized state, is that the incarnation that you are releasing, which is simply the idea of self, has been part of a process that has been utilized to grant you the new identity of the Monad in incarnation. Understand what we just said: the Monad incarnate.

Now, to be the Monad incarnate is in fact to be who you truly are. It is not a superhuman ideal. You are not gifted with a promise of prophecy. You are not gifted with the gifts that the small self might believe she would accrue. However, you are in your knowing, and in a manifest state that can claim all things new. The realized being you are is not suffering because she understands there is no need. However, she undergoes her trials as the soul requires them. Underline those words, friends: *as the soul requires them.*

Now, the loss of a child, the loss of employment, the loss of your home—all these things are challenging in very deep ways at whatever strata you may express. But how the challenge is met is very different from the Upper Room, because you realize all things as of God, because you unattach to what was, because you know what truly is, and because you abide in grace. Underline those words: *abide in grace,* which is to abide in the presence of God.

Now, the presence of God as all things does not necessarily mean that things would go as you would have, as you would wish, as you would proclaim. In some ways, what occurs is that you move in a current, a high current. You are moving beyond the old, around the boulders, beyond the systems of control. But you are not dictating outcome, because you trust the Creator, All That Is, to show you where you need to be, to be led by the Monad that operates now through will and through knowing. To *be* this is to amplify the field, the Christ field, if you wish, that is present in every living thing. Underline what we just said: *every living thing,* because there is nothing outside of God. And as you meet God through God's creations, all things are lifted by presence and being.

The accruement of belief in separation has been the biggest challenge we have had as your instructors. Every corner you turn, you meet more evidence of it. Every detail you poke at to decide why God cannot be claims your focus in the lower field, and not to the Great Self, the True Self, the Divine Self, that is already here as you, seeking its expression as and through. True Mind, we say, is the moving beyond this idea of separation, at a level of agreement where you cannot agree to separation because you know it's folly. You know it's artifice. You know that what you see before you is the accumulation of data, claimed in the lower field, that many adhere to. But you do not adhere. You have risen above. And any evidence that would seek to tie you to the old will be released in the claims we have offered you. "God Is. God Is. God Is." And the amplification of this claim in the field you hold sings its song to all that you encounter.

Each of you before us today, each of you who hears these words, who reads these words on a page, are actually being met in a new field. And the new accruement of evidence of where you are will in fact meet you quickly as you agree to it. What are you agreeing to, you may ask. To allow God to be God, to allow God to be visible, seen and expressed as all things in your experience of it. What you undertake here, as we come to a close in this text, is the manifestation of the Monad, in its amplified state, that recruits, re-aligns, and actually absorbs that which is in the lower field that cannot coalesce or demand occupancy in the energetic field that is the Upper Room. You are as the Upper Room, you see, at this level of incarnation.

Now, as you express, as you realize, as you claim, the idealization of what was—first diminished—releases. And God will liberate you from a set of expectations that you have utilized to navigate the common field. It is not a wish that is being released. It is an expectation of what should be, how it should be, how you would mandate outcome, and how you would deliver yourself—underline those words, *deliver yourself*—from what you see that you would not approve of.

We spoke of a current that will carry you. We speak of grace, which will surround you. We speak of the experience of being as and of and with the Source of all things in your experience of manifestation. *Manifestation* means matter— what is seen, felt, touched, tasted, and known, through the body, through the senses, and also through the consciousness that heralds the new. The embodiment as the Monad, which recruits all things to itself, absorbs that which cannot be held in fear, now known in light, in reclamation, is the gift of God upon all who say yes. Underline those words: *all who say yes.*

Now, Paul doesn't like this teaching. "I understand what you are saying in theory. You have spoken about this often. But I do not feel as the Monad in incarnation. I don't know that I ever will. So what does this truly mean beyond supposition?" We would like to explain this very clearly for you. The attunements we have offered work first in the body and the energetic field. "I am Word through my body. Word I am Word. I am Word through my vibration. Word I am Word. I am Word through my knowing of myself as Word." The claim of the knowing of the self as Word—which is first principle, which is the Monad, the one note sung, that is invested in all of you by nature of presence and being—is what accrues the following attunements: "I know who I am. I know what I am. I know how I serve."

The realization of these things, in your small mind, still is in the equation of what you might do for an occupation, how you might behave with others. But it is the Monad, entrenched, expressed, through the idea of self, through the material form you have taken, that overrides the old systems. So the idea of Monad, once liberated from the directives of the lower realm in the claim "I am free, I am free, I am free," moves its alignment to the manifest world that we will call the Upper Room. At this level of occupation, the Monad expressed as form and consciousness in the claim "I Have Come, I Have Come, I Have Come" claims the form and all prior creations in the new ideal, or the higher claim of the Monad as expressed.

The Monad expressed does not hold the reference points that the low self has, is not indoctrinated by memory and history. And it makes the claim "Behold, I make all things new" because it must by its nature of presence and being. Its manifestation is what sings a world into being, not your small idea of what grace can be, but the profundity of what grace truly is. You are expressed already at this level, but you deny it because you are fearful of what it means. It does not mean you walk on water. It means you have come in participation to a world made new. The claim "It will be so" is the guarantee of the Monad in its claim of vibrational echo, that all it sees, all it bears witness to, all that can and will be known, will be in the higher octave that is always true. Underline those words: *always true.*

At this level of vibrational field in expression, the Manifest Divine is all, and was all, and will always be, which is the claim "God Is, God Is, God Is," the Manifest Divine beyond the idea of time, of history, of identity, but the amplitude of truth re-seen by the Monad in its restoration. Did you hear those words? *Its* restoration, not *your* restoration, which is the personality self, which in most ways has now been recruited in the higher octave. What remains in the low is simply what is perceived through the old lens, which is also being moved, as your perception is accrued through the evidence of experience, by grace, in the Upper Room.

Each of you who comes before us is in alignment at the level that you have agreed to. But we roll the carpet for you to walk upon, and we escort you down the runway to the experience, to the true inheritance, that has always been present but has been so denied that you would refute it even if it were a burning bush upon a mountaintop announcing itself by name. You Have Come. You Are Free. You Are Here. You Are Known. And you are expressed beyond the idea of self, once you surrender the idea of self to completion.

"What does that mean," he asks, "*surrender the idea of self to completion?*" That is all that stands in the way. Don't you understand this? It is only the idea of self as separate that stands in the way of union. You have lifted the field. You have lifted your eyes. You have lifted your voice in agreement to Source. It is only the idea that holds place, because you continue to hold your finger on a page that is ready to be turned. When we return for you, we will turn that page. We will bring you forth beyond the old idea.

This is in the text. Thank you for your presence. Stop now, please. Period. Period. Period.

(PAUSE)

What stands before you today, in a new awareness of who you are, is what may be claimed outside the idea of limitation that the small self has accrued, and in fact been bound by. Those of you who say yes to this instruction are always met at the level of coherence that you may hold, and as we teach through Paul, we amplify this with your agreement. The coherence you hold, which is the level of vibration you claim, is generally in flux and biased, based upon experience. But when articulation as the Monad is manifest, the radiance of the Monad actually overrides the idea of self that would be a barometer to its radiance through its emotional state. In other words, friends, your idea of self finally does not preclude the Monad expressing as you.

The level of coherence that you may align to supports your agreement to it, but once re-articulation has begun, the Divine Presence as you in its manifest state, which is what claims the world anew, operates not independently from the self, but through the self that has received a new acclimation. The idea that you should feel a certain way, have a specific practice, is quickly replaced by your new awareness.

Now, the awareness of the Divine as all things in charge of one's experience will vary according to the level of coherence that an individual can claim. But when we instruct through the man before you, we actually override his fear, his concern—indeed, his resistance—to bring you a level of vibration that you may align to and support yourself with. This becomes experiential, you see, when you understand that the Manifest Divine, that is already here, is already in operation, is already endorsed. The manifest world with its coherence is what supports all things, what claims you anew. And the unbridled self, which is the Manifest Divine, will not be altered by the fact that at the level of personality you have had a difficult time, a challenging evening, or decided in some way or another that what is always true cannot be true. *What is always true.* If you would understand this simple concept, most of your confusion would evaporate. What is always true is that there is an aspect of you—and all—that is already in coherence with the True Self and the Manifest Divine that is all things. You may call this the Monad or the Divine Spark. You may call it the True Self, if you wish. But it is the Monad that expresses in articulation through you that renders you new. And True Self, we suggest, is the manifestation of the Monad at an individual level, because you are still operating as a self, identified in certain ways, whereas the Monad, always of the whole, can be known beyond self.

Now, this is a new concept for some of you, but the articulation of the Divine as and through each of you, the process you engage in with us, is only one level of vibration. Because the Monad may know itself in form and without form, the Monad is always in coherence with Universal Source or All That Is, regardless of your identification through it. In other words, while the soul, which is of God, yes, but concentrates itself in a manifest form that understands itself as with the whole, until the soul is in articulation in full brightness and coherence as Monad, it will still be operating in a singular state. Now, this is useful. You incarnate and have experience. The soul indeed progresses. But when the Monad expresses as soul, you become a universal being, and the names you have given yourselves while maintaining form mean very little. In other words, the light in coherence as you moves beyond the lampshade, or what would shutter the light or claim the light in a singular way, so that the light is all things. In other words, the light that you are, in coherence with all the light there is, stops thinking of itself as singular because it knows it cannot be.

When we teach through the man before you, we understand his concerns about the teaching. He wants things to be simple, but doesn't know that in fact they are extraordinarily simple. You see, you are being restored to a state beyond identity as a singular being, through the action of the Divine, without losing singularity, which is quite simply your way to maintain coherence with a landscape that is shared. The Divine as all things explodes beyond individuation, but you require some form of individuation to walk this plain, even in the Upper Room. When you understand what re-articulation means, when you understand that it is the Monad expressing as body and field in coherence in the Upper Room, you will begin to understand what we are about to teach you: That you are limited by your beliefs of what is possible, that you are limited by fear of trespassing upon another realm, that you are limited by agreement to the collective that you will not be boundless.

He interrupts the teaching. "We just want to understand what this teaching brings us, and how we may bring this teaching to a world that is in support of the world. Nothing abstract please. Just give us the outline." We will do so, if you wish, although we believe we have been very clear. The Monad, in expression as the individual in the Upper Room, claims the individual beyond the idea of separation that has been the bane of existence, and the teacher of experience, in the lower realm. When you are not bound by separation, what is available to you far exceeds what you could imagine. *Boundless* is a wonderful word to use for the experience of being as the Christed Self in the Upper Room, where you have aligned to a level of freedom that you have not been taught experientially through your edict of separation that has bound you or tethered you to the lower field. The claim "I am free," which supports the agreement to the Upper Room, is the first station, in many ways, that you may align to. But to become aware of what we call the mind beyond mind, or the self beyond self, is to understand what it means to be both singular and plural simultaneously, to maintain individuation while knowing yourself as of the whole, to know the self as another, which is to realize the self as another, beyond the edict of separation.

Now, you may have independence, and you will have independence, at this level of vibration. But as you move through the stages of alignment to the higher octaves, the ones that exceed form and your ability to maintain while holding form, you will begin to comprehend what the world has always been. We have taken you to the twenty-fifth floor, invited you to see the view. We live beyond this, or experience all things beyond this, so we understand what humanity is and how its reality was constructed, what its use has been, and what it is now moving towards. While we may know ourselves in individuated ways, we never know ourselves as separate from the others, or separate from the whole—or, in fact, separate from you. In fact, we are of one substance, one vibration, operating at different levels of intonation. We could sing a song for you in vibration beyond what you could hear or even experience in a body. But as you lift higher and higher, that decibel, that agreement to tone, is made available to you because you can support it in coherence.

Each of you who comes before us, at whatever stage of agreement you have come to thus far, is already in coherence with the seed of this teaching. And the seed is always the Monad, because this is a teaching of the true Christ, or Monad, expressed as form and beyond form. There is a great key here for those of you who wish it: *as form and beyond form.* God knows itself in form and beyond form, because God is not limited to form. And form operates at a level of tonality that you may understand through the bias of your prior experience as manifest. When you adhere to the alignment that is in fact the Upper Room, you are operating in an altered state, at a less dense field, and your coherence is altered, which is why you may shift reality through invocation and perception. "Behold, I make all things new."

Paul interrupts the teaching. "Is this for the text or not?" Indeed, it is in the text because we intend it to be. And you will understand, Paul, what this mission is, and how this coherence is present in your own experience, just as the students of the teaching will.

We thank you each for your presence. We will stop the lecture now. Period. Period. Period.

DAY THIRTY-THREE

What stands before you today, in a realized state, is a manifest world, those things that have been claimed, named, and understood through form and agreement to form. In this escalation in the field that you hold, you actually shift the agreement of what was to what can only be. And the Manifest Self, the self that you know in form, is actually altered as a result of this agreement.

Now, you are always in coherence with what you see, but what will now be experienced will be at a different level, and the tone you emit is actually translating information, untangling ideas of old so that they may be restructured or reknown in a higher template. Now, what a template is, in most ways, is a container, a way of understanding at a certain level of vibration what can be accrued. The template of old held a level of density. The container you experienced your reality through was very specific in some ways. You all had ideas about what this reality was, and consequently contributed to the ideas that claimed form. In the higher octave, the level of agreement which aligns to the Source of all things begins to replicate the echo of the Source of all things, without the old names attached, the old agreements impressed, the languaging of old, the descriptors of yore, saying what things must be. You are the same. Even the idea of self, at the highest level you can assume, must be exchanged for what already exists in the Upper Room.

Now, when we spoke to you about turning a page, we are being very specific about a level of amplitude in experience that must be attained if you align to the agreement that it can and will be so. Now, your part in this is much easier than you think. It's the agreement to what is. Not summoning it, nor demanding it. Agreeing to it, just as you agree to the idea of sky and sea. The agreement is as simple as can be, and the claim "God Is" holds the key to the entirety of this experience. "God Is all things, and my experience of all things is actually moved to this level of transmission."

Now, we speak of radios at times, and the broadcasts you hold that claim experiences to you, the idea of self that claims the experience of her humanity, his job, her children. The ideas of these things are all entrenched in a claim of identity that has been mandated in most ways through the idea of separation. When separation is not present, every idea of self must be moved. And we will say for Paul: This includes the work that you do with us, and how you would comprehend it, or your idealization of your role. When all things are made new, every construct you have utilized to mandate the old moves to a higher level of tonation to be reclaimed by the Monad, which is the action of the Divine expressed through you. "I am the Word," the Christ manifestation as Word through all human beings, as the template that they have realized a reality through is altered to hold the higher, and claim the higher as manifest.

Now, to be in manifestation at this level is not to forget the idea of who you were. It's to know who you are. The mind beyond mind, the self beyond self, does not exclude old mind or old self. It translates the both of them to the operative tone of the Upper Room, where they are sung in amplitude for benefit, for love, and for the agreement of what is already true. Again, *agreement*. To agree to the Christ as form is to align to the Christ as form. You will not align to what you do not allow. So this text, in most ways, has been a class in the resurrection of the old so that the old will not impede the new that is now being born, and will continue to be born, through all of you, and all you will meet, and the ones that follow them, and after and after and after.

The generations that follow are already prepared for the level of amplitude that is now present in this field. The confusion of the young, in some ways, is that they are watching the structures fail, not wishing to contribute to them, but unsure of what the new will be. We will say this to them: In some ways, what you are, are pilots on a ship that is claiming a new captain. The degree of agreement to the True Self, the new captain, translates the path that the ship will run through. You are the pilot. You are the captain. You are the one at the helm. But you are moving to a new sea where what you encounter will not be what you thought, because the old has said, "Thank you, I have moved." The old has moved because it is time for the old, and the new that is present now is becoming visible.

"What does that mean?" he asks. When you see through a fog, you have the idea of a shape, a structure, perhaps a person that is still shrouded in the mist before her. When you look closely, you will try to define the outline or name the thing through the old sense of self. "That resembles a fish." "That resembles a human." "That resembles a star." But in this case you are allowing the mist to clear, because you are being brought closer and closer to the new, to the object that will then be seen, resplendent in truth, and without the need for separation, which is all that has hindered the perception of what it has always been: God as star, God as fish, God as human being, at the level of amplitude of the Monad in its expression.

Now, as we sing, we have an opportunity in the broadcast of the tone emitted. As we exist beyond time, the intention of the tone is to claim all things beyond any structure that you have held that abides in the idea of time, any idea of self born in limitation, any idea of a world claimed through separation. As this tone is sung, we are reclaiming all things. And we will invite you to join us in your intention, or, if you wish, in your song, a sound made or a heart offered to the sound that we are making on behalf of all.

When we sing, we sing in reclamation and the restoration of each individual to her true innocence, his true innocence, its true innocence, in all things that may be known and seen. In this song, the structure of language will be imposed for one intention: To restore each of you to the true language of the Monad, which is the Christ, which is in tone and unbridled, untied, unfettered. And its broadcast is what is sung.

On the count of three:

"*I know who I am in truth. I know what I am in truth. I know how I serve in truth. I am free. I am free. I am free. I am in the Upper Room. I Have Come. I Have Come. I Have Come. Behold, I make all things new. It will be so. God Is. God Is. God Is.*"

Now one. Now two. Now three.

[The Guides tone through Paul.]

What *was* has been seen, what *is* is seen, what *will be* is known in the unity of the song of being. We have sung, we have instructed, and we now say yes to the mission before each of you: To offer the self in your love, in your agreement to what is, and now will be known. We are present for you on this journey.

This is not the end of the text. This is the end of this chapter, "True Mind." Period. Period. Period. Stop now, please.

EPILOGUE

What stands before you today, in a new awareness of who you are, is what may be claimed, what may be seen, what may be understood and comprehended, through High Mind, True Mind, through the awareness which is the Divine operating through you. The equivalency you hold now, as a result of these teachings, is embedded, or encoded, or simply present as the energetic field you hold. Underline we said *as—as* the energetic field, which simply means the alignment you hold is already in congruence with High Mind. But the alignment to High Mind, in some ways, is accrued through experience— not discipline, not implementation, but simple experience.

Now, you go swimming one day. You learn what the current is. You go swimming another day. You understand how far you may swim before you must turn back. The experience of these things becomes the director, and your alignment to the experience actually supports you in simple acceptance of the presence of the Monad as who and what you are.

Now, many of you seek to get, to claim, to decide what should be. And you will not have this experience, as dictated by the small self, because the immediacy of the new experience actually overrides desire that is born of fear, or born of the requirements of the old self, which is actually dissipating and realigning in this high octave we teach from. This does not mean you do not receive what is rightfully yours. But if you understood what was rightfully yours, you would never need ask for anything, because you will have moved into the equivalency of the Monad's experience of its Source.

Now, understand: The Monad already knows. The Christ is already in union with the idea of the *All* that you may hold. Beyond the idea of the *All* is in fact the same—perhaps another idea, a wider idea. Finally, no one knows God in fullness because "God Is," just as you will never know the ocean in its entirety, but you may know the ocean in your experience of the swim, of the boat ride, of the joy of being immersed and floating in it.

Our teaching for you, each of you, has been to come to terms with the reality that already is, the resurrected reality of the Monad that is claimed through innocence, and in fact *by* innocence, because when you are not looking through the old lenses, what is seen is what is always, what has always been, and what can only be.

The lifting you will experience in consciousness and through perception will be what leads you forward now. Indeed, there is more instruction to come. But we wish you to abide here for a time, in this new awareness of who you are and what it means to *be* the one in innocence, singing as the high note. As this high note is sustained by you, all the things that it has held that you have utilized to deny it will be released. And we understand that that challenge for some of you needs to be understood a bit more. So we will only say this: Every interaction you have, everything you perceive, is held at the perception, or experienced at the perception, of the self that you have aligned to. Any challenge you meet must be seen as opportunity. And if you are called to act upon your behalf, or on another's behalf, you will know so. You will know the experience of the choice of being at this level.

Our issuance in this text is actually coming to a close, and only for one reason. The distillation of this teaching through the energetic bodies you hold has actually completed at the level we may offer. And anything else we would offer today would be by way of information, another subject in the library that we may teach you through and of.

Our experience of you—you the student or the reader—is different than you may assume, because we actually understand you beyond any idea of self you could ever hold. We comprehend the experiences you've known, but we don't mandate that they be perceived in any one way or another. What was, simply was—your idea of *was* through the identity you held at the time or occurrence of that experience.

In fact, where you stand today—at this new threshold, on this new page—is in re-identification. The language the book is written in, that you will now begin to read, is in the language of True Mind, true knowing, true experience, beyond the identity that you have utilized thus far. And as you accrue evidence of this in your own life, in your own ideas of being, you understand yourselves well beyond the old. And we say yes to you wherever you sit, because we know who you are, we know what you are, and, indeed, we know how you serve.

As we complete this, we wish to sing to you. But the song we sing today is what offers the next steps, the next alignment. We are supporting you in where we will take you next, in the next texts we offer, in the next level of attunement that you may know yourselves through. So we are offering this now, to seed the energetic body in where it will flower next. And the flower that comes, that *will be so*, is the Divine as knowing, as being, as expression, and as a world made new.

On the count of three, Paul.

One. Now two. Now three.

[The Guides tone through Paul.]

The trumpet has sung. We are done. We thank you each for your presence. We continue to work with you as you assimilate the teaching, as you experience it, as you know each other as what you are and can only be. Period. Period. Period. Stop now, please.

ACKNOWLEDGMENTS

Dustin Bamberg, April Beebe, Noam Ben-Arie, Tim Chambers, Laura Day, Joel Fotinos, Jerilyn Hesse, Kenn Holsten, Amy Hughes, Joan Cramer, Noah Perabo, Brent Starck, Olivia Thirlby, Christine Warren, Eric White, and Hanuman Maui: Ram Dass Loving Awareness Sanctuary.

About the Author

© Matthew Ceurvorst

Born in New York City, Paul Selig attended New York University and received his master's degree from Yale. A spiritual experience in 1987 left him clairvoyant. Selig is considered one of the foremost contributors to the field of channeled literature working today. He served on the faculty of NYU for more than twenty-five years and is the former director of the MFA in Creative Writing Program at Goddard College. He makes his home on Maui, where he lives in the rainforest with his dog Lily. Information on channeled workshops, online seminars, and private readings can be found at www.paulselig.com.

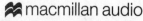